OLD SAWS AND
MODERN INSTANCES

OLD SAWS AND MODERN INSTANCES

BY

W. L. COURTNEY

Essay Index Reprint Series

BOOKS FOR LIBRARIES PRESS
FREEPORT, NEW YORK

First Published 1918
Reprinted 1969

STANDARD BOOK NUMBER
8369-0039-1

LIBRARY OF CONGRESS CATALOG CARD NUMBER
69-18924

PRINTED IN THE UNITED STATES OF AMERICA

PREFACE

A SELF-SUFFICIENT book requires no Preface, still less does it need an apology. It is my misfortune that this book seems to require both.

First, an apology. I am quite aware that I have altered a well-known phrase in using it as my title; and that it should be " wise " saws and not " old " saws that are conjoined with " modern instances." But while I have few pretentions to wisdom, I can at least advance some claims to age; and many of the themes with which I deal are sufficiently old to justify their right to a familiar antiquity.

There is, I fear, much repetition in these pages, and there is certainly some lack of connection and unity. My main desire, however, has been to illustrate modern questions by ancient examples—especially in the region of drama. Thus I have made a study of Brieux in close connection with a study of Euripides, and have contrasted and compared Mr. Hardy's *Dynasts* with the great plays of Æschylus. An inquiry into the conditions and limitations of Dramatic Realism is perhaps the most substantive of my aims in this book, which also includes some purely historical essays.

W. L. C.

London,
August 1918.

v

CONTENTS

OLD SAWS AND MODERN INSTANCES

MR. THOMAS HARDY AND ÆSCHYLUS

I

THE conjunction of names is not arbitrary or paradoxical. There is a great deal of Æschylus in Mr. Thomas Hardy— a certain ruggedness, austerity, elevation, a definite philosophical scheme at the back of all his creations and a gift of high-sounding rhetoric and occasional poetry. As a poet, to be sure, Mr. Hardy is manifestly inferior to Æschylus, who wrote some lines of unforgettable beauty as well as strength. He is also inferior as a dramatic artist, for Æschylus's Oresteian trilogy and his *Prometheus Vinctus* are among the greatest achievements of drama, only to be compared with the biggest work of Shakespeare. But Mr. Hardy has his own qualities of distinction and power; and if he only writes poetry with a conscious effort, as though in answer to Nature's stern imperative " Thou shalt not be a poet " he had boldly and laboriously answered " I will," he has achieved in *The Dynasts* a grandiose exploit which is destined to live. For he has taken the whole period of the Napoleonic Wars and tried to show how much greater and more successfully borne was the labour of England in defeating the enemy than most chroniclers have been disposed to allow; and in the execution of his task he has shown us animated pictures of Courts and camps, of seascapes and landscapes, of capital cities and country villages, together with portraits of generals and common soldiers, kings and peasants— constituting, as it seems to me, a veritable epic of a pro- digious war, rich in artistic colour and imaginative skill, which nevertheless with a certain perversity he has chosen

B

to present in a so-called dramatic form. Actable drama, of course, it is not. It is too cumbrous, too voluminous, too diffuse. Its three parts, nineteen acts and one hundred and thirty scenes, are not constructed as a drama with a single interest and a central unity. It is, as Mr. Hardy himself says, a play " intended for mental performance and not for the stage." And yet we cannot but remember that when Mr. Granville Barker produced selected scenes from it at the Kingsway Theatre, with Mr. Henry Ainley as a kind of Master of Ceremonies and official interpreter, *The Dynasts* created an atmosphere of its own and produced a dramatic effect, which none of those who were present are likely to forget. It is a great piece of work, and even its " disjecta membra " bear the stamp of a great and creative mind.

§ 1

What, however, I desire to examine is not the poetic or dramatic excellence of either Æschylus or Mr. Thomas Hardy. It is their poetic mission, their message to the world. For a poet is not a mere collector of mighty-mouthed harmonies, nor an æolian harp through which the winds of Heaven whistle as they list. He is a bard, a seer, a prophet, who tells us something of an unseen world to which his imagination enables him to ascend and bring down tidings to us dwellers in the prosaic plains. The same thing is, of course, true of a dramatist; indeed, in some senses it is more true. In all drama, it is said, there is divinity—sometimes, it must be confessed, a little be-clouded and disguised when we have to deal with mediocre times, but always visible—like lightning flashes across a black sky—in the great artists. For consider a little. The task of a dramatist is exactly antithetical to that of the priest. The latter's business is to reconcile men to God. God, Goodness, Justice, Mercy are taken for granted, and we must square our conceptions with these primordial axioms. But a dramatist, with his human interest and preoccupations, starts from the other end, the man's side. He does not take anything for granted—except the great broad facts of human nature. Hence, observing how men are hampered and controlled and frustrated by their own passions, or by what we call Destiny, he sees it as his great business to justify God to men. He must show what are the limiting conditions of human activity, how men are helped or hindered by the laws of Nature. He must interpret the scheme of world-governance to the purblind sons of men. Some dramatists are more conscious of this mission : some are almost unconscious of it. Nevertheless, it remains in the background of all their work, as something we, at all events, can appreciate as constituting their rank and value in world-history. Scarcely any dramatist of the first rank has been a less conscious moralist and preacher than Shakespeare. And yet how much we learn from Shakespeare's calm outlook over the world, his dispassionate judgment of men and women, his clear recognition that we weave our own fates, and that for us Destiny is human character ! If he makes his pessimist say

"As flies to wanton boys are we to the gods.
They kill us for their sport,"

he gives to a more manly character the utterance :

"The fault, dear Brutus, lies not in our stars,
But in ourselves that we are underlings."

Goethe was a more self-conscious artist than Shakespeare, especially in his *Faust*. Both Æschylus and Thomas Hardy are very anxious to explain to us their view of the way the world is governed. And sometimes a dramatist will insist on inculcating a patent and obvious moral— witness Brieux in *Les Avariés* and *Les Trois Filles de M. Dupont* and G. B. Shaw in such pieces as *Widowers' Houses* and *Mrs. Warren's Profession*. But to be didactic in this urgent and palpable form is to miss something of the artist's serenity and to injure the dramatic effect by a constant uplifting of the schoolmaster's forefinger. We go to the drama to listen and think and be silent : we do not cherish the prospect of being soundly birched.

§ 2

Æschylus and Thomas Hardy are, as I have said, conscious artists : they feel themselves under a real necessity of accounting for the phantasmagoria of existence in accordance with principles appealing to intelligence. Such a general statement may require some qualification when we come to deal with our contemporary poet, but

with the Greek poet it is abundantly justified. No doubt
there was something in the condition of the time which
seemed to necessitate a reconstruction of man's attitude
to the Divine—something which necessarily laid upon the
shoulders of thoughtful men the burden of explanation.
Views about the God or gods were changing, and had to
be readjusted to known facts. Human daily experience
and rationalised experience, which is science, alike threw
doubts on current theology and mythology. A novel
interpretation was urgently required to save the old faith,
or, if that was impossible, to provide bases for a new faith.
In Æschylus's time the Olympian gods were coming or
had come into their own, and were replacing the old barbaric deities—mainly earth-deities—worshipped with all
manner of superstitions by the earlier inhabitants of the
land. For, of course, Zeus and Athena, Apollo and Ares
and Hephæstus, Artemis and Aphrodite, and the rest were
not aboriginal, but were introduced into Greece as the
bright creations of an artistic race which had got beyond
the stupid worship of stocks and stones. Once established
they had to justify themselves, or rather be justified by
such artists in marble as Pheidias and such artists in verse
as the Attic dramatists. Zeus had, it is true, overthrown
Kronos, but he still had to show that he deserved to rule.
It was at this point that Æschylus took up his burden of
interpretation, being a deeply religious man, versed in the
Mysteries, as well as acquainted with the teaching of
Pythagoras.[1] Sophocles, his successor, was more concerned with man—idealised man. Euripides frankly gave
up the whole business and did not conceal his scorn for the
Gods, until late in life he acknowledged the might of the
newer deity, Dionysus, in that strange play *The Bacchœ*.
But Æschylus, as we shall see, was full of his arduous
mission, working with an uncertain hand in the *Prometheus
Vinctus*, but with assured mastery in the *Agamemnon* and
the *Eumenides*. He was a God-intoxicated poet.
   Mr. Hardy's problem is that which weighs upon us all
in a modern world—to reconcile what Science tells us
about the Cosmos with the revelations of Christianity.
How in a system of things governed by the unalterable
relation of Cause to Effect, antecedent to consequent,
can we find room for a Divine Providence ? In a material-

[1] Æschylus non poeta solum, sed etiam Pythagoreus : sic enim
accepimus.—Cic., *Tusc. II.*, 10, 23.

istic universe is there any place for a God, especially a God who is at once omniscient and omnipotent, infinitely just and infinitely benevolent? It is especially in times of some great calamity, the ruin caused by an earthquake or a pestilence, or the world-wide sorrow of a vast war, that we begin to question the Divine government and ask ourselves how the wholesale destruction of youthful life— the very promise of the future—can be accounted for or harmonised with the notion of an all-powerful God who wills the welfare of mankind. Mr. Hardy, as we know, has been obsessed both in his novels and his long dramatic poem *The Dynasts* with that great European convulsion, the Napoleonic Wars. Indeed, Wessex and the Napoleonic campaign would be a brief summary of his main interest, his chief preoccupation in his work. If, therefore, he is at pains to explain for us in piece after piece the conclusions he has arrived at, his philosophic estimate of ultimate problems is as pertinent and as important in reference to the present tremendous conflict as it is to that which was waged by our forefathers a century ago. And what is his solution of the problem? It is a melancholy confession of Nescience and Agnosticism. Like Æschylus, he will replace an old conception of Godhead by a new one. The God we have to recognise, however, is not a Person, reasonable, kindly, paternal, but an Immanent Will, an abstract energy which works blindly, mechanically, automatically, without intelligence, moving men on its gigantic chessboard as mere pawns and puppets in a game which it does not understand but which it pursues unceasingly. Events happen not because they have been fore-ordained, but purely arbitrarily. Men act not self-impelled, or because they will to act. They dance like figures on a string to a tune set them by a blind Power.

Such in general outline is the position taken up by the two poets—the one a scientific agnostic of the modern type, the other a philosophic advocate of the gods. Both, confronted by similar problems, accept it as their problem to justify the ways of the God or gods to men, the earlier writer by attempting to reform the current conceptions of the Godhead, the other by frankly denying intelligence, pity, providence to that blind but extremely active force which he calls the Immanent Will. If Æschylus gives consolation to his listeners troubled with the enigma of Evil and suffering in a God-ordained world, Mr. Thomas

Hardy cuts the Gordian knot by denying that the world is God-ordained. The first is occupied primarily with an ethical question; the second with a scientific question. What, asks Mr. Hardy, is the ultimate fact about the world? and he answers that in final analysis it is resolved into Force, Energy, Will. But Æschylus's question is different. Is the world, as we know it, constructed and ordered on lines which appeal to human reason? Yes, he answers. Zeus or the Godhead cares for Justice, Goodness, and Truth. He punishes wrong-doing even to the third generation. Ruin, destruction, death are due to men's sins—to their pride, their audacity, their arrogant insolence.

§ 3

In Æschylus's time the Olympian gods had, as we have said, come into their own. It must not be imagined that they were primitive deities, for Greece originally worshipped much ruder and barbarous powers, archaic objects of reverence like sacred stones or trees or certain animals. When the Achæans came down from the north they brought their gods with them and established them on Mount Olympus in Thessaly. Zeus, primarily an air-god, and the rest of his company were never said to have created the world : no, like the men whose highest aspiration they represented, they were conquerors, they took possession of the land and made the original inhabitants captives. Behind the bright figures of the Olympians there is always a dark background of something crude and immature and savage, which they had overthrown. The Gods fought the Titans. Zeus gained his ascendancy by killing Kronos, just as a still more primitive deity, Uranus, had been put out of the way by his successor. In this fashion was pictured the change which had come over the land when brute powers, together with bloody rites of sacrifice, were replaced by intelligent, rational agencies, made after the fashion of men, it is true, but of idealised men. To some extent the Hellenic Pantheon was a literary creation, which we attribute to the times of Peisistratus and to the conscious literary work of Homer and Hesiod. But it was equally a creation of sculpture and plastic art, Pheidias and his associates carving in magnificent outlines the objects which the Greeks were bidden to worship. Mythology, based on local legends, formed the divine annals of Heaven and its rulers. If ever a theology was palpably constructed by men and bore obvious traces of its human workmanship, it was the Olympian. It was framed to make the world intelligible, to improve moral conceptions, and to serve as the recognised creed of the Greek state or polis. But being an artificial structure it eventually perished—because it was " human, too human." It died of its very humaneness.[1]

Æschylus, like the dramatists who succeeded him, ransacked the myths for the subjects of his plays, but being a man of lofty and pious mind he usually tried to lift the stories to his own high level. Inevitably, however, he found the details of the myths clashing with his own moral and religious conceptions, and hence it became his task to rationalise, not so much the fables themselves, as the deductions which men were in the habit of drawing from them. His was essentially a lyrical gift, and the choruses of his plays, in which he gave his lyrical capacity full play, became sometimes, not the comments of a sympathetic observer, but philosophical essays touched with emotion. Whether he was a Pythagorean or not, he was assuredly something of a mystic—which lends colour to the assertion that he was accused of revealing some of the secrets of the mysteries. But if we are tempted to look upon him as a speculative thinker, let us remember that he was also a soldier. He and his brother fought for Hellas in her struggle with the Persian power, and when men wrote his epitaph in Sicily, where he died, they said not a word about his dramas or his poetry : they recorded the glorious fact that he took up arms against his country's foes. And probably Aristophanes's intense admiration for him was largely due to the fact that he belonged to the noble troop of Μαραθωνομάχαι.

When a thoughtful man of this calibre deals with religious faiths he is little likely to leave them where he found them. Throughout all his plays we find constant evidence that the poetic as well as the philosophic imagination is at work in dealing with Olympian theology; but for our purpose in our desire to discover what he thought about the principal God or Zeus, two dramas are of especial importance, the *Prometheus Vinctus* and the *Agamemnon*. Just as the main interest in Isaiah's prophecies is the view he held about Jahveh, so, too, in a dramatist who has

---

[1] See Prof. Gilbert Murray's *Four Stages of Greek Religion*, c. ii.

some of the qualities of Isaiah, the main interest is the portraiture and conception of Zeus.

§ 4

The *Prometheus* is as broad in its conception and as pregnant in its lessons as the Hebraic " Book of Job." It must be remembered that the play which we possess is one of a probable trilogy; it deals with the Titan enchained. The two other members of the trilogy were called *The Fire-bearer* (Πυρφόρος), and *Prometheus Unbound* (λυόμενος). Probably the " fire-bearer " was concerned with the theft of fire from Heaven, and came first. Then followed the play which has been preserved, the *Prometheus Vinctus* (δεσμώτης), and to that succeeded in its turn the play of release and reconciliation.[1] Viewing the trilogy in its completeness, we see that it is, like Job, a drama of human relations to the divine. Man's free will as against God's omnipotence; man's revolt against the arbitrariness of the Divine Rule; man's justification on the score of equity and reasonableness as against such a theory of dependence as is involved in the doctrine of the potter and his clay—such are some of the points involved. Prometheus, the blameless benefactor of the human race (to whom he gave the inestimable boon of fire), victimised and persecuted by the Olympian ruler, bears a colourable resemblance to Job, a just and innocent man, plagued and tormented by the arbitrary will of Heaven in order that his rectitude might be proved to be disinterested. In the long run both Job and Prometheus receive compensation and are restored to their dignities, but only after a wearisome period of physical torture and mental and moral suffering. Or are we altogether wrong in such an analogy, and did Æschylus mean to represent in his hero an arrogant arch-rebel instead of a suffering saint? Is he a martyr or Milton's Satan?

Let us look at the data before us in order to answer this question. We will assume that the first play of the trilogy represented the theft of fire. Zeus and the Olympians were involved in a tremendous warfare with the Titans. Prometheus, himself a Titan (whose name means

---

[1] This is, I think, the natural order. Other theories either place the Πυρφόρος last, or assume that Æschylus competed on this occasion with two plays, not three.

forethought), sided with Zeus, and demonstrated to him that not force but stratagem and cleverness would win the day. Having thus earned the gratitude of the God by enabling him to win, the Titan, grieved to the soul at seeing the wretched lot of human beings, stole fire in a hollow reed (fire was the prerogative of Hephæstus), and thus bestowed the most precious of all boons, the source of all inventions and a very instrument of civilisation, on the miserable inhabitants of earth. For this act of beneficent larceny the Titan is condemned to a severe penalty. Zeus ordains that he shall remain bound in chains on a desolate rock until such time as he bows his head before the sovereignty of the Olympian and confesses his fault. We see him, therefore, at the opening of our play—the second of the trilogy—fastened by iron rivets to his rock and calling heaven and earth and sea to witness to the injustice of his case. Notice in passing how singular this drama is in its immobility. Drama means action, whereas here there is inaction. Prometheus remains fastened to his rock until the very close, when he and the rock are swallowed up in chaos, and the whole play is, as it were, immobilised with him.

But we are not left in much doubt as to the due disposal of our sympathies. I will defy any one to read the *Prometheus Vinctus* without being sorry for the hero and enthusiastically espousing his side of the quarrel. The arrangements and incidents of the drama make this clear. After Hephæstus has done his sorry work and left Prometheus bound, the Chorus enters. And of whom does the Chorus consist? Of the daughters of Oceanus, sea-maidens, tender, emotional, with words of pity and consolation in their mouths, only too anxious to do the hero a service and in such a hurry to get to him that, as Æschylus quaintly says, they had not had time to put on their sandals. The Oceanides are an element of beauty in the rugged, unfriendly scene, appealing not only pictorially to the sympathetic eyes of the spectator, but morally also, inasmuch as they loyally brave the final catastrophe rather than desert their friend. Oceanus himself, when he comes on, mounted on his hippogriff, represents caution and prudence, for he recommends the Titan to make his peace with Heaven; but he does not speak as an enemy, but rather in the language of common sense and compromise. The next visitor is the strange figure of Iô, whose presence here is very significant. She is Zeus's enemy, or rather the victim of his despotic will, tormented by a gadfly because she refused her divine lover's embrace, and therefore naturally attracted to Prometheus as a rebel at heart against tyrannical authority. Even Hephæstus, who might well have considered himself injured by the theft of his special privilege, fire, is sorry for Prometheus; and when towards the close of the drama it is announced that yet more terrible suffering is to befall him—for he is to be cast down into Hades and an eagle is to prey on his liver, which is to be perpetually renewed in order that there may be every day a new feast—we feel that the poet has with direct intention so portrayed his hero's fate that we are full of compassion for the victim, and of indignation against his tormentor. So far as this play is concerned, the Father of Gods and Men is depicted in lurid colours as an unjust and vindictive bully, using his power ruthlessly in order to injure a helper and ally.

Yet this cannot represent a permanent mood in Æschylus. He was, as we know, devout and pious, sincerely anxious to bring into fruitful and beneficent relation humanity and the Godhead. The solution of the enigma is to be found in the third play of the trilogy, which has for its subject the Deliverance. How is Prometheus delivered? We have only a few fragments to guide us, but it is not very difficult to reconstruct the piece. We discover that Prometheus is brought out of Hades and has at his side a friend in Heracles—a lineal descendant from Iô, whose future progeny was foretold by the Titan in the earlier play. The eagle arrives to carry out its dreadful task; Heracles puts an arrow on his bow-string, takes aim, and the eagle falls. The process of reconciliation then proceeds apace. Prometheus was the possessor of a secret affecting the future of Zeus. If the God carried out his intention of marrying Thetis, the child born of such a union was to prove stronger than his father, just as Zeus himself had proved stronger than Kronos. This secret the Titan is now induced to reveal—thus adding a new service to that which he had originally rendered to the Olympian monarch. Therefore he earns his pardon, and when a substitute has been found to go down to Hades in his place, he is restored to favour and given a special festival in his honour at Athens. Throughout the play, apparently, Zeus is portrayed as in a kindly mood, ready to let bygones be bygones.

What are we to make of this contrast? The design of Æschylus is tolerably clear. The Olympian dynasty has to be established, taking the place of the older, more savage Gods, together with their cruel and bloody rites. So Zeus, who has killed Kronos, defeats the Titans. But a young conqueror, who has succeeded by force, is not likely to give up his drastic methods when first he gets the reins into his own hands. He is not sufficiently sure of his position. Against any insurgent or rebel he will act with prompt violence : conspirators, whose ultimate designs are not clear, must be treated as enemies and crushed forthwith. This is the stage of Zeus's rule when Prometheus steals fire for the sake of mankind. The Olympian King will endure no possible rivals near his throne and at once condemns the friend of men to severe punishment. But after a time Zeus's methods change. He has gained the security he desired, his reign is established, and he can therefore afford to be lenient. He is reconciled to Prometheus and forgives him. In this daring fashion Æschylus remodels an old myth in order to satisfy the moral sense. From Zeus the young despot he turns our attention to Zeus the more mature ruler of a better organised Empire, and transforms impatient cruelty into reasonable benevolence. The reformed Zeus can now be an object of reverence and receive the worship which is his due.

Let us not say in a hurry that such a theory is absurd and puerile. I confess that it looks so at first sight—just as though the Greek poet were trying his prentice hand at the interpretation of mythology and leading up to a hypothesis not only inadequate in itself, but disrespectful to the Deity. For the idea of growth and development may be held to be disrespectful to the Deity. It assumes that there was something lacking in him at the start, so that he commenced his career somewhat less than a God in order to grow up to the full stature of his Godhead. Zeus, according to the Æschylean hypothesis, began with crude views as to the necessity of violent methods in governing the world, and subsequently after much profitable experience conceived a more excellent way. Is not such an admission derogatory to the Divine Nature? Can there be degrees of perfection, gradations of omnipotence and omniscience? Curiously enough, however, much the same theory—*mutatis mutandis*—is to be found in Thomas Hardy.   Through nearly all the numerous acts and scenes of *The Dynasts* the Immanent Will is described as proceeding on its dreary path blindly, unintelligently, mechanically.   Its aim is neither Love nor Light.   It has all the stark pitilessness of the Unconscious.   At the very end of the drama the Chorus of Pities is allowed to suggest a new theory.   Is it not possible that Fate or Will, though it does not possess it originally, may develop Intelligence ? May not Consciousness be evolved out of Unconsciousness, as a civilised ruler, in the case of Zeus, was evolved out of a savage despot ?   If such a thing were possible—and Mr. Hardy is clearly of the opinion that it is not yet—we should have a beneficent revolution, a new efflorescence, " Consciousness the Will informing till it fashion all things fair ! "   There is, too, another analogy in a speculative theory which has recommended itself to thinkers troubled with the existence of Evil in a Divinely appointed Universe. How can God sanction Evil ?   One answer is that He does not sanction Evil—that on the contrary He is for ever striving against it, slowly conquering an obstinate material of Unreason and Wickedness and Pain : to which is added the corollary that we can help in the struggle, each in our fashion, by love and self-control and self-sacrifice, extending the borders of goodness and circumscribing more and more the fast-receding continent of Ill.   The underlying assumption here is that though we can ascribe benevolence to the Deity, we cannot ascribe irresistible power.   And this being so, we pray that God's reign may develop and His kingdom be gradually established—" Thy will be done," the process still unaccomplished, though the end be sure.

§ 5

It is time, however, to return from the relatively immature speculations of Æschylus—who being a dramatist was more interested in the psychology of a resisting and suffering Titan than in the economy of Heaven which made him suffer—to the wonderful choruses of the *Agamemnon*. Here we have a series of important affirmations on the character of Divine Government, on the relations of men to God, on human responsibility and the ordinances of Fate. The statements are not very specific nor very consistent; we should hardly expect them to be, as expounded by a mystical poet in lyrical strains.   But if we compare them with the odes of Pindar, which are full of such discussions, we discover that in Æschylus we have a far stronger and clearer thinker. Agamemnon belonged to the house of Atreus, and it was a doomed house ever since the wrong done by Atreus to his brother Thyestes in serving up to him a horrible repast of his children's flesh. Then came the crime of Agamemnon himself in sacrificing his daughter Iphigeneia in order to get fair winds for his voyage to Troy and other crimes such as a conqueror would commit in sacking a captured city. So Agamemnon is killed on his return home by his wife Clytemnestra and her paramour Ægisthus; and a new cry for vengeance is raised on behalf of the murdered King. Orestes, Agamemnon's son, returns from a long exile and puts to death his mother as well as Ægisthus. How is the dreadful vendetta to end? How can Orestes, the matricide, be rescued from the avenging Furies? Only by divine interposition and a formal trial before the Areopagus, when Athene, after the votes were equal for punishment and acquittal, gave her casting vote for Orestes, and the plague of deaths is stayed. This in brief outline is the story, raising interesting problems in metaphysics and theology.

Æschylus in the first chorus of the *Agamemnon* attacks the main problem. What are we to think of Zeus? Let us begin by conceding that no definition of Zeus is possible. " Zeus, whoever he is," cries the Chorus, " if this name pleases him, by this name will I address him. For I can conjecture no other title save Zeus, if it is right to banish foolish imaginings from the mind." [1] The poet suggests that true worship and reverence must be given to a supreme God, without encumbering ourselves with mythological tales. We lose all the majesty of Godhead if we make a human picture of him and construe him to ourselves as jealous and partial and inclined to numerous amours. That is a man-made God, the work of anthropomorphism. What we want is a more philosophical conception, necessarily vague, yet sufficient for our faith and our prayer. Moreover, the Godhead is one—one God, not many Gods. And little as we know about him, we know at least that he is a *moral* force. For he educates man by suffering, teaching even the unwilling to be wise by ordaining pain as the punishment for evil-doing. It is the law of his universe that knowledge comes by melancholy experience of sorrow

[1] Æsch. *Ag.*, 160 *et sqq.*

and suffering. God's punishment is therefore not vindictive : it is educative—opening blind eyes to the realities of things. Zeus's purpose is to make men better. Such is the noble creed, outlined for us in noble language in the first chorus of the *Agamemnon*.

The second chorus starts another problem.[1] Is the ruler of Heaven a Providence, as well as a ruler ? Do the Gods care for mortal things ? It is impious to doubt it. To believe that the Gods are such as Epicurus—at a later period—described them, living in their celestial abodes, unconcerned with human affairs, existing easily because unperturbed with trouble or responsibility, amounts to a disbelief that they are Gods at all. If we refuse to accept an atheistical position of this kind, then the only alternative is to have faith in the wise ordinances of Heaven and to wait for the issue which Providence has decreed. If the mills of God grind slowly, yet they grind exceeding small. Look, for instance, at the career of Paris. Idle, debonair, effeminate, a lover of beauty, he is the favourite of Aphrodite, and as such wins the love of Helen, the wife of his host, Menelaus, and persuades her to elope with him to Troy. But does such traitorous work prosper ? Menelaus, betrayed and forlorn, can find no joy in Art or Life now that the loved one is gone, but he gets his due revenge. Paris involves his city and himself in utter ruin, and on his conscience lies heavy the doom of all the brave men who perished in his quarrel. Were the Gods regardless of human justice in the death of Paris and the fall of Troy ?

Having settled this problem to their satisfaction, the Chorus in their third lyrical ode address themselves to an equally important and difficult question. It was said by men of old time that God is jealous. He cannot brook the excessive prosperity of men, and if Polycrates of Samos is born under a lucky star, he must pay compensation for his good fortune, which, even so, may be rejected of Heaven. Is it true that greatness and prosperity inevitably call down wrath from an offended Godhead ? Such a view involves a mistaken estimate of divine laws and utterly misconceives the true relation of punishment to wrongdoing. " I alone," says the leader of the Chorus, speaking no doubt the mind of Æschylus, " I alone am of a different opinion." [2] It is Sin which is punished, the godless act. The innocent have a fair lot. Observe that the poet tells

---

[1] Æsch. *Ag.*, 355–487.   [2] Æsch., *Ag.*, 750–781.

us especially that his own view is singular, and is not shared
by the multitude.   But he is sure of his ground.   It is not
prosperity as such, it is the mental effect of prosperity—
the arrogance bred in the prosperous and wealthy man—
which ultimately brings down the wrath from God.   The
fatal heritage runs thus.   Affluence breeds insolence
(ὕβρις).   Insolence leads to many evil things—impiety,
hardihood, recklessness—and the evil man spurns with his
foot the altar of justice.   Then comes Nemesis, apportion-
ing to each man the lot he deserves, and therefore overwhelming the confident sinner with ruin.   And so it
happens that wealthy halls in which defiance and pride
and boundless conceit reign are not happy.   Justice shines
in poor men's homes and has no regard for wealth.   Gold
is wrongly stamped with praise.   All this is, the poet
thinks, borne out in the history of the Atreidæ.

> " But Arrogance, in sin grown grey
>   Mid vile men, bears a child at length
>   Like her in name, in lusty strength,
> Or soon or late, when dawns her day;
>
> " Yea, and a brother-fiend, whom none
>   May cope with, impious Hardihood—
>   Black curses twain o'er homes that brood,
> And like their dam each demon son.
>
> " In smoke-fouled huts doth Justice shine;
>   On virtuous lives she still hath smiled:
>   From gold-tricked halls and hands defiled,
> She turns her with averted eyne.
>
> " A guest she is of each pure soul:
>   She on the power of wealth looks down,
>   With all its base coin of renown:
> She guideth all things to their goal." [1]

This is the clearest vindication of the Divine justice
which Æschylus gives us, and it represents the most acute
point of difference between him and a poet like Mr. Hardy.
For with the modern writer, it is precisely the random
arbitrariness of the Immanent Will, which in passage after
passage he emphasises.   If a will is both arbitrary and
reckless, it is assuredly unjust in its effects.   Of its motives
we cannot speak, for, not being conscious motives, they do
not enter into the question.   Even the word arbitrary
connotes a sort of intelligence, and therefore, strictly

[1] *Æschylus in English Verse*, Part III., Arthur S. Way, p. 34.

speaking, cannot be used of the blind purposeless Will. At all events, there can be no suggestion of a nice adjustment of punishment to crime, for neither punishment nor crime has any meaning in an irrational universe in which men are victims of Fate.

Oddly enough, however, we find in the fourth chorus of the *Agamemnon* an allusion to Fate which disquiets us. Fate is declared to be greater than Zeus.[1] Now Prometheus knew that Fate was greater than Zeus, because, as is told in the play, the hero held in his hands a secret decree of Fate which would either doom or save the Olympian God, according as it was obeyed or defied. But if Fate is thus supreme over the Deity, how much more must it be supreme over man? And in that case what becomes of the whole theory of man's responsibility for his action, in virtue of which we call him a sinner or a saint? And how can punishment be just in the case of one who is not a free agent? These, of course, are the never-ending problems which every theology must seek to solve. If man is not free, why is he punished? If he is free, how is his liberty of choice related to Divine predestination and foreknowledge? If Æschylus is not wholly consistent in his handling of the question, we can at least say that he is not more inconsistent than the majority of those who have speculated on Fate, Free Will, Fore-knowledge Absolute. And, so far as the *Agamemnon* is concerned, the poet lays no stress on his doctrine of Fate. It comes in as a casual reflection, unrelated to the main philosophical and religious theory embodied in the choruses of the play.

[1] Æsch., *Ag.*, 1025.

MR. THOMAS HARDY AND ÆSCHYLUS

II

" Let me enjoy the world no less
Because the all-enacting Might
That fashioned forth its loveliness
Had other aims than my delight."

MR. THOMAS HARDY made his reputation by a series of fine novels, such as *Far From the Madding Crowd*, *A Pair of Blue Eyes*, *The Mayor of Casterbridge*, *The Trumpet-Major*, *The Return of the Native*, *Tess of the D'Urbervilles*, and *Jude the Obscure*. One at least, let us note in passing, *The Trumpet-Major*, has a background of war—as a matter of fact, the Napoleonic War, which occupies Mr. Hardy in *The Dynasts*. And all of these novels have certain marked characteristics which are of the greatest significance in estimating the author's work. There is a love of natural phenomena in all their aspects—the storm, the heath, the village; a tenderness for the humbler workers on the land, as well as the yeoman-farmers; a general distaste for the fine ladies and gentlemen, whom Mr. Hardy cannot sympathise with, and therefore cannot draw; a certain view of women, drawn with great subtlety and insight, which makes them almost a dæmonic element in human affairs, and strangely differentiates them from George Meredith's women; and a curious tendency to make use of coincidence in working out the plots. Apart, however, from all these points, which are obvious to most readers, there is a general atmosphere surrounding the incidents which we often find difficult to breathe; or we may call it a background, a *mise-en-scène* in which the stories are set and from which they take a definite colour of sombreness and gloom. Marriages are unhappy, and it is equally unhappy to remain single; lovers do not meet at the close of their long journey of misunderstanding and separation; the cup of happiness proffered to eager lips is ruthlessly dashed away; the rebel against convention is as much a failure as the man or woman who humbly accepts convention as a guide; and, worst of all, there is heard now and again an echo of ironical laughter in Heaven. Jude when he accepted the obligations of matrimony is no more successful than when he broke loose from them. Tess is throughout the sport of unkind Fate—Fate which, described as President of the Immortals, only ends his sport with her when, as a murderess, she dies on the scaffold. Bathsheba, in *Far from the Madding Crowd*, only escapes because of the moral strength and sanity of Gabriel Oak, one of the few vigorous and independent characters in Mr. Hardy's picture gallery. It is impossible to avoid the impression that, in the author's scheme, we are all rats in a trap, doomed to break ourselves against the wires in situations from which there is no escape, victims of a Power which has predestined us from all eternity. In other words, Mr. Hardy's is a fatalistic creed, based on philosophic Nescience, a scientific belief that the Power at the back of things is a blind, purposeless agency, to which we must be careful not to assign human or moral attributes, and which we must be content—with Mr. Hardy—to call " It," and never " Him."

§ 1

Now it is not easy for the ordinary man to understand the mental detachment of the scientific thinker. The attitude of cold curiosity, the exclusion of all other interests except the desire for truth, the rigid employment of analysis, the clear estimation of the relative values of good and bad evidence, the building up of a conclusion based on rigorously sifted data—all these things are uncongenial to the average man, and therefore appear to indicate callousness and inhumanity. The majority of us are apt to look upon the world and all that is in it as they affect ourselves, from a purely human point of view. To regard the cosmos of things as it is in itself, abstracted from the way in which human beings feel and think about it, requires an intellectual effort based on a definite logical training. How shall we illustrate this contrast? Early astronomers thought that the earth was the centre of the universe, the sun, moon, and stars circling round it. Then came Copernicus, Galileo, and the rest to prove that it was the earth which was in continuous movement, travelling in its orbit round the sun. The change in attitude revolutionised astronomy. In much the same way thought is revolutionised when, instead of looking upon our earth as created to minister to our wants and emotions, we carefully exclude the human factor in studying the constitution of the world. Instead of our inquiries radiating in different directions from the Ego or Self as a centre, we now observe how the nature of things, the various properties and powers of the world, full of their own intrinsic energy, impinge and act upon sentient human beings. The first state of mind might be described as anthropocentric, the second as cosmocentric.

But of course it is difficult for a poet and impossible for a dramatist to exclude the human factor. However much a student of science may succeed in riveting his attention on the universe of things, and may refuse to consider man otherwise than as a mere item or element in a cosmos arranged for other ends than man's satisfaction, the claims of the human factor are bound to speak through the voice of the poet and to find a potent advocate in the writer of drama. Lyrical and elegiac pieces are the outcome of strong personal feeling; human emotion rings in the epic; the strong cry of the suffering soul—striving, battling, enduring, dying—echoes through and through every passionate tragedy which ever was written. Mr. Hardy, despite his theory, cannot, however much he tries, remain on the cold, abstract level of science. The world may be the scene of blind energies working remorselessly towards a goal we wot not of, but it is the piteous tale of man which is of absorbing interest to us. Listen to this, taken from one of Mr. Hardy's poems :

> " Or come we of an Automaton
>   Unconscious of our pains ?
>   Or are we live remains
> Of Godhead dying downwards, brain and eye now gone ?
>
> " Or is it that some high Plan betides,
>   As yet not understood,
>   Of Evil stormed by Good,
> We, the forlorn hope, over which Achievement strides ? "

Here is the problem, envisaged quite plainly, though not explicitly, from the human point of view. It may be Nature which is speaking, but it is, above all, human nature. The various alternatives are set out as so many points on which we desire enlightenment. Are we mere puppets dancing to a tune which the Automaton sets ? Or are we the poor wraiths and ghosts of what was once Godlike, but which has now hopelessly deteriorated? Or—and here sounds the voice of Hope, the last thing left in Pandora's box—are we the champions of some mighty project and purpose, for which we must cheerfully give our lives if only those who come after us may win where we failed? Mr. Hardy gives us no answer to these questions. " Earth's old glooms and pains are still the same." But what we catch in these lines is the whisper of that divine discontent, which can never get satisfaction from a purely scientific view of the world, craving, as it perpetually does, for more light and a more comfortable assurance.

§ 2

There is, in consequence, one reflection which inevitably occurs to the mind. A poet with difficulty acquiesces in a soulless Universe. But what of a dramatist who is confronted by the picture of a will-less humanity? So far as Mr. Hardy accepts the scientific view of man and woman as mere automata or puppets, so far must he find his occupation gone, or severely attenuated, as a writer of drama. For drama is action, human action, and the clash of wills is, as we know, the essence of tragedy. But what is the value of action which is purposeless, and what is the interest of conflicting wills in the absence of independence and responsibility? In *The Dynasts* Mr. Hardy paints for us some extremely vivid and dramatic situations. There is, for instance, the death of Nelson on board the *Victory*, the fatal Russian campaign and the overthrow of Napoleon's hopes, the field of Waterloo with all its wild confusion and desperate charges, besides many a stirring little vignette of lowly lives in which eager personalities are seen with their mingled strength and weakness. But what is the dramatic value of Nelson as a puppet, Wellington and Pitt as automata, Napoleon, himself as a pawn in the blind game of chess played by the Immanent Will? Once or twice Napoleon speaks of himself as a mere instrument in the hands of Fate, and therefore not responsible for his actions. But it is only by refusing so to regard him that we preserve his significance in the drama. Happily, in reading these scenes or seeing them on the stage, we ignore or forget Mr. Hardy's own views of their meaning. The human actors in the tragedy appeal to us as warm, sentient, passionate beings, to whom their real fate is their character, and who know what they are doing and struggling for. The background of Spirits, sinister and ironic, leaves, and inevitably leaves, us cold.

As a matter of fact, the invention of a Spirit-world overlooking the play is a concession to our weakness—or, I should rather say, to our not unnatural human demand. Science clearly would not sanction such extravagant fancies as Spirits of the Pities or Choruses of the Years. Let us see what the author himself says about them in the preface to *The Dynasts*. " It was thought proper," he says, " to introduce as supernatural spectators of the terrestrial drama certain impersonated abstractions, or Intelligences, called Spirits. They are intended to be taken by the reader for what they may be worth as contrivances of the fancy merely." He goes on to say that we must not expect from them a systematised philosophy, but he hopes that " their utterances may have enough dramatic plausibility to procure for them, in the words of Coleridge, ' that willing suspension of disbelief for the moment which constitutes poetic faith.' " We may remark in passing that though Mr. Hardy warns us against basing a systematised philosophy on what these Spirits say, such philosophy as we can extract is so precisely that which we gather from Mr. Hardy's novels and poems that we need not hesitate to regard it as the author's own. The only difference is that what was hinted before is now put before us in an explicit shape, and that a creed, which might almost be called systematised, takes the place of casual references and allusions. There is no doubt, therefore, that what the ancient Spirit of the Years says is what Mr. Hardy thinks, and that the general scheme adumbrated by these Intelligences is the most reasonable solution the poet can give of the mystery of this unintelligible world.

But why is the Spirit World introduced at all ? The answer is curious and significant. The author feels the want of something like the celestial machinery we find in Homer, Virgil, and Milton's *Paradise Lost*. Divine personages are very useful to the writers of epics, because they serve as " ready-made sources or channels of Causation." In other words, they explain how things happen by linking them on to the exercise of conscious Wills. But Mr. Hardy's scheme does not admit conscious volition. Therefore, in a world of Necessity and Automatism, he is driven to devise imaginary shapes which have nothing to do with guiding the world on its course, but which may express human feeling or supply human comment. Considering that the panorama we are invited to survey is inhuman, soulless, and will-less, we must find consolation in inventing volatile agencies which are, at all events, lively, active, and conscious of what they are doing. Indeed, one group— that of the Pities—corresponds in some measure, as the author tells us, to the Chorus in a Greek play—the spectator idealised and sympathetic. All drama craves for as much humanity as we can put into it, and it is because Mr. Hardy instinctively feels this necessity that his actual practice in *The Dynasts* is better than his theory. His theory is cold-blooded, but his Chorus of the Pities is warm with human interest and feeling. " Sunt lacrimæ rerum " even in a Monistic scheme of the Universe.

§ 3

It is time, however, to come to closer grips with Mr. Hardy's supernatural apparatus. The denizens of his Olympus, which he calls the " Overworld," are the Ancient Spirit of the Years, the Spirit of the Pities—each with its attendant Chorus—the Shade of the Earth, Spirits Sinister and Ironic, with their Choruses, Messengers, and Recording Angels; while as Zeus, or King of this Divine company, the First or Fundamental Energy, is called " It." Most of these have a specific task. It is the business of the Spirit of the Years to explain; of the Spirit of the Pities to ask questions and complain; of the Spirits Ironic and Sinister to jeer and make satirical remarks. The Shade of the Earth opens the drama with the query, " What of the Immanent Will and Its designs ? " and the Spirit of the Years makes answer :

> " It works unconsciously, as heretofore,
> Eternal artistries in Circumstance,
> Whose patterns, wrought by rapt æsthetic rote,
> Seem in themselves Its single listless aim
> And not their consequence." [1]

" Why this eternal monotony ? " ask the Pities, and we are given two possible hypotheses. Either the Will is tired with this world and is occupied with other worlds,

---

[1] *Dynasts*, Fore-scene.

or else our world lost the Will's original watchful care owing
to the wickedness of early men who contrived to sever us
from Heaven.   But may not some startling event bring
back the old Providence?   No, there is no evidence available to make us think that thoughtful design either is or
ever was part of the scheme.   On the contrary, the data
seem to prove that :

> " Like a knitter drowsed,
> Whose fingers play in skilled unmindfulness,
> The Will has woven with an absent heed
> Since life first was : and ever will so weave." [1]

That is a final verdict, and it is only left for the Pities to
urge how much better it would be for mankind and the
world if, instead of tyrants like Napoleon, they were guided
by merciful and peaceful leaders, " men of deep art in life-
development."   But that is apparently impossible.   " Old
laws operate yet," and men's " dynastic and imperial moils
shape on accustomed lines."   And thus in our melancholy
contemporary experience an Amurath an Amurath succeeds,
and Napoleon is followed by Kaiser Wilhelm.

It cannot be denied that this is a dreary prospect, nor
that our author is one of the most dispassionate of observers.
He often strikes the reader as being only coldly interested
in his themes, like his Spirit of the Years, who, when he
regards dynastic and imperial ambitions, declares, " I care
not how they shape or what they be."   Curiosity, perhaps,
is his chief characteristic—a keen scientific curiosity which
accepts the conclusions to which his logic drives him without
faltering.   His attitude to women is significant in this
regard.   On the whole, I think it may be said that
Mr. Hardy is an apologist for women, but that does not prevent him from being cruel in his analysis.   He looks upon
woman in her humours, moods, and vagaries as being in an
especial degree an instrument through which Fate works
out its schemes.   Fate is, as it were, incarnated in her.
Complicated questions of sex are intensely interesting to
Mr. Hardy; the difficulties of the married state are harped
upon with almost wearisome iteration in most of his novels.
But he draws his pictures without pity; his curiosity is
usually frigid, and sometimes almost morbid.   To a mind
like his, therefore, a huge drama like the struggle of England
against Napoleon is not regarded as a battle-royal between

[1] *Dynasts*, Fore-scene.

rival wills and competing ambitions, with various interludes
in which strength and weakness, passion and frailty, make
their appeal to our sensitive sympathy; but a mechanical
game of celestial chess in which the Immanent Will makes
its blind moves without prescience or purpose, and human
beings are helpless pawns or counters pushed hither and
thither as chance—which is Fate—directs. Look at the
stage direction which Mr. Hardy gives us from time to
time, as if to remind us of the true inwardness of his
drama :
    " The nether sky opens, and Europe is disclosed as a
prone and emaciated figure, the Alps shaping like a back-
bone, and the branching mountain-chains like ribs, the
peninsular plateau of Spain forming a head. . . . The
point of view then sinks downwards through space and
draws near to the surface of the perturbed countries, where
the peoples, distressed by events which they did not cause,
are seen writhing, crawling, heaving, and vibrating in their
various cities and nationalities. . . . A new and penetrating light descends on the spectacle, enduing men and
things with a seeming transparency, and exhibiting as one
organism the anatomy of life and movement in all humanity
and vitalised matter included in the display." The Spirit
of the Pities, looking at the scene, discerns certain waves
" like winds grown visible," twining and serpentining, and
retracting threads like gossamers, which bear men's forms
on their coils. These, says the Spirit of the Years, are
fibrils, veins, will-tissues, nerves, and pulses of the one
Immanent Will, " evolving always that it wots not of."
Men think their deeds self-done; they fancy that they are
acting in freedom. In reality they are but " atoms of
the One, labouring through all, divisible from none."

§ 4

We may shiver at so inhuman a creed, but it does not
overwhelm us, because as man is always and everywhere
better than the tenets he professes to hold, so, too,
Mr. Hardy is far more clement than his doctrine of the
Immanent Will. The essential disadvantage of an abstract
system of purposeless activity, which is to get rid of human
volition and, indeed, destroy the reality of human beings
themselves, is that no one can believe in it for more than
a few minutes together—and then only in a severely logical

mood.   Daily experience is too strong for us, and ordinary
intercourse with our friends seems to give the lie to our
scientific theory.   For we see men acting under the impression that they are responsible for their acts, and we observe
legal punishments inflicted on the assumption that the
individual can sin against the light.   It is a natural inference
that, inasmuch as all life, social and political, is based on
the supposition that men are free agents, we cannot be
far wrong if we take for granted the existence of real
individuals, centres of force and in essence independent.
Obviously, then, it requires a strong and sustained effort
to believe that all these evidences of life are illusions, and
that nothing really moves but a blind and irrational
Immanent Will.   And if this is the case with the ordinary
man, still more must it be so with the dramatist.   For he,
as we have already said, is specially concerned with human
action and with the griefs and joys of self-conscious personalities—all of which tumble into nothingness if only
the One exists or moves.   And here, once more, we may
illustrate the point by a reference to Æschylus, who was
no more consistent with the demands of his lofty theory
than other poets and philosophers.   We have seen that
sometimes he suggests that Fate is higher than Zeus, and
if that be so the whole of his creed of a beneficent Providence
falls to the ground.   There can be no Providence if the
God is overruled by a coldly omnipotent Destiny.   And in
a fragment from an unknown play of his, the *Heliades*,
we have a still more startling theory.   " Zeus," he says,
" is the æther, the earth, the sky; Zeus is everything
that exists, and still greater than these." [1]   This is the
theory of Pantheism ; and it not only makes human liberty
impossible, but it absolutely upsets all that Æschylus has
told us elsewhere about a Zeus who is the son of Kronos
and the last arrived of the masters of the world.

§ 5

It is interesting, as a matter of fact, to observe how here
and there in the course of *The Dynasts* Mr. Hardy gives
us indications and suggestions of dissatisfaction with his

[1] Ζεύς ἐστιν αἰθήρ, Ζεὺς δὲ γῆ, Ζεὺς δ' οὐρανός,
Ζεύς τοι τὰ πάντα, χὤτι τῶνδ' ὑπέρτερον.
A treatise of Philodemus, found at Herculaneum, gives us the title of the
play in which these verses are found.

scientific doctrine of the One. It is the Chorus and the Spirit of the Pities—naturally enough—which voice the human cry. Surveying the course of action from their privileged standpoint, they see the melancholy tragedy of the war, and cry out with Othello, " The pity of it, the pity of it, Iago." Their usual attitude is to disbelieve the grim irony of a Will which knows not what it wills, or, at all events, to hope for some alleviation of the cruel decrees of destiny.

> " This tale of Will
> And Life's impulsion by Incognisance
> I cannot take."

they say in Act I., Sc. 6; and later on, in Act V., Sc. 4, they sympathise with what Sophocles put in the mouth of Hyllus (*Trachiniæ*, 1266–72), when he arraigned the Gods for their treatment of Hercules. The Chorus adds, a little farther on :

> " Why make life debtor when it did not buy ? "

In such criticisms the point is the injustice of a system which after creating human life makes it so helpless and so enslaved. In Act I., Sc. 6, the criticism is pushed home by laying stress on human sensitiveness. It was bad enough to ordain that men should be born into slavery, but it is worse when we remember that these hapless creatures are sentient. Surely it must be a flaw in Nature's handiwork that puppets, driven hither and thither by forces entirely independent of their volition, should also be capable of acute feeling. So in Act IV., Sc. 5, the significant admission is made that " It (the Will) does not quite play the game." If the Will must play with puppets, then by all means let these puppets be merely mechanical toys. To use them as pawns, and yet endow them with a sensitive consciousness, is to act the part of a bully liking to inflict pain. Wretched men, being helpless, are allowed to recognise their helplessness and thus endure a crueller punishment. The slave has all the added misery of knowing that he is a slave. He is in chains and powerless, but not permitted to remain a soulless dupe. That is a strong impeachment of the Immortal Energy, which takes the place of God in Mr. Hardy's system. The only answer is that it knows not what it is doing.

But is it true that it knows not what it is doing? Cannot we detect, now and again, some signs of actual malevolence? We remember the end of *Tess of the D'Urbervilles*, where a reference is made to the " President of the Immortals." He is said to have " finished his sport with Tess " when she finally ends her unhappy life on the scaffold, just as though he took a pleasure in tormenting her. And, indeed, throughout the novel we cannot but feel that the poor heroine is hardly allowed a decent chance, and that the author piles suffering on suffering as though to bring home to our consciousness that Tess and the women like her are born under an unlucky star. We revolt from the picture as too heavily charged with gloom; we resent the doom of the heroine as unjust and unnatural. If, however, we take the book at its surface value, we cannot escape the impression that there is something very like malice in the ordinances of Fate. This is what the Spirit of the Pities feels when in *The Dynasts* it is witnessing the suffering of the poor mad English King (Act VI., Sc. 4). One might almost think, it seems to suggest, that ironical malice has presided over the creation of the world, that men had been created as a jest and scoffed at when they suffer. But here the answer comes at once, whether we accept it or no. The Will is not conscious; it has no intelligence. It is " unmaliced, unimpassioned, nescient Will," and therefore it is impossible that it should enact the *rôle* of an Iago. The One escapes criticism because it is an " It " and not a " He."

§ 6

But later on we get a veritable *cri du cœur*. When the unseen watchers observe the unhappy king fall into one of his paroxysms, the more sympathetic among them cannot restrain their anguish. And it takes a significant form. The Spirit of the Pities feels that the sorrow and desolation of the world are unbearable, unless behind the piteous spectacle there is some Being to whom humanity may make appeal. The Universe must have some presiding Deity—not an unconscious Will, but a conscious Person, warm with love and tenderness.

> " Something within me aches to pray,
> To some great Heart to take away,
> This evil day, this evil day ! "

The mocking reply comes swift and deadly :

> " Ha, ha. That's good. He'll pray to It !
> But where do Its compassions sit,
> And where abides the heart of It ? "

Nevertheless, the Spirit is not abashed or deterred :

> " Mock on ! mock on ! Yet I'll go pray
> To some Great Heart, who haply may
> Charm mortal miseries away." [1]

For the nonce the author of *The Dynasts* is on the side of the angels. In all his references to the mass of men, " the pale, pathetic peoples," " the pale, panting multitudes," who are the victims of despotic kings and the still more despotic Immanent Will, he shows an unwonted tenderness, which goes beyond the limits of his scientific creed. In the passage just quoted he seems to be fully conscious that the human cry cannot be altogether ignored, and that it is an ineradicable instinct which has led men of every variety of race and faith to raise beseeching hands to " Our Father which art in Heaven."

Nor yet at the very end of his drama will he leave us without a gleam of hope. I have before alluded to the passage in which the suggestion is made that Fate or Will may develop Intelligence, as in Æschylus Zeus developed from a tyrant to a beneficent God. Most of the cruelty of the world arises out of the dissociation of primeval Energy from conscious intelligence. If the Will were only aware of what it was doing, it might act from design and even grow to be kindly. At all events, this is the aspiration of the Spirit of the Pities in a choric song which, probably not without intention, is placed in the closing scene.

> " Nay :—shall not its blindness break,
> Yea, must not its heart awake,
>   Promptly tending
>   To Its mending
> In a genial germing purpose, and for loving-kindness' sake ? "
>
>   .   .   .   .   .
>
> " But a stirring thrills the air
> Like to sounds of joyance there
>   That the rages
>   Of the ages
> Shall be cancelled, and deliverance offered from the darts that were,
> Consciousness the Will informing, till it fashion all things fair ! " [2]

---

[1] Act VI. Sc. 5.   [2] After-scene, Act VII. Sc. 9.

§ 7

What are we to say of *The Dynasts* as a whole? From the point of view of drama it is cumbrous and top-heavy; as a study in character-drawing it is exceedingly interesting and suggestive; as a record of events it is very faithful, and keeps close to its authorities. But that, after all, is not what we have been examining in this essay. However rich it may be in eloquent passages of rhetoric, and even in single lines and phrases of real poetry, it will have ultimately to be judged—as, indeed, Mr. Hardy's shorter poems have to be judged—by the philosophy which underlies the whole structure : the theory of the Universe and of the men and women who have to live in it. It is possible, of course, to cut out of *The Dynasts* all the supernatural elements, and the action of the personages and the vivid reality of the scenes will, it may be said, remain much the same. But it will then cease to be the piece of work which the author designed and in which he is interested; it will cease to represent Mr. Hardy's own mind. The Immanent Will is not a conception which appears now and again in these volumes; it runs all through them, it animates and explains the whole fabric. What are we to say of it?

For myself, I confess I should like to adopt the attitude of Epicurus as expressed in a well-known phrase. He, too, saw what we see to-day, that when the gods disappear as objects of worship, the human mind—which is credulous in essence and must worship something—offers its incense to Fate or Will or Chance as the supreme arbiter of the world. Epicurus said : " I would rather believe in all the stories of the Gods than in the Fate of the philosophers." He expressed himself sceptically, of course. What he meant was that he saw no reason in the case of two uncertainties why he should exchange one uncertainty for another. If you can have no certainty about the Gods, you can have no greater certainty about your abstract Fate or Will. Why, then, disturb yourself by a transference from a fairly comforting theory to a distinctly uncomfortable one? We must not, however, put our criticism in so ironic and sceptical a form. Perhaps we may put it thus : The world, as many metaphysicians tell us, arises in consciousness. In other words, all that we can know about the world is due to, and arises from, our mental processes of interpretation—our perceptions, our logical deductions, and our reasonings. If we like to phrase it so, the human mind creates the universe; for only by mental activity can the universe be interpreted and explained. Does it not then strike us as a curious form of suicide or self-stultification that the mind interpreting the universe should interpret it as a mindless universe? Why should we, who look before and after, who are gifted with consciousness and endowed with reason, solemnly fashion as the arbiter of our destiny an abstract Energy or Will which has no consciousness, which does not know what it is doing, and which acts absolutely irrationally? Is not this—I will not say to exchange one uncertainty for another—but to replace God by Mumbo-Jumbo?

As a matter of fact, the present attitude of thoughtful men and women is wholly averse from any such mood of pessimism and despair. Its spirit is rather that of Mr. Britling in Mr. Wells's novel, who at the end of a number of mental changes came to the conclusion that our sons —in the passionate ardour of their self-sacrifice—are enabling us to find God. Let us also add that Mr. Hardy himself has his sunnier moods. The characters of his drama are something more than puppets; and the Spirit of the Pities is at least as notable a creation as the Spirits Sinister and Ironic. Perhaps, after the convulsion of an appalling war, the wounded heart of man may turn for healing and guidance—in all humility and faith—to " a Divinity who shapes our ends, rough-hew them how we will "—a God of Goodness and Justice and Mercy.

ARISTOPHANES, THE PACIFIST

I

ANCIENT ATHENS AND HER PEACE PARTY

WHEN Athens, led by her incomparable statesman Pericles, had resolved to make war upon Sparta, her citizens were by no means unanimous in favour of fighting. There existed strong parties within the State which were especially hostile to Pericles, and there was an organised peace faction which sought various occasions to give effect to its views. Moreover, there was a young, energetic and virile writer, Aristophanes, who took every occasion in his power to prove to his fellow-citizens that their State was not developing in the direction of its best and highest ideals, but slowly deteriorating from what it had been a few years previously. The views of Aristophanes himself were those of the Moderate Party in Athens, whose natural leader was Nicias, a party which occupied an intermediate place between the old thorough-going aristocrats whose memories lay in the past, and the ardent leaders of the democracy who were innovators, and, from a Conservative point of view, destructive revolutionaries. The great merit of Pericles himself was that he, owing to his extra-ordinary strength of character, stood to a large extent above these civic factions. He was technically the leader of the democracy, for he saw clearly enough that the only possible line of development for Athens was to give more and more power to the people. But, as Thucydides tells us, in name Athens might have been a democracy, but in reality it was a beneficent despotism wielded by Pericles. Nevertheless, it was Pericles who had commenced the changes which so afflicted Aristophanes' soul, and though the dramatist is never extravagantly violent in his refer-ences to the great statesman, as he is to his successors, Cleon and others, it is impossible not to see how alien in thought and temper were his political theories from those which had been illustrated by the Periclean reforms.

31

Now it is very remarkable that when Athens went to war with her great rival Sparta she should have allowed her brilliant writer of comedies to abuse the existing government, and to inculcate on every occasion the blessings of peace. It says a great deal for the Athenian democracy that they could thus keep their admiration for Aristophanes absolutely separate from their political convictions. Clearly they did not believe in literary censorship, nor, indeed, in any real censorship in political matters. There is no doubt that Aristophanes was indicted by Cleon on a charge of being unpatriotic, and that this charge was thrown out so that it never came for actual trial.[1] It was a scurrilous age, we must remember, an age in which public figures could be satirised on the stage with impunity, even under their own names. This was the licence enjoyed by the older comedy—a comedy of men like Eupolis and Cratinus and Aristophanes himself. At a later period, when the democracy was less sure of itself, personalities began to disappear, but in 425 B.C. and even before that date, actors could appear representing some foremost figure of the time with personal characteristics duly made patent to the least observant eye.

§ 1

The earliest of Aristophanes' comedies which we possess is *The Acharnians*, but it was preceded by two others, both remarkable in their way as indicating the line which the poet intended to take. The earliest of all, which Aristophanes did not produce in his own name, was called *The Banqueters*, and was a social comedy of much the same nature as the subsequent piece called *The Clouds*. It was an attack on the modern education. A father has two sons, one educated according to the good old-fashioned way of the country, the other brought up at Athens. Naturally enough, when the Athenian-bred man comes back to his father his manners and customs shock the old conservative. He is effeminate in his dress, wearing ringlets—a thing which Aristophanes could not endure— he has learnt to drink and to revel, above all, he has had a sophistical education which upsets the old notions of right and wrong and replaces them by such ideas as convention and expediency. For in the happier age already

[1] *See* Aristoph., *Acharn.*, 377–82.

gone by the type of Athenian " who had fought at Marathon " was a simple creature who loved his farm in the country, worshipped his old gods, thought that the whole object of education was the formation of character, not the development of witty analysis, and believed in the old heroic legends as they were treated by Homer and Æschylus.

After *The Banqueters* Aristophanes brought out a piece called *The Babylonians*, which dealt with a much more daring theme. Here the object of Aristophanes was to protest against the method in which Athens ruled her tributary States. Owing to the valour and energy which she had exhibited in the Persian Wars, Athens was naturally entrusted with the command of the fleet which had to protect the islanders of the Ægean against foreign barbarians. First of all the islands contributed actual ships to the Athenian marine; then it was found easier to contribute money, and a fixed assessment was made of payments to the common treasury held at Delos. It can easily be seen how Athens, from being one amongst a number of States, *prima inter pares*, gradually slipped into the position of a paramount State. The tributes from the islanders helped to make her wealthy; she became a sovereign, or rather a despot city, having a great confederation under her which she soon learnt to tax at her will. Now in Aristophanes' eyes such an evolution was wholly in the wrong direction, and it would seem that in *The Babylonians* he did not hesitate to say that the exactions on tributary States were unjust and excessive, and that in point of fact the Allies, who came over to the great Dionysiac festival at which this comedy was produced, had very reasonable complaints to make against their suzerain. The truth, according to the comic poet, was that Athens, greedy of flattery, listened only to venal and extravagant orators who, praising her to her heart's content, led her along paths fatal to her sense of justice and her older ethical notions.[1] As a mere matter of history, about this time [2] a very distinguished " modern " orator called Gorgias came at the head of an embassy from Leontini and made an extraordinary impression on the Athenian populace by a new kind of oratory, full, as we

---

[1] Aristoph., *Knights*, 1111–19, *Acharn.*, 634–5.
[2] B.C. 427. Cf. Thuc., iii., 86. It is curious that Thucydides does not mention Gorgias, but Diodorus does (xii. 53).

should say, of purple patches. There is little doubt that Aristophanes had this incident in mind when he complained that the Athenian Demos was so easily seduced by new-fangled eloquence.

Here, at all events, was a distinct attack made by a daring young poet against one of the most powerful of contemporary statesmen, Cleon. Cleon so understood it, and because the play was exhibited at the great Dionysia when foreigners were present he indicted Aristophanes for an unpatriotic insult to the Demos and the Council. A charge of treason seems to have been preferred, but the Council refused to entertain it, thinking probably that the satire of a comic poet, even though directed against public measures of the State, was an unfit subject for a criminal proceeding. When later on Aristophanes refers to this matter in *The Acharnians* he refuses to adopt any apologetic attitude, and claims that, so far from being an insult, his satire was most beneficial to Athens. There was nothing really unpatriotic in his attitude, he maintains, because, while so far as Athenian public life was concerned, he aimed only at what was right and just, so far as his ideals went, he longed for that union of all Greeks, that Pan-Hellenic unity, which was in no small measure attained in the great days of Marathon and Salamis. At the same time he does not hesitate to utter his own likes and dislikes. He loathes the demagogues, the informers, the sophists; he cannot endure the War Party any more than he can tolerate the fashion in which Euripides' plays had lowered the old heroic tragedy to the common levels of every-day life.

§ 2

In what has been said we have already anticipated the first Aristophanic comedy which has come down to us—*The Acharnians*. *The Banqueters* (Δαιταλεῖς) was brought out in 427 B.C.; *The Babylonians* (Βαβυλώνιοι) in 426 B.C. The date of *The Acharnians* (Αχαρνῆς) is 425 B.C. From the beginning to end it is a strong plea for Peace. Despite its jesting tone, its raillery, political and social, and an abundance of farcical incidents, it has a very serious undercurrent—as, indeed, was usually the case with the comedies of the earlier period when men were allowed to say what they liked and stigmatise as they chose prominent politicians and the public policy of the State.   The war had now been going on for five or six years, and though the possession of sea-power enabled the Athenians to raid the Peloponnesian coasts, Athens herself had been devastated by the plague—a calamity from which she took long to recover, and which deprived her of her most valuable asset, her statesman Pericles.   Moreover, the citizens, cooped up in the city, had been forced to see their land despoiled by invading armies under the command of the Spartan King.   Bœotia, too, had been the scene of a great reverse which strengthened the hands of the peace party, and probably gave an opportunity for Nicias and the moderates to make themselves heard as against the democrat Cleon and Lamachus, the soldier, whose business was war.   The story of the play is of the simplest. Dicæopolis, an honest countryman, absolutely tired with the war, determines to make terms with Sparta on his own account, and gets an unfortunate man who had been driven out of the ecclesia because he dared to utter the word " peace," to go over to the enemy and get from him samples of the kind of pacification offered—for ten years or twenty or thirty as the case may be.   The men of Acharnæ are very angry with him, because they want compensation for their destroyed vineyards.   But Dicæopolis is quite unmoved by their fury, and when the samples arrive he is so pleased with the flavour of a Thirty Years' truce that he at once concludes a treaty direct with Sparta for himself and his family.   Poor Lamachus is of course left out in the cold : there is no peace for him any more than for the rest of the Athenian citizens.   But Dicæopolis enjoys all the blessings which the others lack and holds high festival as the play ends.

The comedy won a first prize, although it is not one of Aristophanes' best.   But the real interest lies not in the action of the play, but in the circumstances in which it was brought out.   What would be the public attitude in England if some dramatist were to produce a piece strongly recommending an immediate cessation of hostilities and pacification with Germany ?   We assuredly should not be so tolerant as the Athenian Demos, nor should we be at all inclined to admit the poet's plea that he was really seeking the good of his country, and was therefore a better patriot than the advocates of war.   The censor would not permit such a performance; it would seem like treachery to the

Commonwealth. How comes it then that public opinion in Athens allowed in time of war a writer of comedies to pose as what we call a Pacifist ? The answer turns partly on the past history of Athens, partly on the view taken of the social function of comedy.

Let us take the second point first, because it illustrates a deep divergence of view entirely separating a play enacted at Athens from a play in a modern capital. Every one is aware that there were rude merrymakings connected with the Dionysiac festival, out of which probably both tragedy and comedy evolved. But the point about comedy is that it retained throughout its original free-spoken and somewhat licentious character. Rude banter, merciless criticism, flagrant personalities marked all the older comedy which flourished throughout the greater portion of the Peloponnesian War to about 404 B.C. At the time of the festivals of the great Dionysia and the Lenæa the Athenian populace accepted it as their right to see a joyous, irresponsible, and also critical kind of " revue," as we might term it, and since it had many links of connection with their religious worship they were not likely to tolerate much change in its nature or its pretensions. The two characteristic notes which distinguish ancient comedy were, first, the extraordinary liberty allowed to the dramatist for ridiculing and criticising institutions of the State and personages of public importance, and, secondly, an unmistakable serious underplay of thought, the dramatist intending to show himself not only as a critic, but as also a kind of moral reformer—pointing out what, in his opinion, were errors, drawbacks, dangers which affected the community at large and required alteration and reform. Thus Athenian comedy was a thoroughly democratic institution, and, indeed, could only have been possible in a thoroughgoing democracy. The citizens were not at all likely to allow any one to curtail its functions, for it held much the same relation to the life and views of the community at large as modern journalism does to the body politic of modern times. It strikes one nevertheless as somewhat paradoxical that Aristophanes, who disliked the democracy, should use a great instrument of democratic criticism to point out democratic errors. Primarily the object of the poet was to make people laugh; secondarily it was to instruct, to warn, to suggest certain morals. Aristophanes was well equipped for both functions, and hence he was allowed a freedom which was all the more remarkable because we know it to have offended leaders of the democracy like Cleon himself.

But that is not the only ground on which we can exonerate Aristophanes from any charge of unpatriotically recommending peace when his own country was at war. Great changes, social and political, had been going on in Athens since the times of Miltiades and Themistocles. As long as there was a common danger due to the possibility of Persian invasions Greece might remain united, but when, owing largely to the success of her naval commanders, the peril of the Mede was removed, Greece relapsed into that fatal division of State against State, together with all the jealousies that naturally arose between communities at imperfect stages of development, which we know from history to be the main reason why the prosperity of Greece herself was so short-lived. Athens gradually increased her power, to the dismay of Sparta, who thought the supremacy should belong to herself, while gradually, too, the transference of political authority from the old aristocratic families to merchants who had made their money in trade and commerce, metamorphosed Athens herself from a sort of oligarchy to a frankly democratic status.

Thus, instead of leaders like Aristides and Cimon, we get Pericles and Ephialtes as a first stage of democratic development, and then the newer kind of demagogues, such as Cleon and Hyperbolus. Of course, there were many conservatives who deplored these changes. Some, like Nicias, felt them to be inevitable, and believed it to be their duty still to offer their services loyally to the State, while others belonging to a Tory division did not hesitate at times to plot with the enemies of Athens, and especially to intrigue against Pericles, whom they held to be mainly responsible for the change. The outbreak of war between Athens and Sparta gave them fresh grounds for their indignation, and if the later years of Pericles' life were embittered by the constantly repeated attacks of his enemies, no small responsibility lay on the shoulders of the old aristocrats who hated alike Pericles, the war, and the Athenian democracy. Now, although Aristophanes did not belong altogether to the intractable section of aristocrats, he certainly had full sympathy with the moderate party headed by Nicias, and seems honestly to have believed that the hands of the clock could be put

back, and Greece and Athens restored to the position they
occupied at the time of the Persian Wars. He disliked
the idea of Athens as a tyrant State, governing dependencies with an iron hand. He hated the bitter hostility
that had arisen between Athens and Sparta, and thought
that they ought to be united in a Pan-Hellenic community.
Above all, he loathed the vulgarity of the new democracy,
its love of talk, its greed for flattery, its passion for litigation, and the low stamp of public men which it produced.
Holding such convictions with intense earnestness Aristophanes had also the great advantage of being in a position,
as writer of comedies, to inculcate his opinions with the
greatest freedom. Doubtless many of his contemporaries,
especially those who were wounded by his lampoons,
thought him unpatriotic. But the Athenian Demos does
not seem to have cared much whether he abused it or not
so long as he could make it laugh. Nor, indeed, was it
particularly refined in the choice of witticisms it preferred.
There is an immense amount of coarseness in the old school
of comedy, much of which, no doubt, is to be explained
as part of the usual accompaniment of Dionysiac levity.

<h2 style="text-align:center">§ 3</h2>

Aristophanes' fourth comedy, *The Knights* (424 B.C.),
illustrates still more clearly the boldness of the satirist
and the absolute licence claimed for comedy in Athens.
It is an attack—direct, unsparing and bitter—against
Cleon in the heyday of his prosperity, and probably
because it is a fearless challenge it was produced by the
author, unlike the three which had preceded it, under
his own name. In order to understand it, however, we
must refer to events which had occurred a few months
before the play appeared, and which must therefore have
been fresh in the memory of the public. They form an
oddly interesting story.

By a curious concatenation of accidents, Athens had
won one of her greatest triumphs in the war, and Cleon
had attained one of the greatest successes in his career.
There was a daring Athenian commander, full of initiative
and resource, called Demosthenes, who shared with Nicias
the respect of all good citizens. He joined, apparently in
an unofficial capacity, an Athenian fleet which was sailing
round the Peloponnesian coast on its way to Corcyra.

Either because he had a quick eye for good defensible positions, or because he had been advised by some friendly Messenians, he fixed upon Pylos, on the western side of the Peloponnese, as a post it might be worth while to fortify.[1]   In front of it lay the island Sphacteria, leaving two channels of approach, north and south, to the bay which, in modern times, goes by the name of Navarino. The commanders of the expedition would not listen to Demosthenes, but fortune favoured his scheme.   Owing to bad weather the fleet was unable to leave the harbour, and the soldiers amused themselves in the interval by building a rough sort of fort on the mainland.   When the weather cleared the rest of the fleet sailed on their way, leaving Demosthenes with five ships to carry on his project as he pleased.   The Spartans, meanwhile, had received news of this affront to their mainland and dispatched some of their best troops to eject the daring invader.   Demosthenes promptly sent two of his five ships to recall the fleet, and with the remaining three succeeded in holding his own until the return of the main Athenian squadron, which not only drove the Spartan ships out of the harbour, but also managed to isolate and surround a considerable body of the enemy in the island of Sphacteria.   Now the troops imprisoned in the island consisted of the flower of Spartan aristocracy with their attendant Helots, and the peril they were running was so obvious and insistent that the proud Lacedæmonian city felt herself obliged to send envoys to Athens to ask for terms.   Thanks to Cleon, always an ardent supporter of the war, the terms were rejected, and impossible counter-conditions demanded, which, as Cleon well knew, were bound to be refused.

The siege of Sphacteria, however, dragged somewhat, and the Athenians, growing impatient, were inclined to censure Cleon for making them refuse the enemy's offer. But the demagogue was quite undismayed.   " If our Generals were only men," he cried, pointing to Nicias, " the affair would have been over long ago.   If I were in command, I would promise to bring the Spartans captive to Athens within twenty days."   " Then why don't you take command ? " was the quick Athenian retort, and Nicias, making one of the many mistakes in his reputedly blameless life, seconded the request of the Assembly by offering to resign his generalship in Cleon's favour.   Now

[1] Thuc., iv. 3.

Cleon was not a fighter, he was only a man of words, and would naturally decline the dangerous office, but feeling that he was fairly trapped he made the best of what seemed a bad business by asking that Demosthenes should be associated with him in the command. It is possible also that he knew—what the Athenian Assembly did not know [1]—that Demosthenes had already prepared a plan which he was on the point of carrying into execution.

Everything is fortuitous and strange in this curious story, and not the least of the happy accidents was that a mere chance had deprived the Spartans of their best means of resistance. Sphacteria was a densely wooded island, in which the attack would generally be inferior to the defence. But a party of soldiers had landed in order to cook a meal, and the fire, helped by a strong wind, had spread far and near, until the woods were ablaze and destroyed. Thus Demosthenes saw that his opportunity had come, and Cleon on his arrival at Pylos found everything ready for the assault. The island being now bared of its trees the Athenian soldiers, mostly consisting, it would seem, of light armed troops, were in a better position to attack the enemy. Yet even so the resistance was desperate. The Spartan hoplites, although gradually driven to the extremity of the island, fought with all their usual courage, and if it had not been for the good advice of a Messenian leader it is doubtful whether even now Demosthenes would have been successful. But the Messenian suggested to him that there was a practicable path leading round the rear of the Spartan army, and Demosthenes, only too glad to avail himself of the chance thus offered, sent round a small division so as to enclose the enemy between two fires. The result was that the Spartans, exhausted by the protracted struggle of the day and enfeebled by lack of food, were forced to surrender after having first consulted with their comrades on the mainland. So after all Cleon's " insane boast "—the epithet is Thucydides' own—was fulfilled, and the demagogue had the immense satisfaction of returning to Athens within the twenty specified days, bringing his prisoners with him. No event made a greater stir throughout Greece than this victory at Sphacteria, for the tradition was that the Spartan hoplites, like the Old Guard at Waterloo, might die but would never surrender, and the discovery that under

[1] Thuc., iv. 29.

severe pressure they could be conquered by the Athenians was an entire reversal of public opinion. Cleon himself received the honours usually accorded to a benefactor of the State, being presented with a golden crown and given the foremost seat at all public spectacles. So far as we are aware, no similar honours were granted to Demosthenes, although it is clear from Thucydides' narrative that it was his enterprise and forethought which had really secured the victory.

This striking Athenian triumph took place in the late summer or early autumn of 425 B.C., and in the following February (424) Aristophanes' comedy, *The Knights*, was produced at the Lenæan festival. Doubtless Cleon, sitting in the foremost seat, was present on the occasion, and it is not unlikely that Demosthenes also was there, although Nicias had taken an early opportunity of leaving Athens with a fleet, being, as was only natural, disgusted with the turn which events had taken. And it was precisely at the moment when Cleon was at the culmination of his glory that Aristophanes delivered his bitterest attack on the successful demagogue. Nothing could be more directly incisive than the satire of the play. The sovereign State of Athens, the all-powerful Demos, is represented as an old man, almost in his dotage, who has surrendered himself and his household affairs into the hands of a slave. He has, as a matter of fact, three slaves, but only one of these is powerful, the one who goes under the title of Paphlagon, and who is in reality Cleon. The other two are actually given their proper names—they are Nicias and Demosthenes, the tried servants of Demos, who find themselves ousted and bullied by the rascally Paphlagonian steward. In all probability the masks which the actors wore were made up into some easily recognisable presentment of the two generals, while Cleon's mask was more disguised. Aristophanes, however, is not going to allow any one to miss the point of his attack, for he puts into the mouth of a fellow-slave the complaint that Paphlagon had stolen his cake—a direct allusion to recent events at Pylos and the transference of the fruits of victory from the real to the pretended victor. Moreover, the Knights, who form the chorus of the play, were known to be hostile to Cleon, and had quite recently made the demagogue disgorge a bribe offered to him by one of the confederate States in order that he might secure some remission in their tribute to Athens.[1] Every point must have told in this vigorous drama. Nicias and Demosthenes, putting their heads together, discover that the only way to get rid of their pestilent fellow-slave is to secure some rival with a louder voice, a larger vocabulary of abuse, and a more abundant set of oracles to produce at critical moments, than Cleon. The last is a curious personal touch which must refer to Cleon's style of oratory. It was probably his habit to fortify his opinions and judgments by quoting on his side oracular utterances, supposed to support his policy. Fortunately for the two conspirators, a leather-lunged sausage-seller comes on the scene, who is exactly the man they require for their purpose. The sausage-seller defeats Cleon every time, and quickly supplants him in his master's favour. And Demos himself, rescued from his tyrant, at once recovers his youth and regains his normal reasonableness.

We can imagine the feelings of the real Cleon, who began by being a seller of leather, when he not only saw himself travestied as a Paphlagonian slave, but witnessed his oratorical defeat by a vulgar braggart, seller of black-puddings, who could beat him at his own game. But when we reflect that so daring a play, with so stinging a caricature of a prominent politician, could be enacted amidst the laughter of an Athenian crowd, we are forced, I think, to the conclusion that though Cleon might wield considerable power, he had by no means won either the respect or the affection of his fellow-citizens. In other words, Mitford and Thirlwall are more to be trusted when they follow the views of Thucydides and Aristophanes in dealing with these events, than Grote, who in his zealous defence of democratical principles stretches too many points in favour of the ardent demagogue Cleon.

§ 4

Meanwhile the war went on with varying fortunes. Aristophanes, in the year after the production of *The Knights*, brought out *The Clouds* (423 B.C.) and *The Wasps* (422 B.C.). Neither of these is immediately concerned with the course of hostilities. The first is an attack on the modern education prevalent in Athens, and is a continuation, therefore, of the main thesis of *The Banqueters*.

---

[1] Aristoph., *Acharn.*, 6.

Socrates, on whom the attack principally falls, is taken as the type of such different classes of teachers and professors as the Physical Philosophers—like Anaxagoras, for example—and the sophistical instructors in rhetoric, such as Protagoras and Prodicus. The portrait which Aristophanes draws has little or no resemblance to the historic Socrates, who practically confined his teaching to ethics. The second comedy, *The Wasps*, satirises the Athenian fondness for litigation, and is therefore an attack on the paid dikasteries or jury-courts. Both plays have their importance, although not in the connection immediately before us. I pass to the comedy entitled, with Aristophanes' customary boldness, *The Peace*, which was actually prophetic, inasmuch as it appeared only a month or so before a treaty for a cessation of hostilities for fifty years was ratified.

The date of the comedy is 421 B.C., and it was enacted at the Great Dionysia, at which representatives of the Allies were present—a circumstance which would make its bold advocacy of peace with Sparta all the more remarkable. Doubtless pacifist tendencies were prevalent at the time. The various States involved were sick of the war. Athens had not succeeded so well as she had hoped after the brilliant coup at Sphacteria : Sparta, despite some excellent victories due to Brasidas, was anxious to recover the well-born prisoners who were being kept as hostages by the rival city. Brasidas was indeed one of the finest generals whom Sparta produced, and his assaults on Athenian possessions in Thrace made in the teeth of Athenian naval supremacy proved how vulnerable was that maritime Empire which had hitherto carried everything before it on the sea. It need hardly be said that Cleon, who was sent out to oppose him, was no match for the resourceful Spartan, whom Thucydides, with a touch of Attic scorn for a tongue-tied race, described as " not a bad speaker for a Lacedæmonian." But it so chanced that in some rough and disordered fighting near Amphipolis both Cleon and Brasidas were killed. The death of the two prominent advocates of war, representing the martial party in Athens and Sparta respectively, gave an opportunity for peace negotiations, of which Nicias was quick to avail himself, and the fifty-year truce which followed included a definite alliance between the two combatants. Greece, although, perhaps, a little sceptical of the future, was for the time, at all events, able to breathe again.

The *Peace* is certainly not the happiest of Aristophanes' efforts, but at least it put the situation plainly enough before the audience, and carried on the purpose of the earlier comedy, *The Acharnians*. The hero is Trygæus, an unhappy Athenian, who determines to scale the heights of heaven on the back of a beetle. Arrived at the celestial heights he discovers the gods engaged in pounding the Greek States in a mortar. He intends to stop this at all hazards, and therefore releases from the well in which she has been imprisoned the Goddess Peace. Thereupon the gods discard their pestle and mortar, and Trygæus, marrying one of Peace's handmaids, brings her with him home. It must have given sincere pleasure to Aristophanes to find that the object which he had been pursuing for some years past was now about to be realised, and that his satiric dramas had not failed in their mission.

ARISTOPHANES, THE PACIFIST

II

§ 1

THE earlier period of Aristophanes' plays end- with the
" Peace " of 421 B.C.   After that date there is a cessation
of activity on the part of the dramatist, an interval of six
years; and when Aristophanes once more steps upon the
stage his plays exhibit a slightly different tendency.   The
earlier, as we have found, are very combative and satirical,
and are animated throughout not only by a dislike of the
war party, but also by a bitter hostility against Cleon as
leading statesman of Athens.   They are, as we should
term them, distinctly topical plays.   After the peace of
Nicias they became by no means so personal or so pug-
nacious.   For instance, *The Birds*—a comedy which was
enacted in Athens in 414 B.C.—is in great measure an idyllic
piece, as though the satirist deliberately sought to draw
the attention of his audience away from the actual circumstances of the moment to a purely imaginative realm.
We are not, of course, aware why Aristophanes was silent
for six years.   Doubtless he was not inactive, but perhaps
he might have thought that, after the conclusion of a
covenant between Athens and Sparta, there was a real
chance of the spread of those principles which he had
himself espoused—under the assumption that the moderate
party had gained the victory in Athens and that no
immediate disturbance of the peace was to be expected.
If such were his thoughts, he was completely deceived.
But there also might have been other reasons, and not
least the changes in the attitude of the public towards
productions of comedy.   For we know that when, in
414 B.C., *The Birds* was produced, there had come into
existence a new law, said to be introduced by a certain
Syracosius, prohibiting personal attacks on prominent
individuals in the State.   His fellow-dramatists, Ameipsias

45

and Phrynichus, seem to have grumbled at the restriction placed on their activity as satirists. Aristophanes chose the wiser part and altered the character of comedy in order to make it more fantastic and less topical, and to give the Athenians a flight of fancy rather than a diatribe on contemporary events.

Athens was rarely in lack of great men during the Peloponnesian War. She commenced it under the control of one of the greatest of her citizens, Pericles, and though her prestige as a State was decidedly lowered by a man like Cleon, her generals, Nicias and especially Demosthenes, were efficient and, on the whole, fairly successful. And then, after Cleon's death, there arose into power one of the greatest characters in Athenian history—Alcibiades —whose growing reputation fills all the interval from the peace of Nicias to the Sicilian expedition. Alcibiades was a man whose versatile gifts and always juvenile audacity can very easily be misinterpreted, especially if we look only at the character of the influence he exercised over Athens. There is no doubt whatsoever that Athens would have been safer in the hands of a staid and moderate man, less brilliant and less able, but possessed of those qualities of good sense and self-control which would have enabled him to guide his city with reasonable safety through a period of crisis. For in a certain definite fashion Alcibiades was the ruin of Athens. He led her along paths which were exceedingly dangerous for a city in her circumstances; and he abandoned her rather than undergo a charge of impiety which, perhaps, he felt himself unable to meet. He became a traitor when he betrayed her to Sparta, and gave advice to the enemy which enabled him to win success after success. Only towards the close of his career did he manage to atone for his delinquencies when, through the latest period of the Peloponnesian War, he did what he could to enable Athens to carry on her desperate struggle with diminished armies against a circle of foes.

There is one characteristic about prominent Greeks which always strikes one with amazement. They seem to be inspired with the most burning patriotism, but directly anything goes wrong, if they fall out of favour, they do not hesitate to join the ranks of the foes. This had been the case with Themistocles and a good many others of less importance. It was also the case with Alcibiades. One significant exception is furnished by the historian Thucydides. He had failed to arrest the progress of Brasidas in Thrace and had lost his command. But the only form which his revenge took was to write a most dispassionate account of the whole war, in which he does ample justice to his native city and is proudly silent on the subject of his own disgrace. Most of the Greek statesmen were not formed in this mould. If we give the best interpretation to their conduct we shall have to say that they were so enamoured of their native State that they could not bear for a moment the thought that she was listening to counsels other than their own. From this point of view they would act like discarded lovers, with a bitterness as acute as their original passion. For all practical purposes, however, they have little enough excuse for their perfidy, and we can hardly help judging them as we should all traitors who allow personal feelings to overpower their sense of patriotic duty.

§ 2

Alcibiades was a young aristocrat. He had some family connection with Pericles. He was by general consent the most brilliant young Athenian of his day, headstrong, violent, ambitious, lavish in personal expenditure, prodigal in the arts of the demagogue, but with apparently a real sense of the power and dignity of Athens and a genuine desire to see her flourish. But the thought of an Athenian triumph in which he did not share was gall and bitterness to him. For to his eager and wide-ranging intelligence, if Athens was to become the mistress of the Hellenic world he must be the chief man of Athens, an acknowledged despot after the fashion of the older tyrants, whose word was law. His family had some Laconian associations, but when Alcibiades, then quite a young man, made over-tures to Sparta that he should represent her and her interests in Athens, the Spartans very naturally came to the con-clusion that he was too young and too untrustworthy to discharge such important functions. This was an insult which Alcibiades never forgave, and from this moment he took every opportunity of embroiling the relations between the two leading States in Greece.

Rapidly it was discovered that the peace of Nicias was no peace; that it only brought at most a temporary cessa-tion from hostilities. Intrigues began and multiplied, in which Argos and the Peloponnese were largely involved, and though Athens and Sparta were nominally allies this did not prevent them from working with no small amount of energy to do each other the utmost injury in their power. And through it all Alcibiades was the leading influence, or perhaps rather the baleful star. In his wide and lofty imagination the time had now come for a new policy, a policy as far removed from the sage restraint imposed by Pericles as its author, Alcibiades, was from the character of his grave and eminent kinsman. The new policy was, indeed, startling in its audacity. Athens was to extend her conquests in the west, Sicily might be subdued, Carthage might be attacked, the whole coast-line of the Mediterranean, as far as the Pillars of Hercules, might become an Athenian Sea; and then, possessed of this world dominion, Athens might bring a crushing fleet to surround the whole of the Peloponnese, starve Sparta into submission, and become in deed and in name the Imperial power of the Greek world.[1] Naturally a moderate man like Nicias would have nothing to do with such delirious fancies, and it looked for some time as if the old weapon of ostracism was to be called in to settle the differences between Alcibiades and Nicias, in which case one of them would have been forced to retire from active service for the State. But at the last moment popular criticism was turned upon a comparative nonentity, Hyperbolus. Both parties united their forces against this unpopular specimen of demagogue, and Hyperbolus was driven into exile. In many ways it was an unfortunate decision, for it left the city a prey to contending factions. In the older days Athens would have freed herself by a decisive vote; now she accepted a kind of compromise which by no means cured the evils to be feared from two bitterly opposed parties in the State.

The chance for which Alcibiades had been looking forward duly arrived. Envoys from Sicily came to implore the help of Athens in aid of Egesta against a rival city, Selinus, which was being helped by Syracuse. By granting the prayer of the enyoys from Egesta, by sending some assistance to them in their need, the Athenians would at once be involved in Sicilian affairs and find admirable chances for pushing their vague and lofty dreams of conquest. Naturally, therefore, Alcibiades gave strenuous

[1] Thuc., vi. 15, vi. 90.

support to these delegates from Sicily and pointed out to his fellow-citizens at home how great would be the advantage if Athens, using her maritime power, were to extend her empire westward. That empire had, indeed, become a burden heavy to be borne by the islanders and the allies. The tribute from those who were supposed to be associates, but were in reality dependents, had steadily grown from a contribution of 600 talents to more than double that sum, and there was much ground for complaint as to the methods employed by a city who interpreted her Imperial responsibilities in the light of a despotic ambition. There were many in Athens herself who deplored the changes which had come over their position, and amongst them Nicias, of course, urged those principles of moderation which characterised him throughout his career. When his countrymen voted that an expedition should be sent out to Sicily, Nicias insisted that the whole discussion should be reopened on the following day. When even so the decision went against him, he sought to dissuade the Athenians by demanding a far larger force, both of men and ships, than had originally been determined. But the only result of his dilatory policy was that the Athenians granted his requests, and, in accordance with their habitual method of balancing impetuosity by caution, appointed both Alcibiades and Nicias to the command of the expedition. They added a third commander in the person of Lamachus, a brave and vigorous soldier, whose main business was the actual conduct of military operations, and who knew and cared nothing about questions of Imperial policy.

Unfortunately, just before the expedition sailed an unparalleled event occurred in Athens. In a single night the numerous marble Hermæ, rectangular statues to Hermes, which could be seen in the market-place and were erected in front of the citizens' houses, and therefore formed one of the most familiar sights in Athens, were broken and mutilated and the streets littered with fragments. Such an event was all the more mysterious because it could not have been done by a drunken band of revellers. It must have involved a large body of conspirators. Great was the indignation which prevailed at this hideous sacrilege, and Alcibiades himself, rightly or wrongly, was considered to be implicated, mainly on the ground of the reckless character of his customary associates. In the general uncertainty every citizen looked at his

E

neighbour with suspicion and dislike. Some sort of revolution was supposed to be imminent, and the absence of definite knowledge only increased the universal terror. It was a very ominous incident to occur just on the eve of a great adventure, and Alcibiades felt it so keenly that he demanded an instantaneous inquiry, proposing himself ready and anxious to meet all charges levelled against him. But the Athenians would not hear of anything which could possibly delay the sailing of their ships. They allowed Alcibiades to start, still holding his office of general, and only required his future attendance when the formal inquiry should be opened. It was in every way an unfortunate position, for it could not but place their general under the stigma of an unproved crime, a position which undermined his authority with the allies and caused no little discontent in both army and navy. The results were even more disastrous a few weeks later, for, while the generals were concerting their measures in Sicily itself, the Salaminia, or Sacred Vessel, was sent out from Athens to bring back Alcibiades to meet his accusers. So proud and fiery a character could hardly be expected to undergo the humiliation of a trial in such exceptional circumstances, and Alcibiades, perhaps in collusion with the officers of the Salaminia, escaped on his way back to Athens and took refuge in the Peloponnese. There, in order to wreak his revenge on his faithless native city, he stirred up the Spartans to join in the fighting in Sicily, and, above all, induced them to send out one of their most capable generals, Gylippus, whose arrival changed the whole fortunes of the day.

§ 3

Aristophanes' comedy, *The Birds*, is capable of several interpretations.[1] It is a romance, a flight of fancy, a poetical piece of nonsense : but it may also be an allegory and contain many deep meanings, pertinent to the time (414 B.C.) at which it was produced in Athens. The story is quite fantastic, but it is carried out with a wealth of imaginative detail and adorned with several beautiful lyrics and odes which make it one of the most fascinating

---

[1] See introduction to Aristophanes' *Birds*, by Benjamin Bickley Rogers (Bell & Sons), p. xv. Mr. Rogers' edition of Aristophanes (including his translations) are of the utmost value to the student.

of the author's plays. There are two Athenians, Peis-thetærus and Euelpides, who are disgusted with actual conditions and determine to strike out a new idea. They persuade the birds—birds are primeval things, belonging to the early stages of animate life on the globe—to build a city half-way between heaven and earth. It is called Νεφελοκοκκύγια, " Cloud-cuckoo-town." The plan suc-ceeds so well that the new city becomes a menace to heaven, for it prevents the gods from enjoying the sacrifices which come up to them from below and all the rich savours with which humanity is wont to propitiate Deity. So the gods, deprived of the usual offerings, are forced to send envoys to treat with the birds in order to get rid of the untoward menace to their felicity. Peisthetærus, the ringleader in the happy enterprise, receives the hand of Basileia, the daughter of Zeus, and all ends well.

An obvious interpretation makes the play a parable, somehow dealing with Alcibiades and the Sicilian Expedi-tion. Fantastic schemes were no doubt in the air, and the Athenian mind was excited by vast possibilities of empire. But directly we try to apply the allegory it fails us. For if the birds represent the excitable and volatile Athenians, then the gods whom they beleaguer must represent the Spartans, and that does not seem a likely supposition. Moreover, Peisthetærus and Euelpides do not in any fashion—except for their enterprising ardour—resemble Alcibiades. Or shall we say that the piece is a protest against superstition and religious fanaticism? We know that the mutilation of the Hermæ, with which Alcibiades was supposed to be concerned, produced an almost in-describable commotion and much underground activity on the part of informers and spies. It also was the main cause why Alcibiades was recalled from Sicily and thus indirectly invalidated the chances of success. But it is difficult to see any vital connection between Athenian fanaticism and the story of Aristophanes' play unless we force an unreal analogy between Peisthetærus, who defies the gods and succeeds, and the ordinary Athenian, who is a prey to mystical terrors.

Probably there are two different trains of thought recognisable in *The Birds*. There is undoubtedly a satirical element, for Aristophanes seems to be criticising and laugh-ing at the rash caprices of his countrymen, which were often allowed to override the dictates of law and order.

And the play seems, too, to contain or suggest the wistful dreams of the idealist who, instead of turning his thoughts as usual to an Athens of the past, prefers for the nonce to sketch the outlines of a new and wonderful Athens, a city in the clouds which shall be both pure and prosperous. Very likely, however, it only argues dull brains to try to explain an airy exercise of the imagination, a piece of fantasy and romance which defies analysis and is its own best justification. The lyrical motive was always strong in Aristophanes, and the outpouring of song and melody in the chants of the birds lifts the play far above the prosaic level of mere reason or the debates of contemporary politics.

§ 4

The interval between the production of *The Birds* and that of *Lysistrata* represents the culmination of the great tragedy of the Sicilian Expedition. In the autumn of 413 B.C. rumours began to arrive at Athens of the appalling catastrophe that had befallen not only the original expedition under Nicias, but the subsequent one which had been sent out under the command of Demosthenes. The details of the story as they are narrated to us by Thucydides would carry us too far from our subject. In themselves they form a most arresting story, a story in which Fate seems to have decided everything against the luckless Athenians. But, of course, when we look at it more closely the tragedy resolves itself into the failure of individuals, combined, perhaps, with the original impossibility of the whole scheme. In Athens herself probably little was known of the real conditions of Sicily, nor in her confidence in her fleet was there any suspicion that the considerable distance between the actual scene of war and the bases of supply was bound to be prejudicial to chances of victory. Perhaps Alcibiades might have carried the scheme through, but, as we have seen, he had been transformed from an Athenian general into an enemy of his native city, and all his talents, which without doubt made him the most conspicuous man in the Greek world, were employed to help the cause of Sparta. It was, as we have seen, owing to the advice of Alcibiades that the Lacedæmonians sent Gylippus to Syracuse, who, such is the magnetism of a single great personality, transformed the whole situation.

When we have to reckon up the faults of individuals, the glaring incompetence of Nicias must be placed on the highest plane; and it provokes no little wonder that Athens herself refused to mistrust him, declined to recall him when he wanted to be recalled, and persisted in thinking that he was not only a trustworthy, but an energetic commander. It was Nicias' fatal inertia which made Athenian success impossible. To this we must add the Athenian general's insane superstition. At the critical moment of his fate he refused to move the expeditionary force out of the great harbour of Syracuse owing to the fears excited by an eclipse. Delay, procrastination, feebleness, these were the chief marks of Nicias' leadership, and all we can say of him is that, at the end, despite illness and despair, he showed the virtues of a courageous man. Unfortunately, he involved in his own downfall the ruin of a much more efficient general than he was—Demosthenes. Left to his own resources, Demosthenes would at least have been able to carry away in safety the remnants of the expedition, if he had not succeeded in some brilliant attack upon the foe. But, alas! Nicias' counsels were all against activity and daring, and the melancholy result was that, after the destruction of their fleet, the Athenian armies, trying to escape inland, were overwhelmed and forced to surrender. Both Nicias and Demosthenes were put to death while the Athenian prisoners were sent to work as underground slaves in Syracusan stone-quarries.

§ 5

It was the most overwhelming catastrophe which had ever occurred in Greek history. The flower of the Athenian fleet and armies, the most splendid armaments that had ever left an Hellenic harbour, had been annihilated. Political and military leaders alike had perished. The ruin was so complete, so totally unexpected, that at first no one in Athens could believe it. Slowly the truth filtered throughout the population, and Athens woke from her dream of empire to find herself confronted by imminent extinction. The triremes which were left were few and by no means serviceable. Little enough money remained to equip new ones. The allies were everywhere breaking away, rejoicing in the opportunity to break a yoke that had become hateful to them. No city ever had so tremendous a task as Athens saw before her eyes at the opening of 412 B.C. Hopeless and demoralised though they were, the citizens set themselves to do all that was possible. Surrender was never talked about. As Thucydides tells us, they determined that they would not give in.[1] Two of the measures which they undertook were, first, the creation of a sort of Committee of Public Safety, a Board of ten Probuli, an oligarchical institution; and second, the conversion into practical use of a reserve sum in the Acropolis. Happily enough, at the very outset of the war the sum of a thousand talents had been set aside to be used only in the event of an actual attack upon the city by a hostile fleet. If any person suggested a resolution for diverting it to other purposes the penalty was death. But now the moment had clearly arrived when the money had to be forthwith expended; so, at the advice probably of the Probuli, the death penalty was revoked and the thousand talents were to be made available for shipbuilding purposes. It was during the year 412 B.C., the darkest period of the Peloponnesian War —darkest, at all events, before the ultimate disaster— that Aristophanes was writing the *Lysistrata*. It was produced at the commencement of the year 411 B.C., and perhaps the most marvellous thing about it was that it was ever produced at all. For Aristophanes appears once more in his character of the pacifist, suggesting the absolute necessity of peace in the Hellenic world.

In order to appreciate his courage—or, perhaps, his hold on Athenian audiences—let us attempt to realise the conditions of the time. The democracy was in alarm and despair; there was imminent danger that hostile fleets, now supported by victorious Syracusan triremes, would attack Athens in waters nearer home. The allies were everywhere revolting. The best generals, or, at all events, those whom Athens trusted most, had been killed. There was a general lack of money and of most of the munitions of war. I have already referred to two of the enactments by means of which Athens hoped to be able to provide for her defence. I mention them again because they are both alluded to in the *Lysistrata*, and, indeed, form part of the plot. The reserve fund of a thousand talents was to be made use of to build fresh triremes, and a body of ten Probuli had been appointed to watch over the immediate necessities of the State. One of these Probuli is brought

[1] Thuc, viii. 1.

forward as a State officer in Aristophanes' play. We only know the names of two—one was Hagnon, the other was called Sophocles, but whether the latter was or was not the dramatist remains uncertain. It is hardly likely that the Probulos in the play was made up to represent any particular officer, but we observe that both he and Lysistrata are anxious, for different reasons, to get possession of the thousand talents of the Acropolis—the former in order to continue the war and the latter in order to bring it to an abrupt conclusion.

The institution of the ten Probuli was undoubtedly an oligarchical measure. Indeed, one of the anxieties which at this moment was harassing the minds of Athenian democrats was the signs and evidences of an oligarchical reaction. Shortly afterwards the political revolution connected with the four hundred took place, giving a sinister significance to the people's fears. But, however hardly bested, the citizens were in no mood for peace. With the energy of despair the State had resolved on supreme sacrifices. It refused to admit the idea that it was conquered. The general attitude of the people was sullen, savage, despairing, and yet obstinate. With such a temper prevalent it seems hardly credible that Aristophanes should dare to present a farcical play with the satirical thesis that if men could not bring peace to the land, at all events the women could. Peace, urged the dramatist, was the great thing to be desired—peace, almost at any price, even the surrender of Pylos,[1] It is, however, worthy of remark that, though *Lysistrata* was intended to be farcical, both in its general plot and in the incidents it portrays, there is also a deep-lying seriousness, a grave anxiety as to the future, which reveals itself in the argument between Lysistrata and the chief magistrate. In this respect it strongly contrasts with the next play which Aristophanes produced, the *Thesmophoriazusæ*, when, thanks in no small measure to Alcibiades and a few victories of the Athenian fleet, the general condition of affairs was much improved.

§ 6

At the opening of the play Lysistrata, a young Athenian married woman, is standing alone in front of the gateway

---

[1] Cf. *Lysistrata* 1163. The Athenians still held Pylos. *Lysist.* 104.

which led to the Acropolis. She has summoned an Assembly of young married women, not only from Athens, but from Sparta, Bœotia, Corinth, and other hostile States, in order to propound a plan which she thinks will stop the war. Gradually the various deputies come in, especially Lampito from Sparta, who is soon discovered to be very friendly to Lysistrata—an allusion probably to the secret sympathy which all along seems to have existed between the Peloponnesian city and Athens. To the assembled deputies Lysistrata propounds her scheme. All these young married women are to refuse to have anything to do with their husbands until the latter make peace and put an end to the horrible war. Of course, some of the women demur to this project, and Lampito herself, though inclined to support Lysistrata, is doubtful whether peace is possible so long as there are those thousand talents stored up in Athene's Temple. Lysistrata reassures her. While she and the younger women are holding the present Assembly, some older women have been told off to seize the Acropolis where the money is kept. There is, in fact, a thoroughly organised revolt, in which the women have taken possession of the chief points of advantage.

A modern paraphrase of this play was produced in the autumn of 1910 by Miss Gertrude Kingston at the Little Theatre. Mr. Laurence Housman's version was not in any sense a translation from the original Greek, but only an adaptation; but it was very cleverly arranged for the stage, and gave an opportunity for an English audience to get some idea of Aristophanic comedy. Perhaps, therefore, it is unnecessary to enter into any details of the plot. The chorus, consisting of twenty-four persons, is divided into two portions—twelve old men and twelve old women. When they come into the orchestra, representing the supporters respectively of Lysistrata and the Probulos or chief magistrate, they have an amusing altercation, the men trying to set fire to the defences organised by the women and the women retaliating by throwing pails of water over the men. The Probulos himself comes forward at the end of the quarrel and a long debate ensues between him and Lysistrata, the poet, of course, speaking by the mouthpiece of his heroine and describing the reforms which, in his opinion, are necessary in the State. Perhaps because of the exigencies of the time Aristophanes carefully refrains from anything savouring of mere partisanship.

What he recommends is what would be recommended by any patriot—that is to say, the removal of abuses, the suppression of party intrigue, and a union of all loyal citizens in hearty co-operation and goodwill. Then, after the chorus once more have been seen in altercation, an interval of five days is supposed to elapse. By this time the separation of the sexes has become an evil too great to be borne, and there are evident signs that sooner or later one of the two parties must give way. Lysistrata has no little difficulty in preventing some of the young women in her company from being the first to abandon their programme, and a young wife, Myrrhina, has a long interview with her husband—apparently permitted by Lysistrata—which looks compromising. Nevertheless, though she seems on the point of succumbing, Myrrhina finally escapes back into the Acropolis. But the end has already been reached. Deputies come from Sparta meeting deputies also from Athens, and the women have clearly gained the day. Lysistrata, as usual, admonishes both sides, and manages to effect an arrangement which ensures peace, the play ending with the usual festive banquet and general expressions of amity. It is a witty and highly paradoxical play, disfigured by much indecency from our point of view, but in that respect not differing from other Aristophanic comedies. It must have had a curious effect in Athens on the eve of an oligarchical reaction, while the city was strenuously endeavouring, even with her diminished resources, to carry on the war.

For *Lysistrata*, as we have seen, was brought out at the time when intrigues were on foot to replace the existing democracy by other forms of government. Peisander was the leader of the revolution, who, shortly after the play had been produced, came to Athens from the camp at Samos in order to organise the oligarchy. Aristophanes, of course, could not have disliked the tendency of the time, for he was never a friend to the democracy and probably thought that any change might be for the better. But his primary desire was for peace—peace at any price, peace to be obtained by the women if the men were incapable to secure it.

§ 7

With the *Lysistrata*, however, the series of peace-comedies comes to a close, and overwhelming external events seem to have closed the advocate's mouth. The *Thesmophoriazusæ*, which only appeared a few months later than *Lysistrata*, has no politics in it. It is a satire on women and on Aristophanes' old butt, Euripides, but no question is raised touching Athens' policy. Besides, the oligarchical conspirators had begun their reign of terror, and, though the note of the comedy is fairly joyous —for Athens had won some victories—it was clearly not a time to jest with the authorities.

Perhaps, however, the most pathetic of all the comedies, if we look at it in connection with the moment at which it was produced, is the well-known and deservedly popular piece called *The Frogs*. The date was 405 B.C. Athens was entering upon her last agony, making her final efforts to stave off ruin. Eight months later was fought the fatal battle of Ægospotami. Fifteen months afterwards Lysander captured Athens and the Peloponnesian War was at an end. What could a comic poet do at such a time but attempt to turn away men's minds from the terror of approaching defeat, and with a desperate earnestness work to make them laugh ? It was a vain attempt, probably, but Aristophanes did his best. He made his frogs croak their immortal strain, " Brekekekex Koax, Koax." He showed his fellow-citizens how bereft of true poets was their native city and how necessary it was to feed their minds on the great names of the past. Dionysus goes down to Hades to bring back a poet from the shades. For the vacant throne of tragedy Æschylus and Euripides have an amusing contest, and the victory is decreed to the older dramatist—Æschylus, who fought for the Greeks against the Persians and who represented that happier time of Hellenic unity to which Aristophanes' thoughts are always fondly turning. Thus the comedy is in reality a literary criticism and nothing else, in which the poet illustrates once more his inveterate dislike of the " modern " dramatist who had brought down tragedy from heaven to earth. Cleon, the demagogue ; Socrates, the sophist ; Euripides, the realist — these represent the permanent hates of Aristophanes. He certainly could hate well and in all probability he was unjust to all three, certainly to the two latter and perhaps also to the first. In any general estimate, however, of Aristophanes we must not forget that, apart from his strongly-marked satiric tendency, with which I have been principally concerned, he was one of the most indubitable of poets. He sang songs of ethereal beauty, and his " native wood-notes wild " had no little of the unstudied charm and spontaneity of Shakespeare.

DEMOSTHENES AND THE PRINCIPLES OF PATRIOTISM

I

It is one of the strange delusions of " modern " critics, especially if they happen to have a scientific training, that little of real value can be learnt from Greek and Latin classics. The uselessness of Latin and Greek had been the theme of much indignant rhetoric on the ground that the time spent over dead languages might be much more profitably spent over living ones, or, better still, devoted to science. No argument can have weight with those who have made up their minds on the subject on the one side or the other, because the question really turns on a difference of temperament, or, as we used to say, on whether a man is born an Aristotelian or a Platonist. Nevertheless, I have ventured to say that the anti-classical attitude involves a strange delusion, for the simple reason that ancient history and literature are full of " lessons " for the modern reader. Perpetually during the course of the present war we have been reminded of historic examples which seem to illustrate recent events and controversies, and though we are chary now of affirming that history goes in cycles which reproduce one another, and are more inclined to speak of progress in a rectilinear development, it cannot be denied that modern problems often seem to reproduce ancient ones—possibly because human nature remains fundamentally the same.

The questions, for instance, whether democracies can govern dependencies, whether an aristocracy or a democracy is better fitted for carrying on a prolonged war, whether autocracy or a free commonwealth is the ideal constitution for the human race, whether politicians should control generals or generals govern politicians, whether Imperialism in foreign relations is compatible with free institutions or untrammelled Parliamentary debate at home, whether

60

Socialism is or is not a practical polity—on these and many other points too numerous to mention the histories of Greece and Rome shed abundant lights. In the present paper I desire to take a concrete case. We talk a great deal about Patriotism—what it means, what consequences it involves, how it stands related to the wider feelings of what we call cosmopolitanism or internationalism. I know no better or more illuminating material for a study of this kind than is furnished by the career of Demosthenes, the Athenian patriot, in his struggle with the barbarian power of Macedon and the autocratic efficiency of Philip. From beginning to end of his speeches to the Athenian public he is for ever illustrating the claims, the duties, and the rights of a true lover of his country.

§ 1

Three notable figures in Greek history were born at about the same date—Philip of Macedon, Demosthenes, and Aristotle. The last-named was chosen by the Macedonian King as tutor for his son Alexander; Philip and Demosthenes were antagonists during the whole course of their careers. Aristotle represented the scientific and philosophical interest in which Greece was once more to show an example to the world. The sphere of politics occupied the other two men during a period of Athenian decline— which Demosthenes did his best to prevent and Philip his utmost to promote. After the end of the Peloponnesian War Athens never recovered " the first fine, careless rapture " of her prime. She had her brief moments of revival, and, indeed, as compared with the increasing degeneracy of Sparta she showed a high spirit in organising anew her naval power. She also possessed a few generals of no little brilliancy, such as Timotheus, Chares, Iphicrates, Diopithes, Phocion, who gained fitful triumphs in circumstances of considerable difficulty. But her increasing use of mercenaries—instead of native-born soldiers— and her passionate desire to keep intact her Theôric Fund so as to provide for her festivals and spectacular exhibitions when the need of the moment was for munitions of war, told their own tale. Athens had lost her energy, her initiative, her spontaneity; she was, as one of her satirists described her, " an old woman in slippers guzzling her porridge," instead of a Marathon fighter; she had all the lassitude and slackness of one stricken with an incurable and enervating malady. And here we touch the tragedy of Demosthenes' life. Himself a man of unwearied energy, with a patriotic spirit nursed on the heroic examples of the past—having Thucydides at his finger-ends and keeping constantly before his eyes the dominating figure of Pericles —he was doomed to live in an age which had outworn its older ideals and among a people who could only be galvanised by repeated shocks into anything approaching activity. Great men lack some of their greatness when they are deprived of a sympathetic environment. Their own nobility remains the same and shines the brighter, perhaps, because of its singularity. But they lose the comforting assurance of effectiveness; they do not see the results of their labours. They feel all the drawbacks of solitariness : they stand alone. The isolation of Demosthenes is one of the pathetic aspects which strike most acutely the student of his age. For the men who should have worked most closely with him, and helped his ambitions by sharing them, did not possess his large vision and could not see as clearly as he could the signs of the times. Isocrates, for instance, " the old man eloquent," and the honest Phocion ought to have stood by him. But their eyes were holden. They were utterly mistaken about the aims and character of Philip. One thinks at times of a modern statesman, the lonely Venizelos, in the midst of a decadent Greece.

Demosthenes was not a born orator. He laboriously educated himself for his high career in spite of natural disadvantages. Probably he had as a boy some sort of impediment in his speech. His voice was not strong, and we know that his rival Æschines derided him for not being athletic or a sportsman. Numerous stories are told of his rigorous self-discipline. He is said to have shut himself up in an underground chamber, having shaved one side of his face to prevent any temptation to come out in the light of day and to ensure close and continuous study. He put pebbles into his mouth and then tried to speak against the roar of incoming waves, he recited while he ran uphill, and, according to report, wrote out with his own hand Thucydides' history eight several times. We know also that he took lessons from Isæus, an orator of distinction, and there is also a tale that he was an eager listener to Plato. His earlier efforts at oratory were disastrous, and on one occasion after a failure while he was roaming in

the Piræus he was encouraged by an actor, who took him
in hand and gave him some valuable hints.   There seems
no question that he was not born great, but rather achieved
greatness by persistent industry.   His enemies declared
that his speeches were wanting in naturalness and smelt
of the midnight oil.   Indeed, one ancient critic contrasted
him with Cicero in this respect, giving to the Roman orator
the charm of spontaneity and to the Greek the merit of
elaboration and study.   However this may be, there is
no question which was the greater orator.   There is no
oration which is quite comparable with the speech of
Demosthenes " On the Crown " in the perfection of its
style, the sonority of its eloquence, and its graphic mixture
of the narrative and the rhetorical manner.   It is said
that Æschines, his antagonist on this occasion, after he
had retired from Athens, gave Demosthenes' speech for
recitation to his pupils, and when they were loud in their
expressions of admiration, remarked : " What would you
have said if you had heard the man deliver it himself ? "
If the Athenian originally spoke with difficulty, he assuredly
succeeded in conquering all obstacles.   We who only read
his words on the printed page feel the charm of his diction
and the musical rhythm of his best periods.   But his contemporary audience were aware that they were listening
to a man who combined appropriate action with a forceful
oratory which carried them off their feet, a man whose
nervous energy and eager, inspired face added weight and
charm to the noble ethical principles of his political creed.
Thucydides no doubt had taught him much, but he owed
still more to his own character and temperament.   Only
Phocion could sometimes get the better of him by his
rugged simplicity and directness.   " Here comes the man
who can split my harangues in two," Demosthenes said when
Phocion arose to address the Assembly.   It was like the
contest between Brutus and Mark Antony—only in the
reverse order, with Brutus cutting deep into Antony's
flamboyant eloquence.

§ 2

On the other hand, if Demosthenes was not a born orator,
his great adversary, Philip, was a born king and leader of
men, and had a native genius for war.   No one could have
ascended the throne in the midst of more pressing diffi-

culties and dangers than the man who succeeded Perdiccas in 359 B.C. Macedonia was encircled by foes, and the new ruler was only twenty-three years of age. On the north, the Pæonians, on the west, the Illyrians threatened incursions, and in some cases carried them out with the usual ravaging of territory. Moreover, Philip had to face two pretenders, Pausanias, supported by King Cotys of Thrace, and Argæus, who was the nominee of Athens. As against the latter city, Philip was at a great disadvantage, because he possessed no maritime towns of importance, while Athens held at this time Pydna, Methone, Potidæa and some other places in Chalcidice as well as towns in the Chersonese. Islands such as Thasos, Lemnos, Imbros were hers, and she was allied with Byzantium. Along all the northern coast of the Ægean, which has become of such importance in the present war, the influence and power of Athens, based on her fleet, were nearly supreme. Olynthus was the only State in this neighbourhood strong enough to resist her. And yet in twelve months Philip succeeded in transforming the whole situation. He defeated Argæus and the Athenians : chastised the Pæonians and Illyrians; bribed Cotys to give up the cause of Pausanias; and then, after professing friendship with the Athenians and deluding them with vague promises, turned his arms against Amphipolis, a town which Athens had always claimed as her own, and which even now the Macedonian King declared he would surrender to her in exchange for Pydna. He was naturally anxious to prevent the possibility of any armed assistance being given to Amphipolis while he was besieging the town. No sooner did it fall than he forgot his promises, changed his mind and kept both Amphipolis and Pydna for himself. His army had already been brought to a state of high military efficiency. His navy henceforth became an object of close and constant care. Naturally, as against the loose confederation of Athens with her allies, an autocratic despot like Philip possessed great advantages. This is how a little later, in his First Olynthiac oration, Demosthenes refers to this point. " The danger is that this man, with all his cleverness and unscrupulousness—making concessions here, threatening there—may convert and wrest to his use some of our main resources. He has it in his sole power to publish or conceal his designs : he is at one and the same time general, sovereign, paymaster : he accompanies his army everywhere. These are great

advantages for quick and timely operations in war." [1]
The words have a curiously modern ring. One might
almost imagine an Allied statesman in the present war
pointing out how the military autocracy of Germany helps
the Central Powers in their great campaign.

It does not appear that the Macedonian menace was very
quickly appreciated in Athens. Indeed, Demosthenes himself, who saw farther than most of his contemporaries,
hardly realised at first all that it involved. In the earliest
of his speeches to the Assembly—as distinct from his private
and legal orations—he is concerned with another peril,
one which perpetually loomed large in the imagination of
Hellenes, the peril of the Persian King. The speech,
which goes by the name Περὶ τῶν Συμμοριῶν (B.C. 354), is
a very remarkable example of Demosthenes' statesmanship.
As against those who were always preoccupied with the
possibility of Persian designs on Greece, largely on the
ground that Persia was the hereditary enemy, Demosthenes
saw clearly enough that the situation was essentially
changed, and that the clouds on the Eastern horizon no
longer portended an imminent storm. There was no fear
of an attack from this quarter : in point of fact, the Persian
monarch had now become a sort of relieving officer for
Hellenic pecuniary embarrassment, an ally to whom one
or other of the parties—Spartan or Athenian—appealed
for help against their rivals of the moment. It suited
Philip at a later stage to pose as Generalissimo of the
Greek forces against the old foe who had dared to invade
the sacred soil of Hellas, and had been thoroughly well
beaten for his pains. But for the present—at the time when
Demosthenes was speaking—the Persian king was practically harmless. It certainly behoved Athens to prepare
herself for any contingency : she should remain on the
defensive, however, and not attempt any initiative. And
from this point Demosthenes goes on to sketch an outline
of the reforms on which he insisted in many subsequent
harangues—the necessity of rearranging contributions to
the State service, so that the fleet, above all, should be kept
in a position of thorough efficiency.

At this time Philip of Macedon was a cloud no bigger
than a man's hand, and his name does not occur in the
speech. The great enemy, as he became afterwards, was
reorganising his kingdom, training his Macedonian phalanx,

[1] Dem., 'Ολ. I. 4. [The references are to Bekker's edition.]

F

laying the foundation for a navy. Towards Athens he kept the attitude of a friend, and he took care to be represented in the City by orators, who, either through blindness or greed, were devoted to his interests. Eubulus was one, so were Demades and Æschines; and even Phocion, though no one could suspect his probity, often played his game. Afterwards, Philip threw off the mask. He dared to threaten Thermopylæ, but when he found the pass occupied by Athenian troops he thought it wiser to retire. In Chalcidice and in Thrace he adopted bolder tactics. He took pains to secure the wealthy mines of M. Pangæus, and after playing with Athens, and deluding her with the idea that he was going to capture Amphipolis on her behalf, openly showed his hand by advancing on the important town of Olynthus, which he subsequently mastered, helped by the treachery of Lasthenes and the supineness of Athens.

§ 3

I am not concerned in this paper with the incidents of the orator's life, nor yet with the various steps by which Philip—after his victory at Chæroneia—rose to supremacy over the Greek world. I wish rather to indicate the chief features of Demosthenes' policy, and the illustrations he gives of the basic principles of patriotism. Fortunately, for our purpose, there is an inner consistency in his views from the beginning to the sorry ending of his career. Let us remind ourselves that he was a great student of the history of Thucydides and a devoted admirer of Pericles. What was the ideal of Athenian citizenship which the great statesman delineated for his countrymen at the beginning of the Peloponnesian War? It was freedom in the first place, complete liberty under democratic forms. It was culture in the second place, for Athens was the soul of Greece, and her high level of mental attainment was a shining beacon for her age. This culture was alike intellectual and æsthetic. "We love beauty, and yet are not soft or enervated." [1] The Athenians were to be strong, both on land and sea, and yet militarism—such as was to be found in Sparta—was abhorrent to the civic idea. They were to be soldiers, but not pipe-clay soldiers : they were to cultivate intelligence rather than sell their souls to the

---

[1] I refer, of course, to Pericles' great speech over the fallen, as reported by Thucydides. II. 35 *et foll.*

drill-sergeant. Above all, they were to love their native State, which was to be for them not a cold abstraction, but a living and adorable entity. Few things are more remarkable than Pericles' language on this point, as narrated by Thucydides. The Athenians were to become enamoured of Athens, to be her lovers, as though she were a mistress who asked of them their deepest devotion. Patriotism in this sense is not another name for civic duty; it is almost an emotional rhapsody.

To Demosthenes, studying this Periclean idea, several modifications seemed necessary, mainly because the times had altered, but partly because of certain implicit imperfections. The love of Athens was too exclusive an ardour : it was based on the principle that Athens was supereminent in Greece and could tolerate no rivals. There was no Panhellenic feeling in it; as a matter of fact, it was consistent with a duel to the death against another Greek State, Sparta. Demosthenes, indeed, thought that Athens deserved supremacy, but she must deserve it because she was the embodiment of a Panhellenic idea, the natural leader of a Greece which willingly allowed herself to be led. Athens after Pericles had become Imperialist, a despot city, ruling her allies and subject-States with a rod of iron. That must no longer be her policy. She ought everywhere to support Greek communities, help them in their struggles, preserve their independence, above all, render assistance by land and sea, if they were menaced by a foreign and barbarian Power, such as Macedon. Patriotism to the city of Cecrops was to be based on a wider patriotism to Hellenes anywhere and everywhere—very much as love of England should mean loyalty to Great Britain and her sister dominions and commonwealths. Against despotisms and tyrannies Athens, as a true democracy, was always to wage war. If Sparta attempted to domineer, as she did from Ægospotami to Leuctra, she was to be fought down. On the other hand, if Thebes repented of her evil ways, she was to be assisted, despite her long-standing hostility to Athens.

Illustrations of this Panhellenic attitude can be found throughout the speeches of Demosthenes. I take, for instance, more or less at haphazard, the oration " On the Chersonese," which was delivered B.C. 342. The Athenians had dispatched a body of citizens to receive allotments of land in the Chersonese under the command of Diopithes. Disputes arose with the Cardians, who were at once assisted by Philip. But Diopithes held his own, and even carried the war into Thracian territory. The question arose whether on Philip's remonstrance Diopithes was to be recalled. Demosthenes stoutly supported and defended the Athenian general, who in his view was promoting the interests of Hellas against barbarians, and in especial was protecting the Chersonese. It was much to the advantage of Athens to have a permanent force on the northern coast of the Ægean Sea, so that help might readily be given to any Hellenic State which was being menaced by a Macedonian force. " Is it urged," said the orator, " that the Byzantines are infatuated and besotted ? Very likely : yet they must be rescued for all that, because it is good for Athens." [1] They are Greeks, in short, and therefore Athens is their natural protector. Here, too, is another passage to the same effect. " Suppose some god would assure— for certainly no mortal would undertake such a guarantee —that even though you remained quiet and abandoned everything, Philip would not attack you at the last. Yet, by Zeus and all the gods, it would be a disgraceful act, unworthy of yourselves, of the character of Athens and the deeds of your ancestors, if for the sake of selfish ease you were to abandon the rest of Greece to servitude. For my own part, I would rather die than give such counsel." [2] Athens is the city community which is wedded to freedom, and therefore the duty incumbent on her, as a democracy which can never ally herself with despots, is to help other Greek States to remain free. This, too, is the spirit of the oration " On the liberty of the Rhodians " (351 B.C.). Rhodes, whatever her past sins, must be saved from oligarchs and tyrants.

§ 4

But we must get closer to this question of patriotism. Apart from the general allegiance to the Panhellenic idea, there is the duty of the individual to his own State. On what does the obligation of patriotism rest ? On two principles, above all. The first is, that a man does not belong to himself, but to the State which feeds, nurtures, protects him, and assures him in the possession of many

[1] Dem., Περὶ τῶν ἐν Χερρονήσῳ, 16. I use for the most part C. R. Kennedy's admirable translation of Demosthenes' speeches. (G. Bell & Sons.)
[2] Ibid., 50.

civic privileges. This principle is laid down in the oration
" On the Crown "—which is a perfect storehouse of maxims
and principles applicable both to the conduct of politicians
and of individual citizens. Let us observe the bearing of
this principle—or, rather, from Demosthenes' point of
view, this axiom or postulate—of citizenship. An individual citizen does not belong to himself, but to the State. [1]
It follows, therefore, that he has no rights against the State :
if he subsequently earns rights, it is in virtue of his performance of certain duties which—because the State so ordains
—give him privileges. What other consequences can we
draw ? Clearly this : that he has no claim to exercise
his own judgment, as against the superior demands of the
State upon him. He cannot plead " conscience " if he
is wanted as a soldier. As he has no right to a personal
opinion in moments when his city or his commonwealth
is in danger, the " conscientious objector "—of whom we
hear so much in modern times—is ruled out of court.
Demosthenes would have no sympathy with him : probably
he could not even understand him. Individual opinion
is not allowed in questions of Art and Literature, in which
authority and expert judgment alone have the right to be
heard. How much less can individual opinion be permitted
in questions which affect the stability, the continued existence of the State ? Of course, in easy-going times of peace,
we only smile at the vagaries of personal opinion. But
in a crisis, under actual conditions of war, individualism
may be a deadly danger to the best interests of the
Commonwealth.

Let us turn to the second principle of patriotism. If a
citizen does not belong to himself, patriotism must involve
the obligation of personal service. There is no more constant note in the Demosthenic harangues than the necessity
for Athenians to shoulder their own burdens. No man
must delegate this duty to another : he must undertake
it himself. As a matter of fact, Athens after the close of
the Peloponnesian War had adopted more and more the
practice of employing mercenaries to fight her battles for
her, both on sea and land. Her generals, like Timotheus
or Chares, or still more, Charidemus, took with them on
their expeditions hardly any Athenians, but large bodies
of mercenaries and soldiers of fortune. The result was that
when payment was in arrears these men took to plundering

[1] Dem., Περὶ τοῦ Στεφάνου, 260.

and filibustering, and the Allies of Athens learned to dread the arrival of an Athenian force, because it generally meant that they were despoiled by soldiers who, not having regular pay, lived from hand to mouth on whatever they could, lawfully or unlawfully, annex. Demosthenes, though he points out the practical disadvantages of mercenary forces, takes, as we should expect, the higher standpoint that citizens ought themselves to serve in the navy and the army as a matter of duty. Here is a significant passage in the First Philippic (B.C. 352) :—" If you Athenians will only exert yourselves now though you did not before : if every man, where he can and ought to give his service to the State, is ready to give it without excuse : if the wealthy will contribute and the able-bodied will enlist : in a word, if you will become your own masters and cease to think that your neighbour will do everything for you if you do nothing yourself—then, if Heaven so will, you shall recover your own, get back what you have frittered away, and mete out punishment to Philip." [1] Here is another passage from the Second Olynthiac :—" You must show yourselves greatly changed, greatly reformed, contributing, serving personally, acting promptly, before any one will pay attention to you." [2] Or, once more, at the end of the Third Olynthiac :—" How is it that all used to go prosperously and all now goes wrong ? Because anciently the people had the courage to be soldiers and controlled the statesmen. . . . Is there such an emergency as the present ? Far better to be a soldier, as you ought, in your country's cause." [3] Every one, according to Demosthenes, owes something to the State. Let him contribute what he can—money, if he has it to give : taxes which the State imposes on him, let him pay cheerfully. But the greatest of these is Personal Service.

§ 5

Demosthenes rarely allowed himself to utter a single word of pessimism : to despair of the Commonwealth would have seemed to him the rankest treason. But now and again his clear judgment of the signs of the times could not but realise that he was dealing with a decadent Athens which no longer responded to the call of duty. The true-minded patriot was confronted by something more than the

[1] Dem., 'Φιλ., I. 7.   [2] Dem., 'Ολ., II. 13.   [3] Dem., 'Ολ., III. 30, 34.

growing power of an ambitious despot like Philip. He was faced by lassitude, enervation, apathy on the part of his own countrymen—obvious tokens that the heyday of Greek democratic life had passed beyond recall. Perhaps the orator was at times only too conscious that he was fighting a losing battle, but this does not prevent him from doing his utmost to persuade and invigorate his audience, to tell them of their obligations and drive them by every resource of irony, criticism, and abuse, as well as encouragement, to fulfil these obligations to the uttermost. " *Restat amari aliquid* "—even in his loftiest exhortations. Though his courage will not admit it, he is the spokesman of a perishing cause. " Tell me," he says in the First Philippic, " do you like walking about and asking one another, Is there any news ? Why, what news could be more arresting than that a man of Macedon is conquering Athenians and controlling the affairs of Greece ? Is Philip dead ? No, but he is sick. And what does it matter to you ? Should anything befall this man, you will soon create another Philip, if this be your way of conducting business." [1] That the Athenian character has changed is the burden of a passage in the Second Olynthiac : " This, I confess, surprises me, that formerly, Athenians, you fought with the Lacedæmonians for the rights of Greece : rejecting many opportunities of selfish gain, and desiring to secure the rights of others, you expended your property in contributions, and bore the brunt of the battle. Yet now you are loth to serve, slow to contribute, even in defence of your own possessions, and though you have often saved the other city-states of Greece, both collectively and individually, when you are confronted with your own losses you sit still. This does surprise me." [2] The note of disappointment and regret sounds clearer in a passage in the Third Philippic :— " What has caused the mischief? There must be some cause, some good reason, why the Greeks were so eager for liberty then and now are only eager for servitude. There was something, men of Athens, something in the hearts of the people then which there is not now—something which overcame the wealth of Persia and maintained the freedom of Greece, and quailed not under any battle by land or sea. It is the loss of this which has ruined all and thrown the affairs of Greece into confusion." [3] In explaining what this

---

[1] Dem., Φιλ., I. 10, 11.   [2] Dem., 'Ολ., II. 24.
[3] Dem., Φιλ., III. 36, 37.

" something " is, Demosthenes falls back on " nothing subtle or clever," but on the fact that bribery by the aspirants for power or the corrupters of Greece was universally scouted and detested in the earlier time : whereas now it is different. A man who gets a bribe is envied : if he confesses it, laughter is his only punishment; but if any one denounces the crime, then the reward is public hatred. Of course, Demosthenes is covertly alluding to such tainted patriots as Philocrates, Demades and Æschines, who were notoriously in Philip's pay. But the taking of bribes is only the external sign of a deeper-lying malady. It was the low state of public opinion in Athens, the code of morals she accepted, the tarnished ideals of conduct and faith by which she was guided, which revealed the poisoned root of her degeneracy.

PATRIOTISM AND ORATORY: VENIZELOS AND DEMOSTHENES

§ 1

MOST of the sphere covered by the operations in the Near East is classic ground for the scholar. We need not go back as far as the Trojan War to stir a long-dormant interest in the Hellespont. In historic times, when Greece was fighting the Persians, when Athens was struggling with Sparta in the Peloponnesian War, and when in the decadence of her powers the City of the Violet Crown was trying to hold her own against the encroachments of Philip of Macedon, the coast-line of the Ægean Sea, the islands near the mainland of Asia Minor, the Dardanelles, the Sea of Marmora, the Propontis rang with the sounds of strenuous combat both by land and sea. Olynthus, Amphipolis, the river Strymon, the triple promontory of Chalcidice—these the scholar knows as well as the modern historical student knows Salonika. Byzantium, too, was then, as now, a prize worth fighting for, and Athens, nervous about her corn-ships coming from the Euxine and utterly unable to feed her population without their aid, was for ever casting anxious eyes towards the Thracian coast and her possessions towards the north-east. The Hellespont itself saw her despairing efforts against her Lacedæmonian enemy—the victory of Cynossema, the disastrous defeat of Ægos Potamos, the baulked strategy of Alcibiades, the triumph of Lysander. Sixty years later we find once more Athenian navies manœuvring in the same region—Chares, Phocion, and others doing what they could to prevent Greeks from becoming captive to the Macedonian tyrant, and Demosthenes urging his countrymen with all his lofty eloquence to shake off their lethargy and remember the glorious deeds of their forefathers. So far as the city of Olynthus was concerned, Philip succeeded in his objects before the Athenians could be stirred up to action; but

73

between the years 343 and 340 B.C. Demosthenes, at the
height of his influence, checkmated his enemy and, thanks
to the generalship of Phocion, saved both Perinthus and
Byzantium from Macedonian hands. Alas! two years
later the fatal battle of Chæroneia extinguished the liberties
of Greece.

But not only is the soil steeped in classical memories,
which none of us can forget and which make us tender
towards the modern inheritors of a great name. The
circumstances of the time have thrown up a statesman who
seems formed in the ancient mould of an Aristides, a
Pericles, a Demosthenes. It is especially the last with
whom some comparison may be sustained—partly because
both Venizelos and Demosthenes had to struggle with a
very refractory material. It is one thing to lead a nation's
hopes in the spring-time of their vigour : it is another to
instil a decadent race with powers alien from their habitual
apathy. In this sense Pericles had a task as easy as that
of Demosthenes was difficult. The earlier statesman found
a people plastic to his purposes, eager, spirited, virile, full
of ambition, and proudly conscious of their destiny. But
the latter had to flog reluctant and apathetic audiences,
only now and again capable of higher moods—audiences
which were amused by the rhetorical battles of their
orators, but very disinclined to go to battle for themselves.
They preferred to have mercenaries to fight for them while
they enjoyed spectacular displays provided out of the
Theôric Fund. They had no keenness, no native energy—
such springs of action seemed to have been killed by their
melancholy experiences after the fatal expedition to Sicily.
The result is that while Pericles' great speech is buoyantly
alive with untapped sources of strength and a yet un-
developed national spirit, Demosthenes' orations, the
Olynthiacs, the Philippics, and the rest, exhibit the almost
desperate efforts of a man to strike some spark out of dead
matter—to urge, exhort, goad, upbraid, entreat, or shame
passivity into some semblance of life.

Venizelos has much the same task, for his lot, too, has
fallen on unhappy times. To be a Greek citizen in the
modern era is to be conscious of great humiliations. He
must know that he has a poor reputation in Europe, that
the " Græculus esuriens " tradition still survives. The
average Greek appears to be an unstable creature, greedy
rather than ambitious, cunning, and not too scrupulous

in business, and by no means constitutionally brave. He does not remember with any feeling of gratification the war against Turkey in 1897, when his armies ran away, and his country was only saved through the intervention of the Powers. It is true that he fought gallantly and well in the first Balkan War, though probably he had not very obstinate opposition to overpower; and when Bulgaria turned against her quondam allies, in the second Balkan War, Serbia and Greece conducted their campaign with no little success. But the recent history of the Hellenic Kingdom is not altogether a creditable one, and her betrayal of Serbia in that country's anguish and the record of her dealings with the Entente Powers—it was to Great Britain, France, and Russia that she originally owed her independence and her very existence as a kingdom—are not episodes on which a patriotic Hellene, remembering his glorious past, would care to dwell. It is, perhaps, all the more surprising that out of a milieu so unpromising a statesman of the calibre of Venizelos should emerge. There has been no one quite like him in the Near East in his grasp of actual and possible conditions and his far-sighted glance into the future—certainly no politician in Athens who has a tithe of his ability. The Balkan States did, indeed, produce another man of statesmanlike build in Stambuloff, " the Balkan Bismarck," to whom Bulgaria owes more for her existence as a State than she seems ever likely to acknowledge. But Stambuloff was even less fortunate in his conditions and circumstances than Venizelos. And though he had helped Ferdinand to ascend his throne, he had to suffer to the full from the traditional ingratitude of kings, being murdered with Ferdinand's connivance—or at least owing to his studied indifference— in circumstances of peculiar cruelty. Venizelos, as we all know, is a native of Crete, and that island, which originally gave Greece no small measure of her culture, and that early civilisation which goes by the name of Ægean, has given no better present to the mainland in recent times than the personality and influence of one of the most distinguished of her sons. Revolutions in Crete have been a constant feature in modern history, and Venizelos, no doubt, had much revolutionary blood in his veins. But his was not a purely destructive spirit. He bitterly desired the redemption of his native island from the murderous grasp of Turkey; but his thoughts soared beyond the confines of his home to the welfare and glory of Hellas, cribbed, cabined, and confined by Ottoman pressure.

Two ideas, above all, animated his policy, and when he was called to Athens to direct the action of the State he saw some chance of carrying them into effect. One of these was the independence of Greece, viewed in the largest sense—that is, the incorporation within a free Hellenic community of all the scattered elements distributed in Macedonia, the Ægean Isles, and the coastland of Asia Minor, unhampered by the stupid and cruel despotism of the Turk. And to this end he was one of the main agents —if not the principal agent of all—in the formation of the League of Balkan States, which showed to an astonished Europe the marvellous phantom of a united and concordant Balkan Peninsula. It was a grandiose conception only possible to a large-minded and idealistic statesman; but it could not endure, because it was based on the theoretical suppression of scarcely veiled and obstinate rivalries. Nevertheless, it lasted long enough to defeat Turkey—to the surprise and indignation of the Germanic Empires, which assumed that the Ottoman Empire would prevail over its loosely associated antagonists. The second idea of Venizelos related to the inner structure of Hellas herself. Greece was to gain the full development of her polity and the firm establishment of her independence by a monarchy, which was to be strictly constitutional, giving scope and liberty to the will of her citizens. Venizelos, as a matter of fact, saved the monarchy when it was in considerable peril from an arrogant military party, and since the King of the Hellenes owed to the statesman his security, the least he could do to show his gratitude was strictly to abide within the limits of constitutionalism. In the recent struggles Venizelos' complaint against his Sovereign is that he has taken matters into his own hands, against the will of the great majority of his subjects, and events seem to confirm this view. To the mind of the Cretan statesman, the manifest destiny of Greece is to join the Entente Powers and to throw over that superstitious reverence for Teutonic militarism which appears to have so deeply impressed some of the Greek generals—to say nothing of King Constantine. At the moment of writing [1]

[1] Recent events have obviously modified and in some respects improved the situation. This essay was written before the departure of King Constantine.

it looks as if Hellas intended to pin her faith to the
patriotic policy of her great leader, Eleutherios Venizelos. The only point is—and it must be a matter of deep
anxiety for all sincere patriots—whether it is not already
too late. What sort of future Destiny will reserve for Greece,
who is so tardy in her resolve and did not freely give herself when the gift would have been precious, is another
matter.

§ 2

" Too late " is a constant form of reproach in the mouth
of Demosthenes. In the first Philippic he contrasts the
prompt punctuality with which all arrangements are made
for the Panathenaic and Dionysian festivals and the slackness and dilatoriness of the preparations for war. " In the
business of war all is irregular, unsettled, indefinite," " all
your armaments are after the time." [1] " The efforts of
Athens are as awkward as those of an unskilled boxer,
who, when he is struck anywhere, immediately transfers
his hands to the spot where the blow has fallen, and never
watches to see where the next blow is likely to come." [2]
Clever makers of war should not follow circumstances, but
be in advance of them. Or again, in the third Philippic :
" It is disgraceful to exclaim when something has happened,
' Who would have thought it ? We ought to have acted
in this way and refrained from acting in that.' It is
now too late. Many things could the Olynthians mention
now which, if foreseen at the time, would have prevented
their destruction." [3] Possibly similar thoughts have passed
through the mind of Venizelos as he surveyed the pro-
crastinating habit of his countrymen, and the pendulum-
like swing with which they have oscillated between the
Teutonic and the Entente Powers. To be always behind-
hand with their decisions may leave them high and dry,
without friends and without claims, when the ultimate issue
is reached.

Both Demosthenes and Venizelos would accept Mazzini's
definition of a nationality : " The assertion of the individuality of a human group called by its geographical
position, its traditions, and its language to fulfil a special

[1] *Dem.*, Φιλ., i. 40.   [2] *Ibid.*, 46–7.
Dem., Φλ., iii. 81.

function in the European work of civilisation." [1]   That is precisely what Demosthenes believed about Athens. She was called by her past glory, her faith in freedom, her present influence to put herself at the head of the Greek race—wherever they might be located, at Olynthus, Amphipolis, Byzantium or in the Ægean Isles, or on the mainland—and make head against despotism, militarism, barbarism. Philip of Macedon was a barbarian, and barbarians must not rule the free commonwealth of Greece. Philip, too, was an autocrat, and republics must have no dealing with autocracies. There is a striking passage in the second Philippic on this point. Demosthenes is quoting from a speech he made to the Messenians on the occasion of one of his embassies to the Peloponnese to form a combination of States against Philip. " In truth, too close connections with despots are not safe for republics. . . . You behold Philip a dispenser of gifts and promises : pray, if you are wise, that you may never know him for a cheat and a deceiver. There are manifold contrivances for the guarding and defending of cities, as ramparts, walls, trenches, and the like : these are all made with hands and involve expense : but there is one common safeguard in the nature of prudent men, which is a good security for all, but especially for democracies against despots. What do I mean ? Mistrust. Keep this, hold to this, preserve this only and you can never be injured. What do ye desire ? Freedom. Then see ye not that Philip's very titles are at variance therewith ? Every king and despot is a foe to freedom, an antagonist to laws. Will ye not beware lest, seeking deliverance from war, ye find a master ? " [2] The words are singularly applicable to the present situation. Greece is not now a republic; she is a constitutional monarchy. But she desires to be free and independent, to hold her own against the patent tyranny of the Ottoman Empire or the insidious devices of a pan-Germanic league. Can we not imagine a Greek patriot of the present day telling his countrymen that they know Germany as " a dispenser of gifts and promises," and praying that they may not know it as " a cheat and a deceiver ? " Has not Venizelos bidden Greece beware of the gifts of the Danai and cultivate a wise and prudent mistrust ? Above all, is not the warning more than ever

[1] Quoted in *Europe in the Nineteenth Century.* By E. Lipson. P. 264. (A. & C. Black. 1916.)   [2] *Dem.*, Φιλ., ii. 23–7.

necessary in Athens at the present day " lest, seeking deliverance from war, they may find a master?" An excessive shrinking from war, an excessive devotion to neutrality, may lead to something hardly distinguishable from servitude.

§ 3

In a previous article I tried to define what Demosthenes' task was. The main points are abundantly clear, as they are emphasised again and again in the Olynthiacs, the Philippics, the De Chersoneso, and other orations. Athens has the titular right to defend Greece against all barbarians, and especially against the menace of a grasping and ambitious King of Macedon, whose diplomacy is based on deception, on a prodigal use of bribes, and on the sinister service of spies. Athens must also help the Greek States against their own weaknesses, and especially that love of intestine strife which has already ruined so many hopeful democracies. But, above all, Athens must purge herself from her own manifold shortcomings—her want of energy, her love of spectacles, her trust in venal orators, her reliance on mercenaries. She must arm her own citizens, contribute to the equipment of efficient fleets, and rise to the height of her own responsibilities and duties. For patriotism is not only valuable as a material defence against danger : it is an ethical obligation. Indeed, the basing of all political action on morals, the large conception of a free democracy finding its highest spiritual duty in self-development and the guidance of less advanced States, are favourite tenets with Demosthenes, on which he was never tired of laying stress.

It is our good fortune to possess in Demosthenes' *Oration on the Crown* a carefully composed apology, drawn up some time after the actual facts, for the policy pursued by the Athenian statesman. Apology is hardly the right word. It is a proud vindication of statesmanship, of which the speaker has no intention of being ashamed, a string of documentary evidences to prove that what he did was done with the best motives, and sometimes with the happiest results. Ctesiphon had proposed to give a crown to Demosthenes; Æschines opposed the gift on the ground of illegality—for various technical reasons with which we are not concerned. But Æschines also took the opportunity of criticising and abusing his great rival, in order to prove that he was not worthy of such an honour, and that gave the defendant, as we may call him, his chance. Weak, so far as the legal arguments were concerned, Demosthenes was strong in defence of his statesmanship; and no better proof could be given that he retained to the full the confidence of his countrymen than the fact that even after the disastrous battle of Chæroneia he was selected to deliver the funeral oration over the dead warriors. Or, if we need corroborative evidence, it may be found in the issue of the duel between the two orators. Æschines, failing to get the adequate number of votes, went into exile. Demosthenes, securing the verdict for his client, Ctesiphon, won a decisive victory for himself.

What are the main criticisms which might be levelled at Demosthenes' policy? They are tolerably obvious. The policy, whatever might be said of its intrinsic merits, was ill-timed. To bring about a war between Philip and Athens was ruinous, because circumstances made it very unlikely that the democracy would have any chance against the despotic monarchy. What might have been possible in the times of Pericles was impossible after the many disasters which had befallen Athens and had killed her energies and ambitions. Moreover, it was not a good policy in itself. It would have been wiser to keep friends with Philip and make use of him in the quarrels which divided the Greek States. Men like Eubulus and Phocion formed a more correct estimate of the needs of the situation. Æschines was better advised when he tried to establish friendly relations with Philip's Court. Lastly, and most important of all, Demosthenes' policy was an acknowledged failure. It did not keep back the rising tide of Macedonian power. It did not save Athens from defeat. Such are the main counts in the indictment, and it is interesting to observe how the statesman meets them. He lifts the discussion on to a different and a higher plane. He does not so much argue that he was right as that his policy was inevitable, given the past history and the present reputation of Athens. He does not controvert the facts, but maintains that, even if they had been known beforehand, his policy, and every true patriot's policy, would have been unaltered. It is true that he denies in one respect the failure. He points to the successes gained from 343 to 340 B.C., when the sieges of Perinthus and Byzantium

were raised and Philip's forces were driven out of the
Chersonese. But even if all the efforts ended in failure,
that does not prove that they were wrong. Material and
tangible success is not the only criterion; there is a higher
standpoint from which strategy and diplomacy are viewed
in relation to a nation's ideals and not merely in reference
to their immediate results. Besides, the State rewards
its officers because they have done the best they could
under given conditions. Success lies on the knees of the
gods. It is enough for a patriot to do his duty.

Here is an illustrative passage : " What should the
commonwealth have done when she saw Philip establishing
an empire and dominion over Greece ? Or what was your
statesman to advise or move—I, a statesman at Athens,
who knew that from the earliest time until the day of my
mounting the platform our country had ever striven for
precedency and honour and renown, and poured out more
blood and treasure for the sake of glory and the general
weal than the rest of the Greeks had done for their own
special interests ? . . . Hardly any one will venture to say
this : that it became a man bred at Pella, then an obscure
and inconsiderable place, to possess such inborn mag-
nanimity as to aspire to the mastery of Greece and formu-
late this ambition in his mind, whilst you who are Athenians,
day after day in speeches and dramas reminded of the virtue
of your ancestors, should have been so naturally base as
of your own free will and accord to surrender to Philip
the liberty of Greece. No man will say this ! " [1]

Or again : " Mark the line of my policy at that crisis;
do not rail at the event. The end of all things is what the
Deity pleases : it is his line of policy which shows the
judgment of the statesman. Do not then impute it as a
crime to me that Philip chanced to conquer in battle :
that issue depended, not on me, but on God. Prove that
I failed to adopt all measures humanly feasible—that I
failed to carry them out honestly and diligently and with
exertions beyond my strength, or that my enterprises
themselves were not honourable and worthy of the State
and necessary. Show me this and you can accuse me as
soon as you like." [2]

Or once more, with a certain note of passion, as though
success were nothing and policy everything, Demosthenes
utters what he himself calls the paradox that even fore-

[1] *Dem.*, Περι τον στεφ., 80–3.   [2] *Ibid.*, 245.

G

knowledge of the event could not alter, and ought not to alter, what was the right course to pursue. " Never, never can you have done wrong in undertaking the conflict for the freedom and safety of all ! I swear it by your fore-fathers—those who fronted the peril at Marathon, those who ranged themselves in battle array at Platæa, those who fought at sea at Salamis and those at Artemisium, and many other brave men who sleep in the public monuments —all of whom alike, as being worthy of the same honour, the country buried, not only the successful or the victorious ! And justly so. For the duty of brave men had been done by all : their fortune had been decided by the Deity." [1] This is the celebrated oath which has been so much praised both in ancient and modern times, by Longinus as much as by Lord Brougham. The choiceness of the phrasing, the spirit of the rhetoric, and the music of the sentences can only be appreciated in the original Greek.

I must quote another passage, because it succinctly defines the duties of a statesman and constitutes Demos-thenes' justification.

" I do not deprecate," says the orator, " the severest scrutiny in those things for which a statesman is properly responsible. What are a statesman's functions ? To observe things in the beginning : to foresee and foretell them to others. This. I have done. Again : Wherever he finds delay, backwardness, ignorance, jealousies—vices inherent and unavoidable in all communities—to contract them into the narrowest compass; on the other hand, to promote unanimity and friendship and zeal in the discharge of duty. All this too I have performed; and no one can discover the least neglect on my part." [2] If Philip has conquered, his success is due to his army and his wholesale methods of bribery and corruption. Demos-thenes was not a general, so he could not be responsible for the defeat of Athenian troops, while as for bribes, his record was immaculate. And therefore the statesman is able to utter his well-known boast : " Had there been in each of the Greek cities one such man as I was in my station among you; or, rather, had Thessaly possessed one single man, and Arcadia one, of the same sentiments as myself, none of the Greeks either beyond or within Ther-mopylæ would have suffered their present calamities : all would have been free and independent." [3] It was the

[1] *Ibid.*, 263.   [2] *Ibid.*, 306–7.   [3] *Ibid.*, 376.

isolation of Demosthenes which made him so powerless
in the various crises with which he was confronted. May
we not say that Venizelos' impotence—when he has had to
stand aside and let matters take their own course—has
been due to a similar cause? If only there had been
another Venizelos at Belgrade or Sofia !

§ 4

There are, indeed, many valuable points urged in the
Speech on the Crown which make it a storehouse of maxims
and lessons for the statesman and the patriot. Let me
enumerate a few. There is the difference between statesmen true and false, the distinction between the σύμβουλος
and the συκοφάντης. The one pursues strictly selfish ends;
the other aims at the interests of the State. There is
a vivid passage on treachery and its wages; traitors and
their inevitable doom in the contempt of mankind and
the neglect of those who bought them. There are many
references to the higher patriotism, the patriotism of self-
sacrifice, the pursuit of large ideals, as evinced in the
lofty generosity of Athens towards her rivals and the
baseness of Philip. There are the indefeasible claims of a
free State and the rights of a freeman in a republic to die
free. There are useful hints on the real value of an orator,
and the justification of a certain vehemence of speech when
the commonwealth's main interests are in jeopardy. I
have already alluded to Demosthenes' discussion of the
relations between good fortune—a purely external thing—
and the essential merits of a policy, which goes deep into
the psychology of a State and its citizens. Success is only
a very rough test of virtue in a statesman. He must be
judged in the light of his highest aims and his own character. Nor yet is it a fair criticism to compare him with
his predecessors and ask if he is as great or as good as they.
For the circumstances may be so different as to alter all
the values. It is unjust to inquire whether Demosthenes
presented as big a figure to history as Pericles, or whether
Mr. Lloyd George is as great a War Minister as Pitt.

All these points and many others are invested with
the singularly engaging charm of Demosthenes' oratory.
That was no natural gift : it was won by stern labour
and a merciless discipline. He had to struggle against
many disabilities—a weak voice, a not altogether engaging

personality, an awkwardness of gesture and delivery. Like St. Paul, his enemies could say that his bodily presence was weak and his speech contemptible. He was laughed at as a water-drinker by Philocrates and Æschines, and declared on that account to be a churlish and morose fellow. He tells us so himself at the end of the second Philippic, and there is no doubt that many jokes about his abstemiousness were current at Athens. But by dint of hard work he—like Abraham Lincoln, whom in certain points he resembles—conquered all his difficulties of speech and manner, and became, with the aid of one or two friendly actors, the most accomplished speaker of his own and other ages. Demosthenes' high claims to eloquence, acknowledged by every competent critic, rest on certain qualities, of which the chief are naturalness and simplicity. This simplicity is, of course, the last word of art, not the simplicity of poverty or foolishness. When we read the Philippics and the Olynthiacs, and above all the Speech on the Crown, we are conscious that we are in the hands of a master of his craft. When he chooses, the orator knows how to state his case with absolute clarity; and when he indulges in a burst of rhetoric and gives us what we call a purple passage, he realises the effect of contrast by a series of simple sentences, pellucid, straightforward, and without a trace of involution or emotional verbiage. He is an adept, too, in his narrative style— witness the wonderful bit of descriptive prose in the Speech on the Crown on Philip's capture of Elateia.[1] " It was evening, and a messenger came to tell us that Elateia was taken "—a plain statement of fact which is worked up into a passage as vivid and illuminating as anything to be found in Thucydides or Gibbon. There is nothing that is tawdry or merely theatrical in Demosthenes; if we want to find that we must look to other contemporary orators —to Æschines, perhaps, who, though he undoubtedly possessed the grand manner and was an accomplished speaker on the traditional lines, was tempted sometimes to trust to his fine voice and overdo his rhetoric. Demosthenes was disconcerting, because he used original effects; he could be simply conversational in style and make an appeal by unstudied talk, and then, of a sudden, soar into the empyrean. Even the virulent abuse which we find in many of his speeches, and notably in " the Crown,"

[1] *Dem.*, Περι τοῦ στεφ., 218.

and which, without doubt, jars on our sensibilities, probably struck an Athenian audience differently. At all events, it is confined to those whom the orator looked upon as traitors to Hellas. Is he ever high-flown ? Perhaps ; but it is generally for a purpose. And he is always the master of his own rhetoric. He is not " intoxicated with the exuberance of his own verbosity," as Disraeli said of his great rival. He shapes his style to predetermined ends.

§ 5

It was suggested just now that there was some resemblance between Demosthenes and Abraham Lincoln. We must not overstrain such analogies. All the men who work for the redemption or salvation of their countries have certain traits in common, because they appeal to such universal passions as the love of freedom and hatred of slavery. In this sense Mazzini, Cavour, Hampden, Washington, Venizelos, Lincoln join hands with Demosthenes. But between the last two there were—perhaps superficial—likenesses. Both Lincoln and Demosthenes in their training in oratory had to contend against a natural awkwardness of gesture, but, nevertheless, became accomplished orators. In the early life of both there were struggles and difficulties, steadily overcome by a doggedness of disposition, which deepened as experience grew and mastery was attained, into a splendid tenacity of purpose. Demosthenes' policy was thought out from the beginning and remained consistent with itself; Lincoln never wavered in his resolute championship for the Union. Both were misinterpreted and maligned. Both appealed to the highest instincts of the people with whom they had to deal. And both died a tragic death—Lincoln, as we know, succumbing to the pistol of an assassin in a theatre, and Demosthenes taking poison in a temple to avoid falling into the hands of his enemies.

There is no question that, however differently we may interpret Lincoln's somewhat subtle policy as to Slavery and the Union, he looked at all such matters—just as Demosthenes regarded his particular problems—from a high ethical standpoint. The Greek orator might say that a man was not born for himself, but for the State, the highest interests of which he was bound to subserve, and that therefore patriotism was not merely a civic, but a moral obligation. And the American statesman's attitude towards current controversies was equally coloured by the largest ethical considerations. " To him the national unity of America, with the Constitution which symbolised it, was the subject of pride and of devotion just in so far as it had embodied, and could hereafter more fully embody, certain principles of permanent value to mankind. For the preservation of an America which he could value more, say, than men value the Argentine Republic, he was better prepared than any other man to pay any possible price. But he definitely refused to preserve the Union by what in his estimation would have been the real surrender of the principles which had made Americans a distinct and self-respecting nation." [1] " Lincoln's affection for his own country and its institutions is dependent upon a wider cause of human good, and is not a whit the less intense for that." [2] The Declaration of Independence seemed to him to have given liberty, not merely to America, but to the world for all future time. By the inculcation of its principles " the weight would in due time be lifted from the shoulders of all men."

It is this depth of soul, this profundity of character and temperament, which give to Lincoln's speeches a distinction and also a beauty of their own. They are not works of conscious art, though there is every reason for believing that their author spent much time and labour over a discipline in oratory. They carefully avoid all the well-known expedients of a rhetorician on a platform—for instance, they very rarely end with a peroration—and yet Lincoln knew how to appeal to an audience, mainly because he understood the people and had a curiously intimate sympathy with the popular mind. They are full of coarse and common expressions—" the whole thing is as simple as figuring out the weight of three small hogs " is one of his phrases—and still his language can be as austere and stately and graceful as that of any of the practised orators of the world. Here is an example in the First Inaugural in 1861, when Lincoln had just been made President and the burning question was whether there would be war

[1] *Abraham Lincoln*, by Lord Charnwood, pp. 121-2 (Constable).
[2] *Ibid.*, p. 183.

between North and South. " In your hands, my dissatisfied fellow-countrymen, and not in mine, is the
momentous issue of civil war. . . . We are not enemies,
but friends. We must not be enemies. Though passion
may have strained, it must not break our bonds of affection. The mystic chords of memory, stretching from every
battlefield and patriot grave to every living heart and
hearthstone all over this broad land, will yet swell the
chorus of Union, when again touched, as they surely will
be, by the better angels of our nature." [1] Here we have
imagination, grace, a certain amount of conventional
sentiment (as in " better angels of our nature "), but also
a strain of pathos, a touch of delicacy, a high refinement
which are wholly Lincoln's. But Lincoln's masterpiece
is his little speech over the fallen on the field of Gettysburg.
As this article has been occupied with orators and oratory,
it may fitly close with a speech almost perfect of its
kind.

" Fourscore-and-seven years ago our fathers brought
forth on this continent a new nation, conceived in liberty
and dedicated to the proposition that all men are created
equal. Now we are engaged in a great civil war, testing
whether that nation, or any nation so conceived and so
dedicated, can long endure. We are met on a great
battlefield of that war. We have come to dedicate a
portion of that field as a final resting-place for those who
here gave their lives that that nation might live. It is
altogether fitting and proper that we should do this.
But, in a larger sense, we cannot dedicate—we cannot
consecrate—we cannot hallow—this ground. The brave
men, living and dead, who struggled here have consecrated
it far above our poor power to add or to detract. The
world will little note nor long remember what we say here,
but it can never forget what they did here. It is for us,
the living, rather to be dedicated here to the unfinished
work which they who fought here have thus far so nobly
advanced. It is rather for us to be here dedicated to the
great task remaining before us—that from these honoured
dead we take increased devotion to that cause for which
they gave the last full measure of devotion : that we here
highly resolve that these dead shall not have died in vain;
that this nation, under God, shall have a new birth of

---

[1] Quoted in Lord Charnwood's *Lincoln*, p. 206.

freedom; and that government of the people, by the people, for the people, shall not perish from the earth." [1]

Demosthenes assuredly would not have disowned so beautiful a passage. With some such words as these might he have made his funeral oration over the dead warriors on the field of Chæroneia.

---

[1] Lord Charnwood's *Lincoln*, pp. 360-1.

SAPPHO AND ASPASIA

§ 1

SAPPHO AND ASPASIA, learned women of Greece, are not legendary, like the Homeric figures, Andromache, Hecuba, Helen, Penelope, and Nausicaa : they are historical. And yet it is exceedingly difficult to be sure of the precise character which they possess, and the influence which they wield. Alike in many respects—alike especially in this, that they set an early example of feminine enlightenment, of emancipation from prejudice—they are also alike in the fact that they were both the victims of contemporary witticisms. It is too little to speak merely of the gibes of the wits. A kind of crusade was entered upon to destroy their character, to deride their pretensions, to throw scorn upon their names. It was especially the Attic comic dramatists, Eupolis, Cratinus, and Aristophanes, whose trade was to make fun of great figures of the past; and they assuredly did not spare either Sappho or Aspasia. So that when we read about these women, we are trying to delineate their characters as viewed through a veil of prejudice and contumely. Moreover, their apologists and champions have in a certain fashion added to our perplexity, for they availed themselves of the notorious device of asserting that there were, in reality, two, if not more persons bearing the same name. Consequently we find that there is one Sappho who is called " of Mytilene," and another Sappho who is styled " of Eresos," the first being a pattern of virtue, and the second no better than she should be. The same device, also, was practised with regard to Aspasia, although it did not attract quite the same amount of attention. Aspasia, doubtless, was a very ordinary name for ladies who, for whatever reason, might have earned the title of " well-beloved." Thus, though these are real characters, there clings about them a great deal that is legendary. Having earned an unenviable notoriety, the most contradictory assertions became rife among their enemies and their apologists.

But though there is this much in common between
Sappho and Aspasia, that both of them, like some of the
leaders of the Women's Movement in modern times,
attracted unfavourable attention from facile wits, the
conditions under which they lived were essentially different.
In the first case, that of Sappho, we have to deal with the
social conditions of the Æolian Greeks, somewhere in the
seventh and sixth centuries before Christ.   And those conditions are in effective contrast with the times of Pericles
and the beginnings of Athenian supremacy in the fifth
century.   We do not quite know how it came about, but
it is, nevertheless, clear that the Ionian States, of which
Athens was one, took a very different view of women from
that entertained by kindred populations, such as the
Dorians, and the Æolians, both in Asia Minor and the
southern part of Italy, which was called Magna Græcia.
The Ionians kept their women in rigid seclusion, as the
property and toys of their lords and masters; but in some
of the towns on the sea-coasts of Asia Minor belonging
either to the Æolian or to the Dorian family, women were
allowed a very large amount of liberty.   Women met in
frank, free intercourse with men and with one another.
They had their place, not only in social life, but in the
pursuit of philosophy and literature.   They could express
their opinions;   they could also express their feelings
without any fear or shame.   The position of a woman like
Sappho, with her friends and associates, or pupils, was
only possible under the conditions of a social life in which
men and women met as equals.

At that period there existed in Mytilene and the Isle of
Lesbos literary societies under the guidance of one or two
distinguished names in poetic literature, and these literary
societies opened their ranks equally to men and women,
while in some cases they consisted only of women.   Thus,
for instance, Sappho was the centre of a female literary
society, most of the members of which were her pupils—
her pupils, that is to say, in the technical apparatus of
poetic art.   We know the names of some of these associates
or pupils of Sappho—Anactoria, for instance, Gongyla,
Eunica, Gyrinna, Atthis, Mnasidica, Damophila, and
perhaps Erinna of Telos.   The last two obtained a celebrity
of their own for their poetic gifts.   The Greeks, who were
a severely logical race, never made any confusion between
the instruments with which genius works and genius or

inspiration itself. They knew, none better, that in a very true and real sense you cannot teach people to be poets. But you can teach them the technical laws which govern poetic composition. In Sappho's school the aim was, doubtless, to teach technique. Two of her pupils blossomed forth into original creative artists or geniuses of their own, helped, no doubt, by the fact that their teacher had driven them through the mill. To take a parallel case in modern times, it is said that acting cannot be taught. It does not, however, follow that you cannot teach the rudiments or the technique of that art, even though the final inspiration be beyond you. And so, in Lesbos, where they cultivated poetry with all their might, where it was obviously the fashion to write poetry, where poetry was the recognised mode of culture, schools existed to teach and to encourage it; and besides Sappho's school, in all probability there were several others. Gorgo and Andromeda are mentioned in Sappho's poems as her rivals. Very probably they were the heads of other associations of the same kind.

In considering Sappho, we have to imagine a state of society in which it was not considered improper or indelicate to write frankly and openly about emotions, and feelings, and even passionate states. Sappho's poems contain some instances of this frank speaking, and they have been misinterpreted, because we read into the words some of the associations which belong only to a much later stage of civilisation and life. The whole question of the treatment of love by the ancient Greeks forms at once a difficult and interesting chapter for inquiry. It is only necessary here to make one or two distinctions. Compare, for instance, Sappho, with her frank simplicity, and a later poet—only a little later—Anacreon, with his voluptuous sweetness. There is a world of difference in the treatment. There is a world of difference in the tone. It is not exactly an apt parallel, but it may perhaps serve, to think of the difference between Henry Fielding's outspoken language in *Tom Jones* and the style and temper of Laurence Sterne, say, in his *Sentimental Journey*. Again, the early Greeks had nothing whatsoever to do with, and therefore could not understand, what we call the sentimental relations between the sexes. Æsthetic sentiment in this matter is a plant of later growth. For instance, it was made one of the objections to the new kind of drama initiated by Euripides that he had introduced sentiment into the relations between the two sexes; or, more precisely, that in his psychological analysis of woman he had opened the door to sentimental romance. A love story, as such, was never a dramatic theme for the early writers of drama, that is to say, for Æschylus and Sophocles. The whole of the culture connected with Alexandria after the downfall of the Hellenic State system made a great change in this respect. It was at Alexandria that novels were first invented. And so it became possible for an austere classical poet, like Virgil, to introduce into his epical poem, the *Æneid*, a sentimental love episode, quite on the modern lines, between Æneas, the Trojan chieftain, and Dido, the Queen of Carthage. Points like these must be borne in mind in dealing with the love poems of Sappho. Sappho spoke sometimes with unconventional directness, but to argue from unconventional language to disorderliness of behaviour is to go a great deal beyond what the record warrants.

We look back on Sappho through the distorted spectacles of the Attic comic dramatists, and nothing pleased them better, and apparently nothing pleased better the Athenian audiences than that they should poke their somewhat distasteful fun at people whom they did not understand, and who had lived their lives under conditions very different from their own. As if it were not enough that the Attic comic dramatists should have had a good deal to say on the subject of Sappho, we have the Latin licentious poet Ovid concocting imaginary epistles to Phaon.

There is one instance decisive in reference to all this belittlement of greatness. We know what Socrates was to those who loved and understood him. We know how both Plato and Xenophon drew the lineaments of a great moral reformer. Yet how does he appear, even in so comparatively excellent a satirist as Aristophanes? An absurd figure of farce, a corrupter of youth, a moral anarchist—such is the picture drawn by the great comic dramatist of Athens. And if the comic dramatist could deal so hardly with a philosopher who takes so high a place in the history of the evolution of ethics, why should we trust him any more when he deals with a figure like that of Sappho, especially since Æolian society was one thing, and the Attic society something wholly different in its treatment of the woman question?

what would happen if our dramatists in a modern age were allowed the same licence as was permitted in Athenian times ! Would the picture of Mr. Lloyd George, as drawn by a comic dramatist, represent in any respects the truth ? Or would some of the leading ladies in the feminist movement appear as very creditable figures on our stage, if a dramatist were allowed to make all the fun he could of their pretensions and ambitions ? Why should we trust the earlier dramatists any more than we would later representatives of the craft ? But the worst of it is that the early Christian writers accepted and popularised a misrepresentation which the Greeks themselves had invented. Naturally, it suited the Christian writer, in his tirades against heathenism, to follow Greek perversions, and paint a Sappho full of corruption, as a terrible example of the depths to which heathenism could descend. We must put aside all these aspersions and innuendoes, and take the poems themselves, if we want to understand Sappho.

We need not stay long over the actual details of her life. Indeed, it is all very obscure and uncertain, just for the reason already indicated—because later times invented so recklessly stories about the poetess. She was said, for instance, to be married to a man who was called Kerkolas; but the name sounds as if it was an intentional piece of comic chaff. She described herself on one occasion as " the eternal virgin "; but the phrase might have some spiritual sense, and need not be considered to exclude the theory that she had a daughter, Klêis—the name of her mother, according to some, which she then bestowed upon her own child. The date of her birth may be placed at about 620 B.C., and the place, probably Mytilene, the capital of Lesbos. Her father's name is said to have been Scamandronymus, and, according to Ovid, she was left an orphan at the age of six. Other details, more or less interesting, and, alas ! equally uncertain, are concerned with her brothers. One held the position of cup-bearer, a post only conferred on youths belonging to the aristocracy of the Island. Another brother, Charaxus, is mentioned by Herodotus. He was a trader in Lesbian wines, and, having arrived at Naucratis in Egypt, in pursuit of his mercantile occupations, he became so enamoured of a courtesan called Rhodôpis, that he ransomed her from slavery. According to some accounts, he actually married her; but the story goes on to say that on his return to

Mytilene he was violently upbraided by Sappho, and the quarrel between brother and sister was not easily healed. Of the other brother of Sappho nothing is known. For some reason or other, which we shall never ascertain, Sappho had to leave Lesbos, and journey to Sicily. Her reputed death, which is one of the most uncertain things about her, from the Leucadian Rock, connects her with Acarnania; so, she would certainly appear to be a much-travelled lady. But in reality all the personal anecdotes are to be regarded with great suspicion. Of course, she was supposed to have had many lovers. When we discover that amongst them are Archilochus, who lived quite a century before her, and Hipponax and Anacreon, who were unborn when she died, there is sufficient reason for a good deal of scepticism. The personality of Phaon, supposed to be a lover of Sappho, comes to us from Ovid. But there is no mention of such a name in the fragments of Sappho's poetry, and probably the name is an invented one, being similar to Phaethon, another name for Adonis, the lover of Aphrodite. Alcæus, who was also a citizen of Mytilene, and, together with Sappho, a great master of lyric poetry, must have spoken to the poetess in terms of love, for we have a fragment rebuking him : " Violet crowned, pure, sweetly-smiling Sappho," says Alcæus, " I fain would speak with thee a word in thine ear, but shame restrains my tongue." And, according to Aristotle in his *Rhetoric*, Sappho answered, " If thy wishes were fair and noble, and thy tongue designed not what is base, shame would not cloud thine eyes, but thou wouldst freely speak thy just desires." The name Sappho probably means lapis lazuli, just as the name Electra means amber. Perhaps she gave it to herself, or else it was a pet name, just as one of the companions of Sappho was called Gongyla, which means " the round thing," or " a dumpling."

There are many extraordinary things about Sappho. Unfortunately the fragments of her poetry are very few, and yet, on the strength of them, both ancient and modern times have been equally prepared to hail her as an incomparable poet. In Greek times she was, of course, " the poetess," just as Homer was " the poet "—the one unapproachable speaker of inspired things, the Tenth Muse, as Plato called her. And when we look closer at this marvel, we shall find still further reasons for astonishment. Lyrical poetry by its very nature lends itself to a certain extravagance. When we look at it in later times in the dithyrambs of Pindar, we are conscious now and again of a certain pompous artificiality. But the lyrics of Sappho are absolutely unartificial. They have no purple patches, although they make everybody else's purple look grey and ashen-coloured. When critics try to describe the impression which single lines of Sappho, or complete poems, make upon them, they use metaphors derived from fire. " Her phrases are mingled with fire," an ancient critic says. As a matter of fact, fiery is the last word which can be applied to Sappho's poems if we look at their phrasing and their tone. They have a singular restraint of their own. They never run to hyperbole or excessive ornament. They are the essence of refined and cultured simplicity— that kind of simplicity so difficult of attainment, that faultless simplicity which is the last word in Art. Despite the simplicity of the phrasing, they are so full of a subdued yet intense brilliance that, put by the side of them, other lines seem to lose their colour. And, like all the true and genuine phrases of genius, they stick in the memory. You cannot forget them. A grave, clear beauty seems to reign over them, and that is why the only real way of judging Sappho is by reading her poetry, and then judging whether she could possibly have been the dissolute libertine that the Attic comic dramatists represented. Of course, the fact is that a later age, with other traditions and modes of thought, and especially with other views of the position of women, was hopelessly incapacitated from understanding a personality like that of Sappho. She wrote about love, and as it so happens, the longest fragments we possess are about love. But she wrote on many subjects also, and whatever the subject, her lines possess the same translucent quality. " Now I will sing to my fellow-women delightful songs," she says. " The Muses made me of high price, giving me their own crafts." And they assuredly did not narrow their gifts to only love. She speaks of " My joy in the light of the sun, holding within it all things radiant and fair," and it is quite clear that many of her poems deal with the loveliness of Nature. There is her picture of the orchard in summer, " where on both sides cool water tinkles through apple-boughs, and slumber floats down from rustling leaves." And perhaps the best-known passage of all is the one which describes " the apple that reddens on a top branch, atop of the topmost, and the apple-gatherers forgot it—no, did not forget it, but could not reach it." Or, in simpler, more human guise, you catch the note of delicate self-appreciation or self-abasement. " Surely," she sings, " I am not one of those who bear malice in their temper. My heart is innocent." Or there is a wail against ingratitude : " Those harm me most to whom I have done best." Or, again, a little sharp burst of woman's jealousy, " What country girl is this that bewitches your sense ? One that does not even know how to draw her skirts about her ankles." Or the grave reflection, " Mourning befits not the house of the Muses," or the judgment, reported by a later age, " Death is evil, for the Gods have so judged, else they themselves would have died."

The beautiful invocation to evening—" Hesper, thou bringest back all those things which the gleaming dawn hath scattered "—has been imitated by several modern poets, by Byron, perhaps, worst of all. Or the exquisite phrasing of the poem, " He is most blest of mankind who, sitting opposite thee, sees thee with thy sweet smile, and hears thy sweet voice." Or that divine line on which Swinburne plays so many variations, " Yea, verily I loved thee once, Atthis, once long time ago." The subdued passion is just as remarkable as the exquisite literary form, and that is precisely what so many poets that came after her have recognised and sought to reproduce. But it is a question whether any of them really succeeded. Catullus, perhaps, came nearest; and, as we know, Catullus did his best to imitate Sappho. Horace, of course, followed Alcæus, though he reproduced the Sapphic metre. Ovid has some wonderful lines in his Epistle of Sappho to Phaon, lines which redeem the poem from its other aspects of ugliness. There are, perhaps, only two modern English poets who come anywhere near Sappho, or perhaps three, despite the number of those who have tried to imitate her. Byron is bombastic if we put him beside the Æolian singer, but Shelley has the true lyrical note, and Keats some of that chiselled loveliness which makes each Sapphic stanza a masterpiece. And then, last of all, and in some ways best of all, we come, not to Rossetti, but to Swinburne—Swinburne, who has said things about Sappho memorable in their ungrudging enthusiasm, but who himself confesses that the real Sapphic beauty is beyond him. Listen to Swinburne's " Anactoria " :—

" Yea, thou shalt be forgotten like spilt wine,
Except these kisses of my lips on thine
Brand them with immortality; but me—
Men shall not see bright fire nor hear the sea,
Nor mix their hearts with music, nor behold
Cast forth of heaven with feet of awful gold,
And plumeless wings that make the bright air blind
Lightning, with thunder for a hound behind,
Hunting through fields unfurrowed and unsown—
But in the light and laughter, in the moan
And music, and in grasp of lip and hand,
And shudder of water that makes felt on land
The immeasurable tremor of all the sea,
Memories shall mix and metaphors of me."

And this, too, may be quoted, where Swinburne amplifies
the one line of Sappho already given :—

" I loved thee—hark, one tenderer note than all—
Atthis, of old time once—one low long fall
Sighing—one long low lovely loveless call
Dying—one pause in song so flamelike fast—
Atthis, long since in old time overpast—
One soft first pause and last."

The Gods are jealous in their gifts to mankind, and they
give only a few examples of the utterly best.   There has
never been another Homer; nor yet has there ever been
another Sappho—save where certain fragments of her
power and chaste grace survive here and there in the
beautiful poems of Christina Rossetti.

There is a legend connected with Sappho about which
a word or two may be said, the celebrated leap from the
Leucadian Rock, by means of which, according to some,
she ended her stormy career.   An early death, however,
is contradicted by one of the fragments of her poetry, in
which she describes herself as growing old (γεραιτέρα).
The story, as it has come down to us, is something of this
kind.   There was a certain boatman of Mytilene, called
Phaon, who in his old age had the good luck to row
Aphrodite in his boat.   When he refused payment for his
services, the goddess restored to him both youth and
beauty, just as in the kindred legend of Nausicaa the
goddess restored to Odysseus the beauty of his prime.
Aphrodite gave Phaon a magic ointment, so that every
woman who set eyes upon him became enamoured of his
charms.   And one of the earliest victims was Sappho.
Phaon, tired of the gift of eternal youth, and of all the

H

wooing of Lesbian ladies, withdrew to Acarnania, and founded the Temple of Apollo Leucas on a promontory facing the sea. Even in this retreat Phaon was not safe, for the infatuated ladies pursued him, and when he repulsed them each in turn, they threw themselves off the cliff on which the temple was situated, into the sea. Sappho was one of the earliest of these who thus died for the sake of her lover, Phaon.

Now there are many things to be said about this myth. In the first place, Phaon is only a name for the " Shining One," and perhaps has something to do with Adonis, the beloved of Aphrodite. In the next place, this leap from the Leucadian Rock is a very doubtful matter, for, according to some, it was purely symbolic, part of a rite in honour of Apollo, in which, in substitute for a human being, a sack of gold, perhaps, was thrown into the sea. The priests of the Temple undoubtedly earned a great deal of money by the visits of pilgrims, who, for whatever reasons, desired intercession with the god. Perhaps originally men and women did take this leap in real earnest; but the priests took particular pains to have boats to pick up the martyrs and restore them safe to land. The leap may have been a supposed remedy against love, or it might have had other meanings. But, as often happens in the history of ceremonial rites, what was originally a deadly sacrifice becomes a mere symbol, either some substitute being found for the intending victim, or else a sum of gold. To say that Sappho threw herself from the Leucadian Rock might be only another way of saying that she was the victim of love. Or if she actually essayed the leap, instead of allowing some one to do it for her, she was probably saved from the consequences of her rashness, and continued her career as a poetess. The whole question is mixed up with the age of Sappho, which is itself a very doubtful point. Born in 620, she may have lived on to nearly 570 or 560 B.C., and if so, she must have been at least fifty years of age—a somewhat mature woman to have taken to such desperate courses in consequence of a love affair. At all events, there were a number of other people who were supposed to have imitated her in the supposed act of self-immolation, and one of the most celebrated was Artemisia, the daughter of the Queen of Halicarnassus, the lady whose gallant conduct at the battle of Salamis made Xerxes exclaim that the women had behaved like men, and the men like

women. Amazon though she was, she yet was not proof
against the insidious advances of a love-passion, and being
disdained by a youth of Abydos, she, too, hurled herself
from the promontory, to find the release from her sufferings in death. Clearly we are in a very mythical realm
in dealing with events like these. Doubtless Sappho
haunts the cliffs of Acarnania, but she exists solely as a
wraith or ghost for kindred poets, for a poet, above all, so
delicately sensitive and so quickly receptive as Swinburne.

§ 2

When we pass from the times of Sappho to those of
Aspasia, we pass from what Thucydides called " the sphere
of the mythical " to something like the clear light of history.
But even here passion and prejudice have distorted the
facts. Once more we see the evil work of the Attic comic
dramatists, Eupolis and Cratinus, and especially of Aristophanes; for we have, what was wanting in the earlier
case, political rivalries to add venom to merely social
scandal. Indeed, it is difficult to imagine any great and
gifted woman who has struggled against such a mass of
existing prejudices as Aspasia. In the first place, she was
an alien, and there were strict laws in Athens against
aliens, and especially against marriage with aliens. She
came from Miletus, the daughter of a certain Axiochus.
In the next place, she had very high mental accomplish-
ments, and the majority of people are very intolerant of
really able and clever women. Then her very existence
and her position in an Athenian household contradicted
the idea which the Athenians obstinately held of the
proper position of women. Having come to Athens, and
gained the affection of the great Athenian statesman
Pericles, she exercised her influence over him, not more
by her beauty than by her acute intelligence. Now
Pericles was married to a lady of rank whose name, oddly
enough, history has not preserved, by whom he had two
sons, Xanthippus and Paralus, and he seems to have lived
very unhappily with his wife. He parted from her in
consequence, by mutual consent, and attached himself
to Aspasia during the rest of his life as closely as was
allowed by the law.
   The scandal of her existence in Athens was based
especially on the fact that, instead of believing in the

seclusion of women, she held reunions, at which both she and her friends moved with absolute freedom, discussing, with all the most learned men of the day, problems of policy, of philosophy, and metaphysics.   In that extremely amusing, but decidedly improper, comedy of Aristophanes, called *The Lysistrata*, one of the revolting ladies describes the ordinary conditions of an Athenian woman.[1]

> " What can we women do ?   What brilliant scheme
> Can we, poor souls, accomplish ?   We who sit
> Trimmed and bedizened in our saffron silks,
> Our cambric robes, and little finical shoes."

Imagine how Aspasia fluttered the dovecotes of women like these !   Thucydides makes Pericles say, speaking of the proper place of women in a social state, that that woman leads the best life whose name is least commented upon by the public, either for praise or blame.   That, no doubt, was the Athenian ideal; but it was exactly the opposite of the ideal which Pericles aimed at in his own house.   No one was more talked about than Aspasia, and if she was praised by able men, like Anaxagoras and Pheidias and Socrates, because they found that they could talk to her just as if she had been a man, she was right royally abused, not only by the conventional Athenian matrons, but by men like Aristophanes, who attributed to her an evil influence in upsetting a good old social *régime*, and involving their native country in war.

There was a further reason why so much calumny attached to Aspasia's name.   Grave political dissensions entered into the matter, and the enemies of Pericles on political grounds struck at their prominent statesman through Aspasia.   Pericles was the head of the Liberal party.   Together with Ephialtes, he was the man, above all, who developed the democracy of Athens, bringing about that rule of the Athenian people for and by themselves, which made the Attic Demos so astonishing a phenomenon of culture and power.   But the Conservative party, the aristocratic party, were throughout deadly enemies.   Cimon had led this party, and he had been exiled.   To the everlasting honour of Pericles, his political adversary, Cimon, who was a real patriot, was restored to his country by a decree passed by Pericles himself, and a sort of division of responsibility took place

---

[1] Taken from the translation of Benjamin Rogers.

between them, Pericles remaining the great executive Minister of the Republic, and Cimon its chief general, or rather admiral, at the head of the Athenian fleets. Cimon died in the wars, and then the aristocratic party—for, of course, concord did not reign for long—put up against Pericles a certain Thucydides, son of Milesias (not the historian), who fought with all his might on reactionary lines, until the day when it was his turn, too, to meet the doom of exile, Pericles, by the aid of a popular vote, consolidating his exclusive dominion. " It was in name a Republic," says the Greek historian. " In reality it was a sort of benevolent despotism, worked by one man and one man alone—Pericles." But since we have to add to the vindictiveness of an outraged social opinion the bitterness also of party conflicts between the advocates of progress and reaction, it is hardly surprising that the domestic *ménage* of Pericles should be the target for unscrupulous attacks.

This does not exhaust all the various elements in the great conspiracy against Pericles and the democracy of Athens. Social prejudice counted for something; the rivalry of parties counted for a great deal. Some disliked Aspasia because she was an enlightened woman. Many disliked Pericles because he was a democrat. But above and beyond these more or less domestic considerations, there was one power in Greece which had watched with ill-disguised malevolence the steady rise and development of the Athenian Empire. Sparta and the Peloponnese represented a Dorian aristocracy. The Ionians, such as were found on both sides of the Ægean, were not congenial to the lords of Lacedæmon. And when it was observed that Athens, the great Ionian city, had acquired a great fleet, had established a maritime supremacy, had enrolled a great many of the islanders into a Confederation, of which Athens was the head, although the meeting-place was at Delos, Spartan jealousy could be no longer restrained in view of the success of its hated rival. Unfortunately, it was easy enough for the Spartans to act, for the aristocratic and reactionary party in Athens naturally sided with Sparta. They believed in their form of government, which was a curious combination of monarchy and oligarchy, as against the free, democratic institutions of Athens. And despite the glory of sculpture and painting, and the magnificent buildings which made the City of the Violet

Crown the most lovely thing in Greece, these old-fashioned inhabitants of Attica espoused the cause of Sparta rather than of Pericles. Pericles, who was a statesman, foresaw some time previously whither matters were likely to extend. He knew that sooner or later what was afterwards known as the great Peloponnesian War, the war between Athens and Sparta, was inevitable. But meanwhile, while every month brought the conflict nearer, he had to sustain the brunt of attacks upon himself, his policy, and his house, directed, not by internal enemies—though, doubtless, to some extent engineered and aided by them—but by external foes. There is hardly any question that the Spartans had their share in the various petty or great persecutions to which the Athenian statesman was exposed. It was only when each in turn came to nothing, and Pericles still remained the great head, the chief magistrate, the uncrowned King of Athens, that open war took the place of secret and insidious schemes.

Pericles had surrounded himself—and when we say Pericles we mean also Aspasia—with all the most brilliant men of the day. Pheidias, the great sculptor, was one of the most prominent of these. Then there was Anaxagoras, the great philosopher. The leading tragedians of Greece naturally belonged to the same distinguished circle, which was further adorned by the striking personality of Socrates, who, when comparatively young, fell, like every other male, under the charm of Aspasia. The first blow which the enemies of Pericles directed against him was aimed at Pheidias. The ostensible charge against him was that he had used for his own personal profit a large amount of the gold and other materials with which the State had entrusted him, for his great statue of Athene. There were also other accusations against him, probably based upon a large amount of current gossip. For it was said that he had been guilty of a sacrilegious act in representing himself, and also carving a portrait of Pericles, in those combats of Amazons which ornamented the goddess's shield. The result was tragic enough, as far as Pheidias was concerned. He was thrown into prison, and died there, either from sickness or from despair, or, as some said, because he was poisoned. No doubt it was also urged by the unscrupulous that Pericles was not disinclined to get rid, in any fashion that was possible, of the man who was his accomplice in thieving the funds of the State.

Encouraged by their success, the enemies of Pericles next proceeded against Anaxagoras. And here they involved Aspasia also, for it was familiar knowledge at Athens that Aspasia had sat at the feet of Anaxagoras in natural philosophy, and had imbibed the dangerous doctrines with which the philosopher's name was associated. The charge of impiety is one of the most subtle and perilous weapons which any party can use in their intestine squabbles. It may mean so little, and it may mean so much; and always at the background of the charge is that mass of good, honest belief, as well as obstinate prejudice, which constitutes the ordinary instinctive unreasoning faith of the people at large. What precisely Anaxagoras had done did not matter so much as what he was supposed to have done. The philosophical scheme of Anaxagoras was a development of some of the doctrines of the so-called Ionic school, which tried to find an essential principle in the universe to explain its constitution and its growth. The earliest thinkers asked what was the original thing out of which the world developed? Was it earth? Was it water? Was it fire? And to them succeeded a school which turned not so much to material elements as to mental in the explanation of the universe. Anaxagoras declared outright that all these material bodies of which the universe was composed were to be explained as the work of a central spirit or intelligence, Nous, in virtue of which the earth and stars pursued their appointed way. It is easy to see how a charge of impiety could be trumped up against a man who taught so refined and also so esoteric a doctrine. What is this central Intelligence or Nous, and where does Zeus, the father of gods and men, come in on this showing? And what, too, became of all the favourite figures of the Greek Pantheon—Athene, and Apollo, and Arês, and Poseidon? At any rate, it was not difficult to make out a definite accusation against Anaxagoras that he had denied the gods of his country, and that, therefore, he was worthy of death; while those, too, who had listened to him and accepted his subversive doctrines, like Aspasia, must also be held accountable to the law.

The strange part of the matter is that, whereas the law against impiety was, as a rule, directed against overt acts, it was, in the present instance, owing to the proposal of a man called Diopithes, directed against opinions. Who was especially the accuser of Anaxagoras is not quite clear.

It may have been Cleon, or Thucydides the son of Milesias. But the accuser of Aspasia was undoubtedly Hermippus, a comic poet. The two accused persons adopted very different measures of self-defence. Perhaps owing to the advice of Pericles, Anaxagoras quitted Athens secretly, and took refuge abroad; and, according to Plutarch, Pericles accompanied him and bade farewell of him at the boundary of the city. Without doubt the loss of so close a friend as Anaxagoras, coming after the death of Pheidias, struck a heavy blow at the chief statesman of Athens, the more so because he had to devote himself to the defence of Aspasia, menaced by the accusation of Hermippus. The speech which he delivered on the occasion, in strange contrast with anything which could take place in our courts of law, was nothing more or less than an impassioned appeal to the people of Athens to acquit Aspasia, partly on the ground of his own services to the State, and partly on the strength of his confident testimony that she was innocent. And then for the first time Athens saw the portentous and unexpected sight of Pericles in tears. The statesman who was especially celebrated for his self-control, for his Olympian calm and dignity, broke down so utterly, lost so much of his original self-restraint, that his accusers themselves seem to have understood how deeply his feelings were enlisted in the cause of Aspasia. And the judges acquitted her. It was not the only time that Pericles had to face charges of this kind. He, too, was accused of peculation. But, one after another, all these blows directed against him, either by his enemies in Athens or through the machinations of Sparta, met with decisive failure, and at the period when Athens commenced its memorable .war against Sparta Pericles' influence and authority knew no bounds.

It is easy to understand how difficult Aspasia's position was in Athens; how many different forms of criticism she had to meet—if, indeed, criticism be not too gentle a word to describe the attacks, open or surreptitious, of her enemies. There was the social scandal of her position, and then there was the fact that, like Sappho, and, indeed, like Socrates himself, she served as a natural target for the satire and scorn of professional wits. Cratinus, who belonged to the earlier comedy of Athens, has some very bitter words about .her. " Daughter of immodesty," he calls her, " a courtesan with the eyes of a dog." But indeed, for the matter of that, Aristophanes is just as violent in his attacks, only instead of using opprobrious terms, he definitely, in his play called *The Acharnians*, accuses her of having brought about the Peloponnesian War.   In the third place, there was the political opposition —the customary attitude of a reactionary party against what seemed to belong to a dangerous Liberal or even Radical movement.   And in the last place, there was the constant intrigue of Sparta, very obviously making use of the personality of Aspasia, in order to engineer the crusade against Pericles.   It would be wonderful, indeed, if any woman, subject to these diverse forms of continuous criticism, managed to keep her character clear from calumny and insult.

Thus it is a difficult matter to disentangle the true Aspasia from the various caricatures which were rife at her time and at later times.   What precisely did she attempt to do in Athens ?   She came as an alien, was the unrecognised wife of Pericles, and the mother of a son who, until a later date, was considered by the law of Athens illegitimate.   Starting with these disadvantages, she nevertheless made the house of Pericles the meeting-place for men and women, as we should say, of the higher culture, who discussed, on terms of perfect equality, various topics—domestic economy, politics, art, the principles of morals, physics in the largest sense, and probably religion.   Aspasia's home was a salon, in the best sense of the word.   The great artists were there, the great dramatists, the great philosophers.   And, so far as we can tell, some of the more emancipated of the matrons of Athens did not hesitate to join this cultured circle, whatever might be the existing prejudice.   This is especially the point which Aspasia's enemies caught hold of.   They declared that she had induced several of the free-born inhabitants of Athens to forget what they owed to their own position and their own homes; and they did not hesitate to suggest that all sorts of unworthy temptations were held out to the ladies who supported Aspasia's salon. Plutarch gives us a good many details on this point.   He declares that the Athenian matrons went with their husbands, in order to enjoy the pleasure of a really enlightened *causerie*, and the orthodox and Conservative elements in Athens were shocked, while the grosser minds suggested the possibility of base reasons.   All the women throughout the whole course of history who have tried to emancipate themselves from existing prejudice and lead their own lives—who have tried to collect round themselves a company of thoughtful and educated men and women—have invariably found that their best intentions are misinterpreted, and the nature of their reunions grievously maligned by the envious, the spiteful, and the unclean. Aspasia was one of the first—but she assuredly was not the last—to be forced to run through the whole gamut of scorn, satire, and abuse because of her independence, her self-reliance, and her freedom from ordinary prejudice.

If we ask what were the subjects on which she discoursed, and on which she listened to the words of her friends, we discover from Xenophon's *Memorabilia*, and from a fragment of a Socratic writer, called Æschines, about Aspasia, that the constant object of her solicitude was a study of the rights and duties which marriage creates for man and woman. Clearly enough, she recognised that those who entered into a matrimonial contract ought to do so with absolute freedom on both sides. There ought, in other words, to be allowed to women as much as to men a free choice. With conditions like these marriage becomes a union of two thoughtful human beings, who give each other the best of themselves, and therefore help in a partnership of mutual confidence and respect. Naturally enough, the position of woman in the married state occupied the attention of Aspasia, just because she felt that in Athens the wife was not very much better than a chattel and a slave; so that, in thus occupying herself with the circumstances of marriage, she was also one of the earliest of those whom we call Feminists, everywhere upholding the cause of woman as an independent social integer, a definite portion of the State economy. In other words, she revived in the fifth century some of the ideas which, consciously or unconsciously, had animated the earlier centuries. What Andromache had been to Hector, what Penelope had been to Ulysses, what Nausicaa had been as a daughter in the Phæacian Isle, that Aspasia claimed for herself and her sisters in Athens. Meanwhile, her union with Pericles was a very high example, carried out in practice, of those theories which she discussed with her friends in private. And, despite all the controversies of the time and all the oblique references to her fame which we find in contemporary and later writers, let us remind ourselves that the

Athenians themselves made ample amends to Pericles for
whatever ignoble stigma they had thoughtlessly cast upon
the partner of his married life. For when the plague had
taken away both the sons of Pericles, and the statesman
who had toiled so hard for the supremacy of Athens was
left without a single representative at home to discharge
sacrificial duties to the shades of his ancestors—when the
family of the Alcmæonidæ had no heir to carry on its fame
—the Athenians determined to legitimise the youthful
Pericles, who was the son of Aspasia. Now it was quite
open for Pericles to have adopted some boy in order to
keep up the honour of his name. The fact that he did not
do anything of the kind, combined with the recognition
on the part of his fellow-citizens implied in the act of
legitimation of Aspasia's child, surely proved that in the
better judgment of Athens Aspasia's life had been so pure
and noble as to redeem her from all the base charges of
ignoble wits.

Thus in the long run truth prevails, and strength of
character will win its legitimate triumphs. Aspasia was
a great woman, full of quick natural intelligence, adorned
and fortified by a steady, organised system of culture.
Socrates, in his laughing fashion, declares that she taught
him how to speak, and going even further than this, tries
to make out that it was Aspasia, and not Pericles, who
wrote the Funeral Oration which was delivered in Athens
shortly after the beginning of the war, and reported so
fully by Thucydides. This, which we find in the Platonic
Dialogue called " Menexenus," is clearly Socrates' joke,
and we must not for a moment take it seriously—any more
than we can take seriously the report that after Pericles'
death Aspasia married a common cattle-dealer called
Lysicles. So prominent a figure naturally attracted to
itself every kind of floating gossip, complimentary or
malevolent. For ourselves, one or two things, amongst
many that could be cited, are quite sufficient to keep the
memory of Aspasia at the high level which her intellect
and her virtue deserved. A pretty story tells us that
Pericles, every time he left her for his ordinary avocations,
and every time he returned, kissed her—a fact which must
have been sufficiently remarkable to be worth chronicling,
and for this reason obviously a very unusual indication
of affection. We have said also that when he was defending her before the Athenian judges, Pericles, despite his

Olympian calm, burst into a flood of tears.   Points like these only illustrate how extraordinary was the devotion which united the first statesman of Greece with the most brilliant woman of her time.   But when we find that Athens could give up all its old prejudice, could turn its back on ancestral customs and conventions, and recognise the legitimacy of Pericles' union with an alien; and when we have to add to that this second fact, that Plato, who did not like Pericles, because he represented a political ideal different from his own, could yet venture to make his great master, Socrates, sit at the feet of Aspasia, in order to learn of her the arts of discussion and oratory, we can hardly be wrong in the conclusion that the Milesian woman, the daughter of Axiochus, Aspasia, the well-beloved of Pericles, stands in the very front rank of the great women who have adorned the pages of ancient and modern history.

A PHILOSOPHIC EMPEROR

Marcus Aurelius Antoninus

§ 1

The perennial charm which surrounds the *Meditations of Marcus Aurelius* is explicable on several grounds. Perhaps in the first place we should put the fact that the author of these thoughts was an Emperor; that is to say, a man who was every day face to face with all the problems of government, and who had to lead his soldiers against outlandish tribes—the Quadi, the Marcomanni, and others. In his busy career of practical industry one would hardly expect such a man to find opportunity or leisure for the kind of diary, in twelve books, which he has bequeathed to us. Another point of interest is that, though he had the inestimable advantage of a father by adoption, Antoninus Pius, to whom he pays a remarkable tribute in his opening chapter, he was himself surrounded with figures of the ordinary imperial depravity. His wife, Faustina, had no particularly good character, although probably some of the stories narrated of her by Dion Cassius and others represent nothing more nor less than the scandal of the time. At all events, it is certain that his son, Commodus, was a brutal ruffian, and it is difficult for us to understand how so gentle, so cultured, so philosophic a father should have left such few traces of his personality on the upbringing of Commodus. But a third and still more important element in our interest in the writings of the Emperor Marcus Aurelius Antoninus is that he was so near to, and yet so untouched by, Christianity. If we take the series of his thoughts, which he put down, apparently, day by day, as a kind of private commentary to guide his own career, we are struck over and over again by their likeness to and their difference from Christian tenets. The thoughts remind us of the *Imitation*, especially in their constant enunciation of the necessity for a definite purpose for human beings, some specific goal or object, which is to save men from stupid and idle vacillation.

109

Yet Marcus Aurelius' reflections are not Christian in spirit; they are Stoic. Together with the writings of the enfranchised slave, Epictetus, they give us the best possible picture of what Stoicism had become in the second century A.D.

Stoicism was a creed which especially recommended itself to the Romans from the very earliest time of its introduction, because in many ways it corresponded with the stout and intolerant Roman spirit, with its natural love of independence and its valiant endurance of suffering. Stoicism was assuredly not Greek in spirit, but rather the antithesis of the Greek idea. To the best Hellenic writers, ethics—that is to say, the private morals of an individual —were inextricably bound up with politics, the laws and conditions by which States preserve their integrity. When the Hellenic system was broken up, two forms of philosophy appeared, both in a manner dependent on the new fact that a man was bound to regard himself not as a citizen of a given State, but as a citizen of the world. One was the Epicurean philosophy, which taught the calm and dignified pursuit of cultured happiness. The other was the Stoic, which laid stress on the manly virtues of independence and strength of will. In the breakdown of the old constitutional forms, in the misery and unsettlement of the times, the Stoic philosophers invited men to fall back on their own natural powers and capabilities, to face the problem of life by a resolute assertion that within the four corners of his own consciousness man was free, and the proper master of his fate. Roman Stoicism, of course, took various forms. In the writings of the Emperor Marcus Aurelius these tenets are represented in the gentlest and most appealing way, albeit that they are not divorced from the fundamental principle that a man must find within himself the sources of his own strength. And so we come to what, apparently, has been looked upon as a paradox— the picture of an Emperor, with all the weight of a great kingdom on his hands, recommending himself, in aphorism after aphorism, to retire within the citadel of his own soul, and find peace and comfort in the knowledge that reason governed the universe. For that is the keynote of the Emperor's acquiescence. The principal part of a man's individuality is his reason, and the chief principle of the universe is reason also. Whatever happens to a man must be what is best for the whole system of things, and he must extract what consolation he can from the recognition that he is part of a universal rational order.

And this is the man who possibly had an unfaithful wife, and certainly had a brutal son, and who, above all, consented to the persecution of Christians. Two persecutions, at least, of Christians happened in the reign of Marcus Aurelius Antoninus—one in which Polycarp suffered at Smyrna, which may have taken place in A.D. 167, and the other the notorious trials at Lyons in A.D. 177. It is difficult for us, at the first blush, to understand how so gentle and so humane an Emperor could sanction tortures for Christians. Perhaps we shall never quite understand the mystery, for we cannot put ourselves back by any feat of imagination into the second century, and we cannot realise that the religion which has meant so much for a modern world should have been regarded at that time as a pernicious and detestable superstition. Trajan and Hadrian both laid down certain rules, coming practically to this : that if a Christian would recant, he should, of course, be left alone. If he persisted in his errors, he must suffer the penalty for his contumacy. One feature about the Christian communities, which is constantly being asserted by contemporary authorities, is their obstinacy. Mild and humane men like our Emperor were, of course, latitudinarians. They accepted the established paganism. They gladly gave as much liberty as they could to other faiths, so long as these other faiths did not attack the recognised orthodoxy of Rome. And they could not understand why the Christians were so contumacious, why they so strenuously put forward their own faith as that which must, in the long run, conquer paganism, and prove that the Roman deities were either devils or nothing. We now put our finger upon the main reason why the Christians were persecuted. From the Roman standpoint they were a sort of religious anarchists. They would not be content with cultivating their own faith in secret. They were militant and polemical. They wanted to destroy the established creed. To these considerations we must add the fact that there was a very large amount of ignorance about the exact tenets of Christianity, and that a number of Latin authors saw no difference between them and the Jews, who were always seditious and always troublesome. One thing, at all events, is certain : the ordinary population conceived the most violent hatred of Christians and Jews alike. It was the people who forced the hands of their Governors. They insisted that these seditious sects should suffer the penalty for their supposed crimes. It was in order to stop menacing revolutions that the Governors not only exercised their own authority, but appealed to the Emperor to sanction their legislative acts against the Christians. Of two things, one: Either the Empire must go on, with its established faiths, and in that case Christianity must be put down with all the severity that flows from the *odium theologicum ;* or else the frank admission must be made that paganism was effete and out-of-date. No one can expect the ordinary Roman Governor, or even an ordinarily enlightened Emperor, to assent at once to the latter alternative. After all, the real excuse of the authorities in this matter is that conventional excuse for harassed authority—that the business of the Imperial government must go on.

§ 2

The first thing to say about the philosophic system of Marcus Aurelius is that it is not a system at all. There is nothing systematic in the occasional and discursive remarks of the Emperor, except so far as we can fit them into the general framework of thought provided by the Stoical philosophy. The circumstances under which these reflections were composed, the fact that they were occasional notes, written very likely when the Emperor himself was engaged in his campaigns—the general nature of a private diary, which is always present to our minds when we read the *Meditations of Marcus Aurelius*—preclude the notion that we have to deal with a formally constructed treatise on themes connected with God, the world, and man. One or two points, however, must be remembered in order to explain the general attitude of the thinker. The Stoics believed in a division of knowledge between dialectic or logic, ethics, and physics. Later on, probably by Cleanthes, each division was subdivided; and thus we have a classification yielding physics and theology, ethics and politics, dialectic and rhetoric. There was obviously a gain in clearness by this subdivision, for we now know that, according to the Stoical point of view, physics, in the largest sense of the word, includes theology, or the constitution of the universe as a divine system; and that the proper and legitimate notion of the duties incumbent on a human being involves also his relation to a given state or constitution. Dialectic or logic we may put aside, for it makes but little appearance among the *Meditations of Marcus Aurelius.* Another point material to our inquiry is the recognition of the Stoical principle that man ought to live " conformably to Nature." Nature is, of course, an ambiguous term, and may mean either the normal or the original. It may mean the material, or, from a more enlarged standpoint, the material as ordered and arranged by a divine intelligence. When the Stoic teachers recommended men to live conformably to Nature, what they meant was, that man should so guide his life that he, a part of the universe, should move in unison and harmony with the totality of things. They meant, also, something more. They intended to indicate that, man's nature being modelled on the larger nature, the same principle of governance or direction should be used by man in his own concerns, which is acted on by Nature herself on the larger scale. Thus, for instance, man is composed, roughly, of two parts—spiritual and material; and the Cosmos, too, is composed of two parts—material, which the Greeks called ὕλη, and the informing reason or intelligence, to which they give the name of νοῦς. Now we know the world as a determined order of antecedents and sequences, of causes and effects, of something settled and arranged by a guiding spirit, which makes for harmony and order. Here is a model, then, for our own careers. The reason should guide; the physical properties of the human being should obey. But there must be a settled purpose in man's life, some goal to which he directs his efforts, some ideal which he seeks to realise. If in the conduct of his life he obeys the leading principle of reason, then he is acting conformably to Nature, which also, as experience shows us, is arranged on lines of providence and thought.

So far we move without any difficulty, because we are dealing abstractly with general and easily understood principles. But, as Marcus Aurelius is always keen to tell us, life is not theory but action; and it is, of course, action, experience, the daily conduct, which are of the greatest importance. One or two simple rules we may take for our help. The first thing to remember is, that man is intended to be social; that is to say, he is one unit in a society

I

bigger than himself, and he must learn the lessons of
unselfishness. He cannot pursue his own good to the
exclusion of that of his neighbour. He has hardly any
individual rights, apart from those which spring from the
social constitution to which he belongs. He must not
attempt to divorce himself, by a life of seclusion, from
the life of the community at large. As the Scripture reminds us : " We must bear one another's burdens," " We
are members one of another." In such maxims plainly
speaks the voice of an Emperor only too conscious that
upon him rests the imperial duty of governing his kingdom,
of discharging tasks not for his own individual aggrandise-
ment, but for the benefit of the whole. Other salutary
maxims are of more personal application. We have discovered that the guiding principle in human beings is
reason, from which it follows that we must not yield to
the persuasions of the body. We must not be conquered
by the passions, for all these are material. We must be
swayed by the spiritual or intellectual elements within
us. We must acknowledge the superiority of reason.
And the third maxim is, that so far as lies within our power,
we must free ourselves from deception and error. The
senses are always deceiving us. So, too, are the vague
opinions of men. Just as we must not mistake the mere
impressions on our senses for truths established by reason,
so we must not be led astray by the general estimation
which men place on what they call things of importance.
If we trusted our senses, for instance, we might suppose
that a mere pleasurable gratification, the chance offspring
of a momentary temptation, was preferable to the ordered
discipline of experience. Or, to put it in our modern way,
if we trusted our senses we might think that the sun rose
every morning and set every evening, and that the dew
came down from above instead of rising from below. We
might think, in short, that the sun went round the earth
instead of the earth round the sun, and that the stars in
the heavens at large were made for the use of the inhabitants of our petty world. Intelligence, thought, science,
correct vulgar errors. And, in precisely the same fashion,
we ought each of us to be able to correct vulgar errors
about the objects of human pursuit. What is the good
of worrying about wealth, or reputation, or even sickness,
or even death itself ? Some of these things belong to
the class of what Marcus Aurelius calls the indifferent,

ἀδιάφορα. Others are beyond the range of our own power, and must come upon us, whether we will or no.

The wise man will not disturb himself about indifferent matters, or the things outside the range of his own control. What he is concerned with is the ordering of his own soul, so that he may win for himself recognised virtuous states—courage, justice, temperance—and obtain the tranquillity which is the reward of philosophic self-control. Everywhere our knowledge is limited by our ignorance. We do not know very much—or rather, we know very little—about the ultimate constitution of things. It is enough for us to realise that we are in the midst of a world which is not accidental or haphazard, but which evolves or develops, as we should phrase it, according to a settled plan. We are in the hands of reason, of a providence which is intelligent, and if we train ourselves properly we shall be masters of our own soul, so as to order our lives rationally and intelligently. Some men will say (so Marcus Aurelius argues in one passage), How do you know there are gods, when you do not see them? And to this he answers that in the first place you do see them, for the universe at large shows you in the laws of Nature the existence of divine foresight. In the next place, you do not see your own soul; yet every rational man believes that he has within himself an individuality of his own, and that he can guide his affairs with discretion. Whether God created the universe at any given moment, or whether it has existed from all eternity, are unprofitable questions. We do not wholly understand how the universe of things is kept together—whether by a constant assertion of divine power, or by the establishment of " seminal principles," which ever afterwards carry out their own effects. But it really does not matter very much. Everywhere there are gods. If we live, we are surrounded by them, and wherever we go when we die, there, too, will be gods. Death itself is not a formidable thing—no more formidable than birth. We were nothing, and we became something. We cease to be something, and become nothing. Everywhere throughout the universe there is change, dispersion of elements, and fresh aggregation of elements. Things fade, and die, and revive. It is the idlest of all stupidities to fret or worry over the way in which the universe has been made. Thus the philosophy of Marcus Aurelius is, above all, that which is suited to harassed men.

§ 3

In his brilliant article on Marcus Aurelius in the *Essays in Criticism*, Matthew Arnold makes some remarks on the contrast between the Emperor's ethical position and that of Christianity. Such comparisons are not altogether profitable, for the respective principles are not to be compared. The primary appeal of the Stoical philosophy is to the head, the brain, the reasoning powers. The Stoic wise man is he who, through sheer strength of intelligence, having discovered all that is of consequence in life, and put aside all that is unessential, dominates himself and his fate, and lives the complete master of his own life. This tenet about the wise man brought the Stoics into a good deal of criticism and ridicule, because such an ideal person has never existed, and never could exist, and, as Horace laughingly remarks, if he had a cold in his head, his ideal dignity would be very largely impaired. But the picture which Marcus Aurelius tries to present is more human, and more sensible. He does not claim such masterful authority for the wise man. In the simplest conceivable fashion he goes through some of the ordinary difficulties of life, and shows how a philosopher, by dint of his reasoning powers, by going back in every case to first principles, manages to carve out for himself a career not absolutely happy, but at least contented and estimable. Happiness as such was not the object of the Stoic philosophy. Contentment, the absence of worry, the power of self-control, complacency, decorum, self-respect—these are the things at which the Emperor aims, and which, so far as we know, he attained to a large extent in the course of his life.

But it is obvious, of course, that this picture of humanity can only be realised on the ground that the ordinary feelings and emotions are either sacrificed or ruthlessly kept under constraint. The primary appeal of Christianity is not so much to the head as to the heart. The first principle of the Christian religion is the power of love; and at once we are conscious that we are in a different domain, with appeals of a very different kind of cogency, and an ideal which, so far from obliterating feeling, purifies and ennobles it. Neither Christianity nor Stoicism would assert that happiness was the end of life. The Christian relegates it practically to another world. But what we notice is, that whereas the ideally good man of the Stoic is a slightly inhuman creature, the ideal figure of the Christian is a thoroughly and completely human being, who, believing in self-sacrifice, devotes himself, through sheer love, to the good of his brothers. Of course, for this reason Christianity can powerfully affect the average man, whereas the doctrines of Stoicism are, at the most, for the elect and the thoughtful.

There is another point which arises out of Matthew Arnold's discussion of the *Meditations*. He notes in the Roman Emperor a certain wistfulness, as though, when all was said and done, something more were wanted to satisfy the ordinary needs and aspirations of the soul. Every reader of the *Meditations* will judge for himself whether this criticism is justified or not. For myself, I do not see the wistfulness so much as an occasional uncertainty. For the most part, Marcus Aurelius lays down his opinions before us as though they reconciled him to life. Now and again it is not so. Occasionally he is invaded by a distinct phase of scepticism, as though what had hitherto seemed clear had suddenly become obscure, and he was not quite sure whether the first principles to which he throughout trusted were in every respect trustworthy. A very significant passage of this kind is to be found at the end of the seventh book, in the last paragraph. The passage itself is somewhat obscure and probably corrupt, but the general meaning is tolerably obvious. The things which make for man's peace are the assurances which we derive from study and experience that the whole constitution of things is governed by reason, that the chains of cause and effect go on in accordance with a settled law, and that whatever the end may be of the whole development, it is not inconsistent with such reason and intelligence as exist in us. But there is an alternative supposition, and it is one to which, in moments of weakness, vacillation, and doubt, the thinker is sometimes tempted. Perhaps, after all, reason does not guide the universe. Perhaps the whole Cosmos is the result of chance, a fortuitous concourse of atoms, the final end of which no one can foretell. And perhaps men are not rationally directed, but are mere puppets, drawn this way and that—automata, whose very consciousness of their fate only makes their automatism the more pathetic. This is not a mood which is in any sense habitual to Marcus Aurelius, but it is discoverable sometimes. The extent of our knowledge is only very small. We do not know how God exists, or how He works, and the aspirations of faith are not always borne out by the operations of thought. Perhaps this is what Matthew Arnold means by "wistfulness"; but it seems more like that kind of uncertainty which besets any thinker when he gets near ultimate problems.

On another feature belonging to the Stoical system Marcus Aurelius lays down no precise judgment. The Stoic thought that it was one of the privileges of the wise man that he should be able to take himself out of existence by his own act whenever he found life intolerable. Some of the Stoics thanked God for the eternal law that, though we are only given one way of entering into life, there are many ways of going out of it. Such was Seneca's view; and one or two Stoics committed suicide for reasons which seemed satisfactory to themselves, but which hardly produced conviction in others. On the whole, it would seem that the Emperor does not encourage suicide. On the contrary, the general trend of his remarks is, to induce a man to wait for the end patiently and with tranquillity. As long as he lives a man can do useful acts. He ought not to abridge his possible usefulness by a hasty departure from the scene of action. Still we find a significant sentence which we may, if we like, interpret as a recommendation to suicide : " The house is smoky, and I quit it." But suicide is not quite in conformity with the general notion that a man is part of a social state, that he has his *rôle* to play—from which it follows that it must be something like a clear dereliction of duty if he takes himself away. Nor yet is Marcus Aurelius quite clear as to what happens to us after death. He cannot assent to the doctrine that the soul, which is part of the Divine, should perish utterly, for no portion of the Divinity can perish. But what form of existence the soul enjoys after human life is a matter which cannot be solved by philosophy, and which, therefore, the philosopher wisely leaves alone. A man need not worry, however. God or the gods will do whatever is best or most consistent with the whole Cosmos of things. In the next world there are gods quite as much as in this.

After all, that which gives Marcus Aurelius his immortality is the fact that the book of his *Meditations* is one to which we turn again and again in the certain hope of finding consolation and help. It is a bedside book, if ever there was one—a book not to be read through at a stretch, but to be taken up when occasion serves, full of wise and grave maxims, which never lose their pertinence or value. And it is not only because the reflections themselves have such philosophic weight that we take them to our hearts; it is because the author has revealed his own nature in all he has said, and the character of Marcus Aurelius is one which it is good for us to know. In this Emperor, with all his grave responsibilities of empire, we find a temperament of rare sweetness and humility, of tender affectionateness, of unfailing sympathy, of the most strenuous and unwearied effort towards an ideal goal. Other men may do good because they think that good will be done to them. Not so the Emperor. Goodness is never on the look-out for any reward. Take, for instance, this—

(V, 6.) One man, when he has done a service to another, is ready to set it down to his account as a favour conferred. Another is not ready to do this; but still in his own mind he thinks of the man as his debtor, and he knows what he has done. A third in a manner does not even know what he has done; but he is like a vine which has produced grapes, and seeks for nothing more after it has once produced its proper fruit. As a horse when he has run, a dog when he has tracked the game, a bee when it has made the honey, so a man when he has done a good act does not call out for others to come and see, but he goes on to another act, as a vine goes on to produce again the grapes in season. Must a man then be one of these, who in a manner act thus without observing it? Yes.

Or as mere current maxims to help us through the weary day, read the first section with which the fifth chapter opens—

In the morning when thou risest unwillingly, let this thought be present— I am rising to the work of a human being. Why then am I dissatisfied if I am going to do the things for which I exist and for which I was brought into the world? Or have I been made for this, to lie in the bed-clothes and keep myself warm? But this is more pleasant—Dost thou exist then to take thy pleasure, and not at all for action or exertion?

Or again, in the same strain—

(II, 1.) Begin the morning by saying to thyself, I shall meet with the busybody, the ungrateful, arrogant, deceitful, envious, unsocial. All these things happen to them by reason of their ignorance of what is good and evil. But I who have seen the nature of the good that it is beautiful, and of the bad that it is ugly, and the nature of him who does wrong, that it is akin to me, not (only) of the same blood or seed, but that it participates in (the same) intelligence and (the same) portion of the divinity, I can neither be injured by any of them, for no one can fix on me what is ugly, nor can I be angry with my kinsman, nor hate him. For we are made for co-operation, like feet, like hands, like eyelids, like the rows of the upper and lower teeth. To act against one another then is contrary to nature; and it is acting against one another to be vexed and to turn away.

Other maxims of a like import may be cited—

(IV, 24.) Occupy thyself with few things, says the philosopher, if thou wouldst be tranquil. But consider if it would not be better to say, Do what is necessary, and whatever the reason of the animal, which is naturally social, requires, and as it requires. For this brings not only the tranquillity which comes from doing well, but also that which comes from doing few things. For the greatest part of what we say and do being unnecessary, if a man takes this away, he will have more leisure and less uneasiness. Accordingly, on every occasion a man should ask himself, Is this one of the unnecessary things? Now a man should take away not only unnecessary acts, but also unnecessary thoughts, for thus superfluous acts will not follow after.

Or this—

(V, 11.) About what am I now employing my own soul? On every occasion I must ask myself this question, and inquire : What have I now in this part of me which they call the ruling principle? And whose soul have I now? That of a child, or of a young man, or of a feeble woman, or of a tyrant, or of a domestic animal, or of a wild beast?

Or once more—

(V, 16.) Such as are thy habitual thoughts, such also will be the character of thy mind; for the soul is dyed by the thoughts. Dye it, then, with a continuous series of such thoughts as these : for instance, that where a man can live, there he can also live well. But he must live in a palace;—well, then, he can also live well in a palace.

Are you afraid to die? Listen, then, to what the Emperor says—

(X, 36.) Thou wilt consider this, then, when thou art dying, and thou wilt depart more contentedly by reflecting thus : I am going away from such a life in which even my associates, in behalf of whom I have striven so much, prayed, and cared, themselves wish me to depart, hoping perchance to get some little advantage by it. Why, then, should a man cling to a longer stay here? Do not, however, for this reason go away less kindly disposed to them, but preserving thy own character, and friendly and benevolent and mild, and, on the other hand, not as if thou wast torn away; but as when a man dies a quiet death, the poor soul is easily separated from the body, such also ought thy departure from men to be, for Nature united thee to them and associated thee. But does she now dissolve the union? Well, I am separated as from kinsmen, not, however, dragged resisting, but without compulsion; for this, too, is one of the things according to Nature.

After all, it is almost inconceivable that if the world be

ruled by Divine Providence, goodness should be destroyed
by death.

(XII, 5.) How can it be that the gods, after having arranged all things
well and benevolently for mankind, have overlooked this alone, that some
men and very good men, and men who, as we may say, have had most
communion with the divinity, and through pious acts and religious ob-
servances have been most intimate with the divinity, when they have once
died should never exist again, but should be completely extinguished?

And the *Meditations* end on a fine note of philosophic dignity, wherein Marcus Aurelius resumes all that he
has felt about the shortness of life and the necessity for
contentment.

(XII, 36.) Man, thou hast been a citizen in this great state (the world):
what difference does it make to thee whether for five years (or three?) for
that which is conformable to the laws is just for all. Where is the hardship, then, if no tyrant nor yet an unjust judge sends thee away from the
state, but Nature who brought thee into it? the same as if a prætor who
has employed an actor dismisses him from the stage—" But I have not
finished the five acts, but only three of them." Thou sayest well, but in
life the three acts are the whole drama; for what shall be a complete
drama is determined by him who was once the cause of its composition,
and now of its dissolution: but thou art the cause of neither. Depart,
then, satisfied, for he also who releases thee is satisfied.

Such was the gentle and philosophic Emperor, a model
for all men in whatever condition of life they may find
themselves, giving apt consolation to those who are per-
plexed, and always suggesting fine ideals to those who know
how to be humble and simple. Simplicity, indeed, is one
of the Emperor's chief recommendations, for, as he says,
after telling us to be just, temperate, obedient to the gods,
we must do all this with simplicity, because " the pride
which is proud of its want of pride is the most intolerable
of all."

THE IDEA OF COMEDY.—I

§ 1

SOME years ago I wrote certain essays under the title " The Idea of Tragedy." I want in the present and the succeeding paper to say something on the corresponding subject of " The Idea of Comedy," my effort being to disentangle from the variety of different plays which have come under the general head of Comedy the essential idea of this form of dramatic work. And it is by no means an easy thing to do, because the very meaning of the word has changed in different periods of history, and the term has been taken to cover a wide range of theatrical work. There is only one way to proceed in a case like this. We must determine in our own mind what is the highest specimen, the finest flower of the comic spirit, and when this has been settled we shall be able to appreciate the various approaches made to it, and estimate the success or failure, from the point of view of the supreme excellence. Where shall we find the highest examples of the comic spirit ? I do not think there is much doubt that the real writer of comedies, the man who discovered the proper formula of this kind of work, and left imperishable examples of his dramatic skill and aptitude, was Molière.

In George Meredith's well-known " Essay on Comedy " —an authoritative work which no one would omit considering in this reference—the whole idea and stamp of what comedy means is founded on the polite and distinguished plays of Molière, and also of Congreve, types of that kind of work which is only possible in a highly civilised society of men and women of taste and breeding, met for the exchange of verbal wit and fashionable intrigue. This high comedy is, of course, essentially different from the lower types, descending into the region of farce, which often usurp its name. George Meredith gives us a definition which it will be useful to remember, for its value will be apparent later, when he says that the kind of comedy to which he is referring is that which produces " *thoughtful laughter.*"

Thoughtful laughter—it is a good phrase.   We laugh at a farce, we laugh at all kinds of burlesque entertainments, we laugh at pantomimes, we laugh at the grotesque humour of some of the artists in a Revue.   But this kind of laughter could not possibly be called thoughtful; it rather rests on the absence of all thought, and comes more naturally from a vacuous mind.   It may be irresistible, but it is not dignified.   Thoughtful laughter is a different experience, which does not come to us often.   It is an inner experience —a sort of internal chuckle—which does not display external manifestations.   It is the enjoyment of the intellect when situations, or characters, or, sometimes, phrases strike one as happy exhibitions of humour.

The distinction between comedy and farce is in some cases not easy to make, but as a general rule we can apprehend the fundamental difference between the two in the following fashion.   In a farce the situations are the main thing, and they condition character;   or, in other words, character is a negligible thing if the situations are amusing.   In comedy, on the other hand, the character of the personages conditions, or creates, the situation.   The situation does not exist for itself, but in order to illustrate the personages involved.   But comedy itself has different types.   There is comedy which is a form of burlesque; comedy which is a department of romance; comedy whose main subject is the succession of comic incidents; comedy which deals with manners—changing manners and fashions of a time- - and comedy which deals with character.   A comedy which is for the most past burlesque extravaganza is exemplified, let us say, in Aristophanes; romantic comedy is the especial gift of Shakespeare; for comedy of incidents we look naturally to the Italian school, verging on farce; for the comedy of manners let us select our own Restoration dramatists.   The comedy of character remains, which we naturally attribute to Molière.   As a matter of fact, Molière's comedies are typical of their class, because they combine earlier varieties.   You have a comedy of manners and also a comedy of incident, but these are made to serve the main purpose, which is to exhibit character.   In pieces like *Les Femmes Savantes, Le Misanthrope, L'Avare,*

Tartuffe, and others we have a full and complete exhibition of the comic spirit.

I have said that it is not easy to disentangle the idea of comedy. Why is it difficult? The first thing to notice is that comedy has been found difficult by writers. One would be naturally inclined to say that comedy must be easier to write than tragedy. As a matter of fact, history seems to prove that it is more difficult. Almost everywhere tragedy comes first in literature. Æschylus, Sophocles, and Euripides in Greek drama, produced their tragedies, carried to a high level and pinnacle of excellence their tragic plays, before comedy began. Aristophanes is supposed to have turned the attention of the Athenian public to comic themes. That, however, is what is known as the older comedy, succeeded by the middle and the new. The man who discovered the true formula was Menander. He belongs to the new comedy. We ascribe, without much hesitation, to him this honour, because he was so extensively imitated and admired in subsequent times. Terence, the Roman dramatist, was his constant imitator. Without Menander, apparently, there would have been no Terence, though there might have been Plautus. Of Menander himself, unfortunately, we know but little. I am not sure that he could have been very much appreciated during his lifetime. He lived between 342 B.C. and 291 B.C. He wrote one hundred comedies, and only gained the prize eight times. He had a rival, not only in dramatic art, but also in personal affection towards a lady called Glycera—the writer Philemon, who probably was more popular than he was. The story goes, which is repeated for us by Aulus Gellius, that Menander used to ask Philemon, " Don't you feel ashamed whenever you gain the victory over me? " Philemon's answer is not recorded. Subsequently Menander became the idol, the superlatively favourite writer of antiquity. Even St. Paul quoted him. In the First Corinthians, fifteenth chapter, verse 33, is found the text, " Evil communications corrupt good manners." This was one of the moral maxims of the dramatist, moral maxims of which he was fond, apparently, such as these : " The property of friends is common," and the much-quoted " Whom the gods love die young."

Lately we have discovered a little more about Menander, for between the ten years—1897 to 1907—certain papyri were found in various parts of Egypt containing large fragments of Menander's comedies. Even now, however, we do not know much about him, but enough to be pretty sure that he achieved in his day what Molière achieved many years later—the comedy of manners in the first place, and also of character exemplified in manners. Perhaps the slow growth of his frame was to be explained by this very fact which is occupying our attention, namely, that the discovery of the essential idea of comedy is of a late growth. Do we wish for another example of this in our own literature? There is none better than is furnished by Shakespeare himself. Shakespeare seems to have found no particular difficulty in arriving at the idea of tragedy. Perhaps he found the form all ready for him, in this respect—in Christopher Marlowe, for instance; but there was no form ready for him in comedy, and therefore he made a series of different tentative efforts in this direction, not always with success. We find much the same result if we look at the history of dramatic literature in France. Corneille achieved his tragedies before the time when he made some hesitating advances in the direction of comedy, and only after many efforts did Molière succeed in achieving his splendid representation of manners and morals and character.

§ 2

Thus comedy, it would seem, is a late and difficult acquisition. Let us ask ourselves why. One obvious answer is, that comedy deals with everyday life, with which we are all familiar, and about which we all claim to be judges. Tragedy introduces standards which we cannot always verify out of our own experience; therefore, we do not claim to be adequate judges, and the writer of tragedy escapes a censure which is only too ready and waiting for the writer of comedy. If I write a novel of which the scene and the characters are in some fanciful region, there is nothing to curb my invention. But if I write a novel dealing with everyday life then my condemnation is easy in the mouth of those who say that I have betrayed remarkable ignorance of actual facts. We can get another reason for this superior difficulty of comedy in the fact that the best and most perfect specimens of comedy depend on a large amount of contemporary culture and civilisation.

Society must be pretty well fixed in its prevalent characteristics before men are in a position to treat it lightly and to allow themselves to laugh at some of its forms. You must be tolerably sure of your religious faith before you can afford to be humorous about it. You must be equally certain of the main principles which underlie both ethical and social structures before you dare to be humorous about them. So, too, a real comedy of manners and character combined can only be the product of a tolerably advanced civilisation which is so convinced of its real stability that it is not shocked by the gay points of witty and cynical humour expended on its satirical illustration. " It is a strange enterprise," said Molière, " to make honest folk laugh." Why is it strange? Because it is arbitrary. Comedy is in its essence a purely arbitrary product. If you take life simply and naturally, you will readily discover some of its grave and menacing problems. You will find out the tragic elements in existence without much difficulty, and you will feel your mind depressed with the burden of things, and write, if you have the dramatic gift, studies exhibiting to the full the perplexities, the high emotions, the profound love and equally profound despair which such problems involve. And now look at the procedure of the comedian. He is going to try to make you laugh at the very things which would naturally urge you to tears. He is going to abstract from the panorama of existence certain types of human character which he insists on regarding as occasions for mirth and laughter. Sometimes, it is true, the laughter is nervous enough, so nervous that we suspect that the author is in a hurry to laugh for fear that he should cry. Sometimes his comic spirit is the issue of a really philosophic complacency, won after much effort. Life is a terrible tangle, he seems to say; you had better treat it gaily, or otherwise you might go mad. Sometimes, again, being himself of a light disposition, he insists on looking only at the superficial aspect of things. Above all, the comedian has discovered one thing which is of enormous value to men in this vale of tears—the real ethical and social value of humour, as a preservative, as a gift of sanity to save us from exaggeration. And therefore the comedian will be neither optimist nor pessimist. He will laugh equally at both creeds. The arbitrary character of comedy is sufficiently shown in the various aphorisms that are used about it. For instance, Horace Walpole's " life is a comedy to those who think, a tragedy to those who feel," or the indubitably sage comment that if your comedian were to extend his play beyond the recognised number of acts it would be the commencement of a tragedy.   But he is in a hurry to bring down his curtain, because if we gazed more intently at his pictures we should find our laughter fading away.   Why do most comedies end with marriage?   The answer comes pat : Because the sequel is too depressing. And is not Malvolio a really tragic character when Andrew Aguecheek and Maria and Toby Belch have worked their wicked will with him, and consigned him to a dungeon, which assuredly he does not deserve?   Is not Molière's Alceste equally tragic?   Comedy is, as it were, the flower that grows on the edge of a precipice, which we gather with a fearful joy; it is the butterfly which alights on the barricades, the bright gleam of sunshine irradiating the dark clouds which seem to menace a coming storm—an artificial piece of work representing an arbitrary and artificial point of view.   It is at his own peril that the comedian says, like Puck, " Lord, what fools these mortals be ! " because it is an assumption of superiority easy enough for an elf, difficult for any of us who may all be involved in the same condemnation.

§ 3

The slow growth of comedy, the actual steps in its history, serve to illustrate its artificial character.   We must take note of some of the changes which it underwent before we can understand the form in which it appears in Shakespeare, in Molière, and in the Restoration dramatists.   At its origin—as, indeed, one would naturally suppose—comedy aimed at a humorous delineation of individuals.   In a city like Athens, given over to a good deal of unrestrained mirth, which also after the triumph of the democratic influences under Pericles and Ephialtes was the home of liberty in its widest aspects, Athenian comedy began with a bold and vigorous satire on some of the personages who were actually directing its civic development.   When Aristophanes laughed at Cleon and the Knights, when he instituted a mock trial between the two tragedians Æschylus and Euripides, when he turned the points of his satirical humour against a strange contemporary character like Socrates, it is as though some modern wag, let us say Mr. Bernard Shaw, were to allow himself to represent in laughable guise Mr. Asquith, Mr. Lloyd George, or Lord Haldane. Even in Athens the licence of the dramatists was found intolerable, partly because it destroyed all respect for leading personalities, partly because it was so hideously unjust. No one, for instance, would for a moment imagine that Aristophanes, the prince of these early comic dramatists, gave a faithful presentation of the Athens of his time. He made downright mistakes, where his knowledge was not equal to his satiric talent. Thus, for instance, he presents before us a Socrates engaged in the problems of physical philosophy—exactly that department of research with which Socrates had nothing to do. Socrates was a moral philosopher above all. Be that as it may, the earlier form of comedy, which was aimed at individuals, and was, for the most part, burlesque extravaganza, very speedily gave way to other kinds of comedy, technically called Middle and New Comedy, which created comic types to take the place of the earlier subjects of criticism. You will find in the period of middle and new comedy most of those types of character invented, which afterwards play a great part not only in the comedies of Rome, but also in the comedies of modern Italy and Spain. Standing types, such as boastful soldiers, parasites, courtesans, revellers, self-conceited cooks, above all cunning slaves, these were the things which helped to amuse the Athenians, specially at a time when the clouds were gathering fast round their beloved city, and there was every reason why their mind should be distracted from the calamities which threatened them on every side. A farce called *Gigantomachia* was actually being played when the news arrived in Athens of the destruction of the two Sicilian expeditions.

And so, gradually, a comedy of manners was instituted, not a comedy of manners as it was understood in a later age, but of a conventional kind, dealing with recognised and conventional figures. Over Roman comedy we need not linger, because it was purely derivative. It is true that a distinction was drawn in Roman comedy between that which treated of Greek subjects and imitated Greek originals, and that which professed at all events to have a native character. The first was called Palliata, the second Togata. But, as a matter of fact, both were dependent largely on Greek originals, and the spirit they had introduced. Plautus and Terence, of course, were the distinguished dramatists of the time who devoted their talents to comedy. Of Plautus it is probably true to say that he had certain originality and a genuinely national, as well as popular, element. Terence, a finer and more cultivated writer, was almost entirely indebted to Menander, both for plot and treatment.

We have already observed that most of the types commonly used by writers of comedy were taken over in modern times, when Italy, above all other countries, was inspired by the spirit of the Renascence. Perhaps the invention of Harlequin was the great addition made by early Italian comedy. But it is to be noticed of Italian comedy as a whole that its most popular form was the so-called " Comedy of Masks," a collection of recognised characters, most of whom wore masks in order to indicate the class and type to which they belonged. So artificial and yet so popular was it, that, though Goldoni strove vigorously for originality of treatment he yet was unable wholly to withstand the influence of tradition in many respects. In Spain, in similar fashion, comedy revolved round certain fixed types of character. The soldier was the great figure in the dramas of Lope de Vega. For the most part these comedies dealt not with common life, but sometimes with episodes in the national annals, sometimes with contemporary or recent events. But they almost always had for characters the upper classes, the class that wore cloak and sword, from which the comedies themselves—" de capa y espada "—took their name.

The sum total of our observations, so far, is that we have a comedy of intrigue, a comedy of fixed characters, to a large extent traditional and conventional, and therefore also, within these limits, a comedy of manners. But a comedy of character in the true sense of the term, a piece which is to reveal the intricacies of some human personage freshly observed and studied, so that we recognise him as belonging to our human brotherhood, for that we look, for the most part, in vain. The problem which is left for the later writers is how, with full recognition of the artificiality of the framework, to find room for a real psychological study, and that is a problem which was not perfectly nor fully solved until Molière came on the scene.

K

§ 4

Meanwhile, Shakespeare provides us with an extremely interesting chapter. On the whole, it must be said that Shakespeare as a writer of comedies was a good deal inferior to Shakespeare as the author of tragedies. That is to say, the things which matter to us most in Shakespeare, the things by which he lives and in which his astonishing range of poetry, philosophy, and psychology is best illustrated, are seen in pieces like *Romeo and Juliet, Hamlet, Macbeth, Othello*, and *Lear*. Nevertheless, his comedies are very interesting, because he is evidently trying to elaborate a formula of his own, and to achieve this, apparently, without any help rendered to him by his predecessors. I have already suggested that the form of tragedy was pretty well fixed by Marlowe and others. But the formula of comedy was by no means fixed. And thus we see Shakespeare groping after different forms, essaying tentative experiments not always too successful.[1] He first of all seems to have thought that he ought to invent characters by the aid of his own fantasy or imagination, and to invent his stories also, a matter in which he was certainly not an adept. *Love's Labour's Lost*, for instance, supposed to be the earliest original piece of Shakespeare, is, in all probability, a story which Shakespeare made out of his own head. His knowledge of human nature was not at that time profound, nor was he perhaps altogether inclined to rely upon it. And the result is a kind of comic opera, superficial and mechanical, just the sort of thing which a clever young man might put together, including certain stage types like the braggart and the pedant and the clown, which he might have taken over from the Italian comedy. Then he bethinks himself that he might as well serve Plautus as Plautus had served his Greek originals, and in *The Comedy of Errors* he is merely borrowing from the *Menæchmi*. If the result attained in the earlier instance was polite comic opera, now the result is pure farce. Then he turns to something which is more or less a comedy of intrigue, in *The Two Gentlemen of Verona*, not a very plausible piece of work, and not nearly so well constructed as, for instance, *The*

[1] See Prof. Brander Matthews' *Shakespeare as a Playwright* (Longmans), a work of no little value to all students of the craftsmanship of plays.

Comedy of Errors. Observe, in passing, that Shakespeare always provides parts for clowns, and the clown of the Elizabethan theatre was descended almost directly from the Vice of the mediæval stage. Perhaps, as has been suggested, there were two low comedians in Shakespeare's company, for whom parts had to be found. At all events, the clowns run in pairs in these earlier comedies—Costard and Dull in *Love's Labour's Lost*, the two Dromios in *The Comedy of Errors*, and Launce and Speed in *The Two Gentlemen of Verona*. I need not mention *A Midsummer Night's Dream*, because it is more of a masque than a comedy.

Now what is the great advance we discover when from these dramas we turn to the romantic comedies, to *The Merchant of Venice*, to *Much Ado About Nothing*, to *As You Like It*, and to *Twelfth Night*? First of all, it would seem that the dramatist has made the discovery that he need not trouble himself to invent characters, but has only got to open his eyes to the numerous characters that existed in his time. Who can doubt that his wonderful heroines—Portia, Beatrice, Rosalind, Viola—were studied on the spot, taken from some of the personages who moved in the court, distinguished ladies who, though they allowed themselves a certain amount of freakishness, and even sometimes buffoonery, yet preserved the essential lineaments of gentlewomen? Nor was there any greater necessity to invent plots. They could be found anywhere, especially amongst the Italians or the French. The rudiments might be taken from these sources, but Shakespeare found out that his best talents could be exhibited in the fashion in which he reconstructed these dramas, sometimes taking two sources for one play and welding them together into a more or less successful unity. Lastly, Shakespeare, in his search for a formula for comedy, came to the conclusion that if you wanted pleasurable and cultivated romance it had better be exhibited as contrasted with a background of something sinister and menacing, involving elements of serious tragic interest. This is the point which is most significant in Shakespeare's romantic comedies. You have a pair of sparkling lovers, sometimes two, or even three pairs, on whom Shakespeare expends all his pains, and then you have an underplot which serves to show up by force of contrast the brilliance of these happy lovers. They are plucking safety and happiness out of circumstances which in themselves look dangerous. They win in the end because, otherwise, the play would not be comedy at all; but their victory is all the more conspicuous and significant because at one time they appeared to be threatened with imminent disaster.[1]

And now we see the value of that definition which we have borrowed from George Meredith, that comedy involves thoughtful laughter. We smile at some of the airs and graces which these gay, romantic personages assume; we smile at the wit combats between Benedick and Beatrice; we smile at the braggadocio of Bassanio, who thinks it necessary to assure Portia that he is a gentleman. We note also the careless assumption of superiority of Antonio in *The Merchant of Venice* which, because he is over-confident in his commercial success, puts him into the hands of Shylock. But our very laughter makes us serious and thoughtful when we discover that these happy creations of the dramatist's fancy are playing with edged tools, and in some cases are almost courting disaster. Behind Bassanio and Portia rises the sinister figure of Shylock; underneath the witty badinage of Benedick and Beatrice lies the cruel plot, the wanton misbehaviour of Claudio, and the tragic demand which the heroine makes on the hero at the very crisis of their fate : " Kill Claudio ! " In many of the older philosophies happiness is represented as being a boon of the gods, for which we ultimately have to pay. The gods are jealous; they do not like human prosperity; they, apparently, are even made uneasy by human light-heartedness and laughter. So, too, the writer of comedy seems to remind us that smiles are purchased at the cost of tears, and that good luck and prosperity are rare and unusual things, for which some recompense or ransom will, ultimately, be exacted. Shakespeare, as well as Beaumarchais, seems to recommend us to make haste to laugh lest we should begin to cry.

The Merchant of Venice is especially significant in this respect. Shakespeare has now got his formula, such as it is, that comedy involves two, or it may be more, lovers, who are to be joined together in the end in complete happiness. It also involves—because true love never did run smooth—the intrusion of some elements of danger, or, at all events, difficulty, threatening at times to interfere with the bright elements, but kept for the most part as a back-

[1] Cf. *Shakespeare as a Playwright*, by Prof. Brander Matthews, chap. viii.

ground in the form of a sub-plot. As to the origin of these stories, Shakespeare at this period of his development will take them from anywhere, take two together, interweave them, despite their obvious diversity of feeling, and make of them a single consistent play. For the dramatist has discovered wherein his chief strength lies. It is in so arranging his materials drawn from different sources as to exhibit in full light the main character, or characters, in which he is interested. Invention, which was, perhaps, his earlier method, he has already discovered to be barren in his case. He does not possess much invention, but he is a rare hand at working up materials gained elsewhere. And he has discovered that the business of comedy, quite as much as the business of tragedy, is to educe, in one way or another, a real study of character, albeit that for the purpose of romance the characters are more slightly drawn. Still, let us not forget that in this earliest of his romantic comedies, *The Merchant of Venice*, Shakespeare has drawn a complete portrait of the Jew—a portrait so acute, so thorough, so absolutely unlike anything which his contemporaries could have drawn, that the Jew threatens to usurp the main interests of the play and turn the comedy into a tragedy.

Let us linger a little over this point, for it is a curious illustration of the way in which a maker of comedies seems to find it necessary to have dark clouds round the horizon, in order that we may better appreciate the sunshine that bathes the forefront of the scene. Let us ask ourselves what was the original intention of Shakespeare. Clearly he wished to put before us the wooing of Bassanio and Portia, repeated over again, as is his wont, in the wooing of Gratiano and Nerissa and that of Lorenzo and Jessica. Portia is the conspicuous figure, from the point of view of the dramatist. Portia appears early in the play, and has the fifth act almost entirely to herself. The other characters, as it were, group themselves round her transcendent charm; they form a court retinue at Belmont, where she reigns as queen. And Belmont, too, is absolutely the place of romance. It is like those Ruritanian countries with which *The Prisoner of Zenda* made us acquainted, a country precisely like the Forest of Arden, or Messina, or Illyria, or wherever Shakespeare chose to place the scenes of his comedies. They have no geographical boundaries. They are, if we like to phrase it so, a cloud-cuckooland where marvels happen. We see this in many ways, especially in the fact that Shakespeare is at no pains to make his characters belong to the locality he has chosen. Perhaps he is more successful with Venice, but who, in *A Midsummer Night's Dream*, thinks for a moment of the neighbourhood of Athens? Who looks upon Bottom as a Greek? How could Dogberry and Verges possibly appear in Sicily? Or Sir Toby Belch, or Andrew Aguecheek, or the inimitable Maria in Illyria? These come of an English stock, from Warwickshire perhaps, because Shakespeare is no pedant in the matter of his scenery. And just as his Romans are Englishmen, so, too, is the nurse who serves as go-between in *Romeo and Juliet* constructed on a solidly British basis.

The essence of the romantic comedy remains with the lovers in the fairy home of Belmont. But what has happened to the play in later times? Any actress is proud to assume the part of Portia, but in a modern world she knows perfectly well that her interest is subordinate to that of the actor who plays Shylock. And even with regard to this character we are conscious of a change from an earlier conception. Shakespeare, undoubtedly, meant us to hate and loathe Shylock. He spares no opportunity of holding him up to derision. He wants us to laugh at him as well as to spurn him, for in this matter he is faithfully reproducing the feelings of the time, which regarded the Jew, as money-lender and usurer, with absolute abhorrence. If we want a proof, we need only turn to *The Jew of Malta*, by Christopher Marlowe. In this we have a sinister figure of rapacity and evil, a man designed to exhibit some of the worst vices of humanity, and called Barabbas as though to suggest at once that he is the born enemy of all followers of Christ. Shakespeare probably started with the same intention as Christopher Marlowe, but what is the curious result? He is such a born psychologist that he must needs do justice even to Shylock. He cannot help but make him human. He makes us feel how largely his malevolence was due to the most un-Christian conduct of the Christians. He gives him the noble speech which commences " Hath not a Jew eyes? " involving an appeal to our generous feelings of compassion for one who was at least as much sinned against as sinning, All the waves of calamity beat against this solitary figure. His servant derides him, his daughter runs away from him, he is robbed of the jewels of which he made great store. Finally, he is even robbed of that revenge which, according to his interpretation of the law, was his due. And when he leaves the scene at the end of the trial, bankrupt in hope and prospects, forced to become a Christian, with all the edifice which he had so laboriously built up in ruins around him, he becomes a figure of absolute tragedy, so tragic, indeed, that Shakespeare is in haste to tack on a fifth act in order to restore the balance of his play. It is doubtful whether Shakespeare ever saw a Jew, for they were not allowed to live in England. Most likely, however, this law was evaded. But the extraordinary thing is the ability with which the dramatist gets hold of the essential features of a characteristic Jew, who uses imagery derived from the Old Testament, insists on the absolute letter of the bond, and shows throughout that intense pride in his race which has kept the Jew a thing apart through centuries alike of prosperity and failure.

Shakespeare becomes a little more sure in his procedure in each of the ensuing romantic comedies. Clearly he was feeling his way in *The Merchant of Venice*. He is aware that a mere love-story is not sufficient, not even when the lovers are doubled and trebled. Something more is required to stiffen the plot, and it is probably with some such idea in his head that Shakespeare added the Antonio-Shylock story to the Bassanio-Portia story. What is the result? The background overpowers the foreground, the sinister figure of Shylock dominates the whole play, and what ought to be sub-plot comes to be the main intrigue. He does not make quite the same mistake again. He still believes in the necessity of some mutterings of storm, in order to give due contrast to the sunlight, but he will see to it that the importance of the serious elements does not overpower the lighter intrigue of his lovers. In the next, therefore, of his romantic comedies, *Much Ado About Nothing*, we still find much the same formula as that which dictated *The Merchant of Venice*—two pairs of lovers at least, and behind them a dark intrigue which threatens to mar their felicity. We have also in *Much Ado* the same kind of interaction of two plots which we have already observed in *The Merchant of Venice*. There is the story connected with Beatrice and Benedick and the story connected with Hero and Claudio. But the menacing figures of evil, Don John and Borachio, are not really very formidable; indeed, such villainy as they are on the stage to express is more than a little artificial, and we are not inclined to take it very seriously.

Melodramatic figures like Don John and Borachio are themselves made use of to lead up to the more purely comic factors of the play. The broad comedians, Dogberry and Verges, for instance, justify their existence, because Borachio gets drunk, is apprehended, and gives the whole secret away.

Meanwhile, more than ever before, Shakespeare expends his whole force over the two characters which stand well in the forefront of the action—Beatrice and Benedick. We are to suppose that they were, more or less unconsciously, attracted to one another, even before the story opens. We observe that they begin to bicker as soon as the curtain goes up, and inasmuch as this bickering is sheer word-play and of no particular use to the action, the audience at once understands that these gay fencers have entered the lists more than once before and know to a nicety the length of each other's weapons. Beatrice is one of the most commanding figures which Shakespeare ever drew. She is stronger all round than Portia, stronger, I mean, intellectually. She has not the winsome grace of Viola, nor the quiet, demure fun and humour of Rosalind. Into Beatrice's composition comes something of the nature of the shrew. We can quite imagine that if she had not been given free play and not been surrounded by all the tender affection of those who knew her and loved her, she might have become Katherine the Curst. Whether in that case Benedick would have been able to manage her, as Petruchio managed Katherine, is a doubtful matter. Like all comedies, the curtain falls on the happiness of the lovers, and we are expressly debarred from wondering what happened afterwards. The married life of Benedick and Beatrice we should not like to be too sure of, although they began their career so gallantly. Shakespeare has now, however, discovered that he is at his best when he is amalgamating different stories, bringing them together with that touch of supreme theatrical genius which is his most distinctive characteristic. The procedure is just the same as in *The Merchant of Venice*. How are the two widely different stories, of how Portia was wooed and won, and how the wiles of Shylock were defeated, to be amalgamated in one plot? How, again, was the story which involved the fates of Hero and Claudio to be reconciled and made one with the flashing wit encounters of " Dear Lady Disdain " and her much-derided and much-loved soldier? In each play—*The Merchant of*

Venice and *Much Ado*—we get a sort of critical scene in which this union of diverse elements is consummated. In *The Merchant of Venice* it is the trial scene, in *Much Ado* it is the church scene. Very artfully and ingeniously does Shakespeare work to get all the due effect out of his two stories in *Much Ado*. As we all know, the church scene consists of two superficially contradictory episodes. The repudiation of Hero by Claudio is so bitter and so unpleasant that only a Shakespeare could have tacked on to it without fear that little scene between Beatrice and Benedick. In truth, the marriage ceremony is the device which is to bring the two lovers together. Hero is Beatrice's friend, Claudio is Benedick's friend. Hero has been disgraced publicly; Claudio has shown himself contemptible in the harshness with which he has pursued his vengeance. And out of this imbroglio comes the strange discovery that Beatrice is in love with Benedick, and that Benedick is quite prepared to overthrow all his old friendships for the sake of Beatrice's beautiful eyes. Left together, after all the others have gone their respective ways from a desecrated ceremony, the pair of lovers have their brief, poignant talk, and the central moment for which Shakespeare has long been preparing is reached when Beatrice flashes upon Benedick her two words : " Kill Claudio ! " Both she and he knew how much she was asking. It was a supreme test of the love that was greater than mere friendship. Does Benedick like her well enough to renounce all his old associations for her sake ? And the answer comes at once. From that moment Benedick is Beatrice's sworn knight, ready to fulfil her lightest, as well as her sternest, behest.

As to the figures which surround the principal actors in his play, Shakespeare is, as ordinarily happens, supremely careless. He does not even try to be convincing. The plot against Hero is as stupid as it is malicious. It is impossible to believe in Don John's absurd villainy. Nobody cares, however, because Shakespeare looks to it that we should be so much interested in the main incidents that nothing else matters. Fortunately, as we have seen, the villains give an opportunity for the illustration of two characters of downright comedy—Dogberry and Verges. What business they had to be in Messina is another question. They are, of course, purely English, drawn from some of those rustic types which our dramatist had before his eyes in his Warwickshire home—incomparably stupid and incomparably funny, much better than the two Gobbos of *The Merchant of Venice,* or the two Dromios of *The Comedy of Errors.* Nor let us omit, before we leave this play, to notice one feature which connects it with Shakespeare's later work. As distinct from Portia and Bassanio, who remain at the end of the play pretty well what they were at the beginning,[1] we observe a distinct development of character in Benedick and Beatrice. We watch them, as it were, growing before our eyes, out of two witty combatants becoming two ardent and affectionate friends. Development of character in the course of a play becomes a keynote of Shakespeare's later work, as we see in *Hamlet* and *Othello* and *Macbeth.*

When Shakespeare, at a later period, after writing *Hamlet* composed such pieces as *All's Well That Ends Well, Measure for Measure,* and *Troilus and Cressida,* he wrote so-called comedies, which cannot possibly be included in any real definition of the comedy spirit. No one pretends to like any of these three plays. They are all full of a kind of bitterness, which is very far removed from the usual Shakespearean tolerance and broad-mindedness. *Troilus and Cressida* is the strangest piece of all. Some of us are inclined to say that Mr. Bernard Shaw travesties the early heroes and antique forms of heroism in such plays as *Cæsar and Cleopatra* and *Androcles and the Lion.* But his irreverence—if, indeed, that be the right term—is as nothing compared with what Shakespeare did in *Troilus and Cressida.* Perhaps, because he was angry with his so-called rival poet, the classical Chapman, he set himself to work to belittle all the old Greek heroes, as though he were running a tilt against classical types. Ulysses, Agamemnon, and the rest cut strange figures in his play. And never was a bitterer thing created than Thersites.

It must not be supposed that romantic comedy is only to be found in Shakespeare. It runs through all the history of the art, and our modern age affords us many illustrations. It would seem that most dramatic writers, although they try in a truly logical spirit to exhibit the humour of the situations they describe and the humour of the characters which they are illustrating, are tempted now and again to abandon such points of irony and satire as they may deem necessary for their task in order to indulge in some frankly

---

[1] I am not sure, however, that Bassanio has not gradually learnt a good many lessons about " gentlemanliness."

ideal and imaginative production which will be of the essence of romance. It is very rare indeed that you get a man like Mr. Bernard Shaw, who, disbelieving in romance, keeps his comedies free from romantic entanglement. And yet there is *Captain Brassbound's Conversion* to make us pause.[1] Sir Arthur Pinero gives us a romantic comedy in *The Princess and the Butterfly*, and Sir James Barrie gives us very little else. How otherwise are we to describe pieces like *The Admirable Crichton, Little Mary, What Every Woman Knows*, or even *The Adored One*, except as romantic comedies, in which the circumstances are often ideal and the characters possess ideal excellences?

It is more important, however, for us to determine in brief and summary fashion why Shakespeare's conception of comedy falls short of the real range and value of the comic spirit. Why does it not amount to comedy as we have learnt to understand it? For one reason above all others. Comedy is, and must be—at least, as we judge from having read the best examples—a humorous criticism of life. There is no lack of humour in Shakespeare, but there is no criticism of life. You cannot have a criticism of life, and therefore no criticism of contemporary manners, if you insist on putting your chacacters into a purely ideal scene. Belmont is unreal; so is Messina; so also is Illyria; and most of all ideal is the Forest of Arden. We are asked to see play-acting under conditions which do not obtain in the life we know. There is a study of character, it is true, and there are also contrasts of character, but a comedy of character—character as educed out of the clash of real living personalities and vital incidents—cannot be found in the Shakespearean comedies. They are delightful exercises of wit and fancy, and they please us perhaps just because they are not altogether real. They are artificial in the sense that they are purely fantastic, whereas characters of true comedy are artificial because they are abstracted as types from the actual circumstances of the real world in which the dramatist moves and has his being. The world as pictured by the true writer of comedy is the real world, though heightened and adorned by his comic humour. The characters he portrays are real men and women, albeit that for the purposes of his wit their lineaments are exaggerated.

[1] And shall we add *Pygmalion*?

THE IDEA OF COMEDY.—II

COMEDY OF MANNERS—HIGH COMEDY, OR COMEDY OF CHARACTER

§ 1

A WELL-MARKED division of comedy is that which is generally called the Comedy of Manners, of which the best representatives for our purpose are the Restoration dramatists. We need only be concerned with two of these —Wycherley and Congreve. A predecessor of Wycherley's — Etherege — and two successors — Vanbrugh and Farquhar—need not occupy us, because there can be no manner of doubt that the two principal dramatists—the one who by his contemporaries was called " manly Wycherley," and the other " friendly Congreve, unreproachful man "—represented the culmination of the period, and are therefore best fitted for our study.

Criticism has always been busy over these Restoration dramatists. The one thing which is absolutely certain is that they wrote, not so much a comedy of incidents, or even intrigue, still less that they wrote a comedy of character, but that with conscious art they devoted themselves, and with no small success, to a Comedy of Manners. Perhaps it is unnecessary to say what this involves. It means that both Wycherley and Congreve were occupied with the life of their times, as a pageant, as a show, a panorama which should exhibit the various foibles and fashions of society, which should give a picture, including peccadilloes, failings, sins, as well as occasional merits, and never be concerned with any deeper implications which men of a different order of intellect might find interesting in the condition of society. What does this resolute adherence to a Comedy of Manners signify? It indicates, clearly enough, that the authors did not intend ostensibly to be critics. They may be betrayed into occasional satire and irony, but they are not inspired as a rule by a lofty moral

indignation. Indeed, morality as such was not their job.
It is quite true that Wycherley sometimes, as in his *The
Plain Dealer*, seems to show a certain moral bitterness of
his own, as though he almost hated the characters whom
he was portraying. But that is by no means the general
attitude. As a rule, if we take any of the plays of these
men, *Love in a Wood*, *The Country Wife*, *The Gentleman
Dancing-Master*, *The Old Bachelor*, *The Double Dealer*,
The Way of the World, it is tolerably clear that all that
the authors intend to do is to present the gentlemen and
ladies of their time with a mirror in which they can see
some of their worst follies reflected. Lest the picture
should be surcharged with black, the various *dramatis
personæ* are shown to possess a witty epigrammatic style;
sometimes it is affected, or false wit, sometimes it is real
wit. But anyway there is a superficial brilliance, the sort
of brilliance that would belong to a highly civilised social
state which cares more for verbal felicity and the clever
conduct of an agreeable conversation, the turn of a phrase,
the ingenuity of a repartee, than anything else in the world.
Thus Mirabell and Mrs. Millamant in *The Way of the World*
are the ripe flower of Restoration comedy, as brilliant in
their ways as Benedick and Beatrice in Shakespeare's
comedy.

We have said that criticism has been very much concerned with the Restoration dramatists. The most
tremendous condemnation was passed by Jeremy Collier,
an extremely formidable attack, which probably had a
lasting influence on the fortunes of the English stage.
For if we ask why Puritanism took up arms against the
drama, the answer must inevitably be that the Restoration
dramatists outraged the feelings of society, or, at all events,
a large and respectable portion of society, and that Jeremy
Collier, running atilt against the licence and indecency of
the stage, was to a considerable extent justified by the
sympathy of honest men. The attitude of critical condemnation is to be found also in Steele, Addison, Macaulay,
Thackeray, and even Meredith. The defence of the
Restoration dramatists was undertaken by Leigh Hunt,
by Charles Lamb, and Hazlitt. Naturally, too, the
dramatists themselves had something to say. Wycherley
wrote an answer to Jeremy Collier, and Congreve made
some observations in answer to his critics in his essay on
" Humour." In quite modern days you will find an

extremely clever and ingenious apologist in Mr. John Palmer, who has written a valuable history on *The Comedy of Manners*.[1]

Inasmuch as Lamb is perhaps the best of the apologists, it is as well to remind ourselves of what he actually said. Here is a significant passage :—

" I confess for myself," says Elia, " that (with no great delinquencies to answer for) I am glad for a season to take an airing beyond the diocese of the strict conscience, not to live always in the precincts of the law courts, but, now and then, for a dreamwhile or so, to imagine a world with no meddling restrictions, to get into recesses whither the hunter cannot follow me—

> . . . . Secret shades
> Of woody Ida's inmost grove,
> While yet there was no fear of Jove.

I come back to my cage and my restraint the fresher and more healthy for it. I wear my shackles more contentedly for having respired the breath of an imaginary freedom. I do not know how it is with others, but I feel the better always for the perusal of one of Congreve's—nay, why should I not add even of Wycherley's—comedies. I am the gayer at least for it, and I could never connect those sports of a witty fancy in any shape with any result to be drawn from them to imitation in real life. They are a world of themselves, almost as much as fairyland. The Fainalls and the Mirabells, the Dorimants and the Lady Touchwoods, in their own sphere do not offend my moral sense ; in fact, they do not appeal to it at all. They seem engaged in their proper element. They break through no laws or conscientious restraints. They know of none. They have got out of Christendom into the land of—what shall I call it ?—of cuckoldry—the Utopia of gallantry, where pleasure is duty, and the manners perfect freedom. . . . We are not to judge them by our images. No reverend institutions are insulted by their proceedings— for they have none among them. No peace of families is violated—for no family ties exist among them. No purity of the marriage-bed is stained—for none is supposed to have a being. No deep affections are disquieted, no holy wedlock bonds snapped asunder—for affection's

---

[1] *The Comedy of Manners*, by John Palmer. (G. Bell & Son.)

depth and wedded faith are not of that soil. There is
neither right nor wrong—gratitude or its opposite—claim
or duty—paternity or sonship." A brilliant defence,
truly, to which we shall return presently.

As happens in most controversies, the attacking and the
defending party are not answering one another so much as
developing their own respective standpoints. What is it
that Jeremy Collier assumes? He takes it for granted
that the office of comedy is to do men good, by showing
the ruinous character of vice and the saving grace of goodness. Oddly enough, Wycherley accepted this standpoint.
He even went so far as to maintain that a pure woman
could keep his comedies side by side with her Bible. But
if one begins with the principle that the office of the
dramatist is practically that of the moralist, then there
can be no reasonable doubt that all these men—Etherege,
Wycherley, Congreve, Vanbrugh, and Farquhar—lament-
ably fail in their task. If we talk like ordinary men of the
world, and use words in their conventional sense, all these
comedies, without exception, are full of indecencies,
especially, perhaps, *The Country Wife* of Wycherley.
The men are rakes, and successful rakes; they boast of
their conquests; the women are willing accomplices, they
exist to be wooed and won. But, of course, the real
question is whether a dramatist, as such, ought ever to be
a moralist, or, to bring the matter to a more definite point,
whether a writer of a Comedy of Manners is ever concerned,
or ever should be concerned, with the moral implications
involved in the action of his characters. Clearly, a great
painter has every right to paint a distorted and ugly face,
if it happens to be true, and a literary man may describe
a scene full of ugly things, or depict a period in which the
standard of living is deplorably low. And in precisely the
same fashion the writer of a comedy may show his personages guided by disreputable motives if he is sincerely
trying to give us a veracious tableau of the times. There
is one quality, however, that we require, and that is an
absolute sincerity. When a man draws what he sees
around him with sincerity of this kind, we may dislike the
result, we may call him all manner of injurious names for
being interested in wrong things, but he may quite well
remain an artist, because the moral point of view is never
obtrusively before his eyes. In the long run, too, it will be
found that sincerity of purpose will not be prejudicial to

the higher interests of morality. But the man is not consciously working towards a moral end. What is his aim? It is to express the values of life and character, values not in an ethical, but in an artistic sense. If he is sincere he brings out the inner meaning of it all, and in this roundabout fashion he can actually be said to be working in accordance with the great moral laws which condition the universe. If we apply these considerations to the case before us, we shall probably have to allow that some of these Restoration dramatists were sincere, and are therefore to this extent justified, and that others were not. It is generally conceded that at all events Vanbrugh and Farquhar were not sincere students, but purely imitative, but that Wycherley and Congreve were sincere. The latter tried to draw what they saw before their eyes. We may hate the result—perhaps they hated it also. Certainly in *The Plain Dealer* it looks very much as if Wycherley did. But they accepted the task which they had set before their eyes, and wrote comedies of manners.

There are two considerations, however, which make one pause before attempting to whitewash these dramatists. In the first place, they one and all affected the extremely disingenuous pose of being fine gentlemen first, and only as a sort of amusement writing the plays by which they lived. When Voltaire came over to visit Congreve he was naturally indignant when he discovered that Congreve wished to be regarded as a gentleman first and as a dramatist afterwards. "If I had come merely to visit you as a gentleman, I would not have taken the trouble : I came to see you as an artist." There is, assuredly, something insincere in the pose of men who profess to belittle the work to which they are devoting their talents. If they write comedies with their tongues in their cheeks, we cannot give them the respect due to those who plenarily acknowledge the high office of literature.

The other consideration is, that we never discover in the work of these men that most gracious quality which so often appears in Molière, comedy with thoroughly healthy laughter. It is not laughter that comes from these comedies—not laughter in Bergson's sense as society's vindication of itself against follies and artificialities—it is a snigger or a sneer, a polished irony not always very honest or clean. There are times when we would wish them to be less polished and more vulgar, if only they would consent to have a downright masculine laugh at the hypocrisies of their period.

§ 2

As a matter of fact, the only two real antagonists on this question are Charles Lamb and Jeremy Collier, and because the point raised is one which is interesting and important with regard to art in general, and to the art of comedy in particular, it is worth examining it a little more in detail. I have already quoted a paragraph from Charles Lamb's essay on " The Artificial Comedy of the Last Century." His argument is that it is often a positive relief to turn away from the dull things of life to an artificial realm, where current rules and laws do not obtain, and where men and women can do whatever they like without fear of the magistrate or the police constable. Now, it is this sort of pleasure which men like Wycherley and Congreve can give. We do not make the mistake of taking them too seriously. We assume that they are speaking of an artificial condition of society, and therefore their worst characters—Mr. Horner, for instance, in Wycherley's *Country Wife*—need not be regarded as of flesh and blood, but more or less as fairies. I may remark, however, in passing that the idea of turning so extremely material a person as Mr. Horner into a fairy certainly appeals to our risible faculties. Indeed, this is the weak point in the whole of Lamb's position. If the men and women who live and move in the comedies of Wycherley and Congreve are to be regarded as fairies, we may dismiss them from the things which matter, even though we may still have to object to their conduct as fairies. They do not matter, I say. Unsubstantial denizens of an unsubstantial world, they have to appear in a very different kind of framework from that provided by comedy. What was the criticism that I ventured to offer on the Shakespearean comedy? It was that, being throughout of a romantic texture, it had little or nothing to do with the actual life of the age in which it was produced. And in the same way Mr. Horner and his worthy associates are, according to Lamb, to be excused because they, too, do not belong to the world as we know it. In other words, Lamb's apology delivers them from censure just in proportion as it removes them from the actual condition of

L

things. But it is surely obvious that if Wycherley and Congreve were not writing about the men and women of their time, with whose characters and principles of life they were intimately acquainted, the whole value of their comedies, as comedies of manners, disappears. Either Mr. Horner was modelled on a real prototype, or he was not. If he was, he was an indecent libertine. If he was not, he may take to himself all the credit of being a denizen of a fairy world, but we are still entitled to add that he lives in a fairy atmosphere which it is a little difficult to breathe.

Let us turn to the other figure in the controversy. Jeremy Collier produced, in 1698, his *Short View of the Profaneness and Immorality of the English Stage,* " a book which threw the whole literary world into commotion," as Macaulay remarks. In 1698 the world was different from what it had been under Charles II. The excesses of the Restoration period are to be excused mainly on the ground of an inevitable reaction against a one-sided and extreme austerity. The nation had, however, now recovered from the effects of Puritan rigour. It had recent experience of the profaneness and debauchery which accompanied the return of the Stuarts. The profligacy of the Revolution still remained, and maintained its hold in certain parts of society where men of wit and fashion congregated. Above all, the theatres were its chief stronghold. The most brilliant of Congreve's comedies, *The Way of the World,* was not produced till 1700. Collier's notorious Tract was published two years before.

The author was a remarkable man, of great independence and originality, not in any sense a bigot as we understand the term. He had an extensive knowledge of books; he is even said to have possessed grace and vivacity in conversation, and he undoubtedly wielded a most powerful pen. He was a Tory of the Tories, and so far as his religious opinions were concerned, he belonged to that section of the ecclesiastical world which Macaulay describes as " furthest from Geneva and nearest to Rome." He was constantly in trouble with the authorities. Two men who were intimates of his—Sir John Friend and Sir William Parkins—were tried and convicted of high treason for planning the murder of King William. Collier did not hesitate to administer spiritual consolation to them, accompanied them to Tyburn, and just before the execution laid his hands on their heads and solemnly absolved them. It is easy to conceive the indescribable scandal which so overt an act inevitably created. Indeed, so furiously did the storm rage that Collier, described as a rebel against his Sovereign Lord the King, found it advisable to withdraw from the kingdom, and was outlawed. Incidents of this kind are sufficient to prove that the author of the famous Tract was a man of great courage as well as independence of mind. Indeed, if we remember that his political sympathies were with the Stuarts, and that the Stuart King had thrown his ægis over profligacy in the court, while decency was associated rather with Conventicles and Dissenters, it will be understood that in publishing his book, girding at the indecency of the stage, Collier was criticising that cavalier party to which by sympathy he belonged.

The Tract is a spirited attack on the whole of the literature of the time, and more especially on that part of it which was occupied with the stage. The author may or may not have been a Jacobite, but in this work at all events he only remembers that he is a moralist, a Christian, and a citizen in what ought to be a well-ordered commonwealth. Not only does he deliver his trenchant blows at Wycherley, Congreve, and Vanbrugh, but he strikes without fear at the most towering figure of all—the great Dryden himself, who, I may mention in passing, never replied to his attack, although every one in England expected him to do so. Of course, Jeremy Collier's book has many faults. It is much too violent; it tries to prove too much; it takes for granted that the object of a comedy is to improve public morals. In his anxiety to prove his victims the guiltiest of offenders, he brings into his charge against them things quite trivial, and, indeed, quite innocent. On this point Macaulay makes some undoubtedly just remarks. "He blames Congreve for using the words 'martyr' and 'inspiration' in a light sense, just as if an Archbishop might not quite innocently say that a subject was 'inspired' by claret, or that an Alderman was 'a martyr' to the gout. Sometimes, again, Collier does not sufficiently distinguish between the dramatist and the persons of the drama. Thus he blames Vanbrugh for putting into Lord Foppington's mouth some contemptuous expression respecting the Church Service, though it is obvious that Vanbrugh could not better express reverence than by making Lord Foppington express contempt." In short, the Tract had many of the demerits which usually attach to violently polemical literature. I have already suggested that its general standpoint completely mistook the nature and purposes of art. Nevertheless, it is quite clear that the honours of the fray, at the end of the seventeenth century and the beginning of the eighteenth, rested with the ecclesiastic, and not with the dramatist. Collier had a pretty wit of his own. Congreve had remarked of his play, *The Old Bachelor*, that it was a trifle, to which he attached no value. "I wrote it," he said, "to amuse myself in a slow recovery from a fit of sickness." Collier's repartee was brilliant. "What his disease was," he replied, "I am not to inquire, but it must be a very ill one to be worse than the remedy." Probably in the long run the real, perhaps the only, defence of the post-Restoration drama was that it was adapted to the age and period in which it was produced. The case stands as it does with those Sophists of Greece, of whom Plato remarked that it was not they who were to blame, but the society which produced them. In the same fashion we might say that censure should attach, not to the comic dramatists, but to the public of the day which applauded their efforts.

§ 3

I turn to Molière.[1] I have said more than once that Molière represents the ideal writer of comedies, and that perhaps there is no one—with the possible exception of Menander in Greek comedy—who so perfectly realises the conditions of his task. There are many considerations to be borne in mind in arriving at this conclusion. Let us try to summarise some of them. In the first place, Molière, like Shakespeare, is a workman who knows his tools. He studies his actors; he studies his audiences; he studies the kind of theatre in which he is to represent his plays, and lastly, being himself an actor and an extremely good one, he has a thorough inside and outside experience of what he has to do. We never welcome the idea of a dramatist who composes characters suitable for particular actors and actresses, because we suppose that this is a limitation of

[1] In this matter I obviously follow a logical rather than a chronological order.

the free and independent workmanship of the author. Yet it is abundantly clear that most dramatists not only have studied their actors, but are bound to do so. We are pretty certain that Shakespeare did. He had Burbage before his eyes when he composed some of his heroic parts. The comic men of his company also were studied, as was remarked in the preceding essay. And if Hamlet, besides being " the glass of fashion and the mould of form," is described as " fat and scant of breath," the suggestion has been made that the line was written in because Burbage was beginning to put on flesh.

Now when we get to Molière we move on much more certain ground, because we know a good deal more about the company of Molière than we do about the actors who surrounded Shakespeare.[1] First of all, we know that Molière wrote parts for his wife, Armande Béjart, who was a most competent actress, and who appeared as Elmire, Célimène, Henriette, and other characters. So, too, her elder sister Madeleine Béjart, had parts provided for her to suit her capacity, such as Dorine in *Tartuffe*. Argan, in the *Malade Imaginaire*, has a cough : Molière wrote this part for himself after the time when his cough became troublesome. La Flèche, in the *Avare*, is lame : the character was written for Molière's brother-in-law, who was also lame. Tartuffe, we know, has abundance of skin on his bones, and the character was composed for Du Croisy, who was plump and well-favoured. Doubtless, many other indications could be found of the way in which the dramatist availed himself of the existing resources of his company.

Then, too, Molière was, in a real sense, the first of the moderns, primarily because he does not write for a mediæval theatre, as Shakespeare does. In Shakespeare's time, as we are aware, the roof only covered part of the theatre, the lighting was most indifferent, there was practically no scenery, and the apron stage ran down amongst the audience. But Molière's transformed tennis-court was roofed and lighted, furnished with scenery, and, indeed, so far as it went, belonged much more to the theatre of a modern time. This is one reason why the dramatist began to work out his ideas in comedy. He could anticipate a stage-form practically identical with that used by such

[1] See *Molière, his Life and his Works*, by Brander Matthews. (Longmans.)

late dramatists as Ibsen, for instance. Either he fell back on the old Italian plan of having an outdoor scene, with houses on either side to serve as a meeting-place for the characters, or else he had an interior in which, without change, he could make his story unroll itself in the fortunes and adventures of a single family. Then, too, it is quite clear that Molière studied his audiences with uncommon care. If he had to please the King and his courtiers he knew he could devise the kind of thing—half farce and half ballet—which would suit the occasion. But with regard to his own public we get in him a tolerably plain example of how a man of genius can not only educate himself in the performance of his dramatic tasks, but can also educate his audience.

What, roughly, is the history of the Molière comedy? Let us remember that he was only fifty-one when he died, and that all except two of his thirty plays were written in the last fourteen years of his life. From 1659 to 1673 he was very fertile, in some years bringing out as many as three pieces; and he not only was stage-manager and general director of his company, but generally took a part himself. During these fourteen years he gave examples of most of the different kinds of comedy to which we have already alluded. He began with a form entirely borrowed from the Italians, the so-called comedy of masks, with stock characters, such as the " wily valet," the " prig," the " boastful soldier," the " braggart," and the like.[1] *L'Etourdi* is entirely on the lines of a comedy of masks. Molière was quite well aware that the average audience for whom he had to cater liked its farces in this form. It was fond of seeing amusing situations, whether probable or not did not very much matter, and the personages who had to be subordinated to these situations were for the most part artificial characters—both artificial and unreal. We get to a comedy of manners in the *Précieuses Ridicules*. Then in the *École des Femmes*, which is a comedy of manners, we get also a comedy of intrigue. In *Le Mariage Forcé*, which was enacted some time ago by Mr. Granville Barker's company at the St. James's Theatre, Molière wrote what ought to be described as a comedy ballet, and which still preserves its laughter-provoking qualities,

---

[1] It is interesting to discover from Dr. Cornford's *Origin of Attic Comedy* (Arnold) that these stock characters serve as a foundation also for the Aristophanic comedy.

quite apart from its association with the ballets in which
the King and the Court delighted. And then, leaving out
many intermediate steps, we arrive at comedy of character
in such pieces as the *Misanthrope*, the *Avare*, *Tartuffe*, and
the *Femmes Savantes*, models of high comedy, plays which,
in the early period of his career, he would hardly have
dared to produce, because they asked more of the audience
than the audience was generally prepared to grant. The
audience desired to be amused, and Molière was bound to
amuse them, and, indeed, it is wonderful to observe how
he makes us laugh at characters and situations which,
directly we begin to analyse them, reveal elements almost
of tragedy. Tartuffe remains a comic character, even
though we have found occasion to loathe his hypocrisy
and pretensions. So, too, we laugh at the miser Harpagon
almost as much as we laugh at M. Jourdain in the *Bourgeois
Gentilhomme*. But characters of this kind, whether they
represent miser or hypocrite, misanthrope or learned prig,
or pretentious doctor, have now, as Molière is able to draw
them, achieved a really solid character for themselves, and
the play exists for them and for the exhibition of their
characteristics. The incidents of the play are made to
reveal and bring out the special traits of the individuals
involved. We obtain, therefore, something more than a
comedy of intrigue or a comedy of manners, and we have
left the comedy of masks a long way behind us. We
have got to high comedy, a rare and special product, a
comedy of character, of which Molière alone is able to
present us with the highest examples. It is a very delicate
fabric which he has been able to construct. A little less
analysis of character and we should get down to the
comedy of manners; a little more tension in the conduct
of the plot and we should leave the range of comedy
altogether and get into something which could hardly be
distinguished from tragedy. Molière knew how to make
painful situations amusing, and how to draw characters
we instinctively dislike and repudiate in such a fashion
that they seem to draw out of us a large amount of interest
and, perhaps, even a certain amount of sympathy.

Now Aristotle saw, clearly enough, with only the Greek
plays before him on which to base his conclusion, that in
the case of a tragedy the story is at least as important as,
if not more important than, the characters. It can never
be the same with comedy. With comedy the story is

relatively unimportant; everything turns on the delineation of the men and women whose mutual relations determine the plot. Probably this is due to a certain extent to the fact that comedy originated with a certain fixed set of characters, as we find in the later Greek comedy, and early Italian and Spanish comedy. If you examine many of the plays of Molière, you will come to the conclusion that the story is of a somewhat thin and unsubstantial character. In the comedies of Wycherley and Congreve the stories are wholly unimportant; indeed, it is difficult to see with regard to some of them what the story is. So, again, if we take a comedy like that of *George Dandin*, we end precisely at the point where we began. So also in the *Misanthrope*, when we have been introduced to the chief characters of the comedy, and studied their peculiar characters, the comedy ends. And it is precisely here that we become aware, I will not say of one of the chief defects, but of the chief danger of high comedy. The principal characters tend to become typical rather than individual. Harpagon, for instance, is the embodiment of avarice itself. He is also—because he happens to be drawn by an accomplished artist—an individual whom we can recognise. Nevertheless, his main object in the play is to be a type, just as Tartuffe has become absolutely typical of all hypocrites. Molière, though generally careful to show us the social conditions in the midst of which his plays run their course—differing in this respect from Shakespeare, who never gives us a hint of existing social conditions except in *The Merry Wives of Windsor*—tells us very little of the principal characters of his best comedies. We ask, for instance, where Alceste came from, or in what social rank he is to be found. We may make a guess, but the dramatist does not help us much. Orgon has practically no name at all, only a sort of character-label. Tartuffe again—we should have liked to have known what his early experiences have been, where he came from, had he been unmasked before, or had he been invariably successful in his intrigues? But Molière does not help us. These great figures of his stand in a sort of isolation, typical of certain vices and failings, existing for their own sake as part of the machinery wherewith your true comedian will mark out for you the kinds of temperament or personality to accept or to avoid. But it is, of course, only of these main characters that this criticism is true. Molière has known well enough how to surround his most typical by his most individual personages. And as he was always learning by experience, he could go back—if expediency so suggested—from his highest achievement to a piece like *Les Fourberies de Scapin*, which is a mere farce. So, too, when he discovered that the *Misanthrope* was unpopular because it hardly had a story to tell, he was careful to supply the *Femmes Savantes* with a much more regular plot, so as to win the interest of his public. And if we need any other example of the way in which Molière was constantly educating himself, let it be discovered in his abandonment of tragedy—or rather heroic comedy—when *Don Garcie* failed to win the popular approval. The people loved Molière as a humorist, as a comedian of rich and versatile gifts, and though once and again he tried to prove to them that he was capable of other work, they refused to accept it. For the public of Paris Molière was a comic actor, and nothing else. But he also happened to be a genius who represented some of the highest achievements of French literature. Such a truth probably never occurred to his admirers. Nor need we be surprised at this. Shakespeare, too, was known as a popular playwright, as a good business man, and as an indifferent actor. His contemporaries would have opened their eyes in wonder if they had been told that he was also a consummate poet, and the greatest figure in English letters.

§ 4

Masterpieces, evidently, are not only difficult to compose, but are very difficult to get published. Molière wrote three masterpieces at least, of which the most significant is the well-known *Tartuffe*. The first three acts of *Tartuffe* belong to the date 1664. They at once fell under the interdict of the authorities, and it was not till 1669, five years afterwards, that the performance of the complete play in five acts was finally authorised. There was an abundance of reasons for this long delay. But, meanwhile, let us see in what respect the play itself represented a certain novelty, whereby Molière established his position as the greatest comic dramatist of his time, and, perhaps, of all time. *Tartuffe* is a masterpiece because it represents the culmination of the development of comedy as the more or less light and laughable treatment of themes serious in themselves. Comedy—as Meredith taught us—creates thoughtful laughter, the laughter that does not end in and with itself, but suggests trains of thought in the mind and leads to certain conclusions. How to treat grave subjects and devise complex characters, and yet retain the comic framework, is Molière's own secret, and it has been shared by very few among his fellow dramatists. In his case it was the ripe fruit of years of work. Abundance of laughter could be extracted from the valets, who were the heritage to him of the Latin stage; abundant laughter also from the serving maids, the clever and sharp-tongued soubrettes, who were in especial Molière's invention; abundant laughter also could be created by the traditional types of character—the fool, the braggart, the stupid lover, the empty-headed pedagogue. But now, slowly, dawns before Molière's mind a larger task. The play ought to arise from the clash of character with character. It ought to follow naturally the relations exhibited between the different personages. The characters themselves need not be of a conventional type; though typical, they must be real and human. They must be such characters as we are able to meet every day, easily recognised, well marked in their characteristics, and rounded figures, so to speak, complex beings so essentially human that we can laugh at and with them, and even forgive them where they go wrong. Moreover—and, perhaps, that is no slight advance—the scene must be laid within a single family, whether of bourgeois or of aristocrats, and the plot must be unrolled before our eyes within the four corners of an ordinary sitting-room. No longer are we to have a public square, flanked by the houses in which the principal personages live. It must be just an ordinary interior, the living-room of a family. This is what Molière did in his *Tartuffe*, and in his *Misanthrope*, and in the *Femmes Savantes*, three high specimens of his dramatic skill. And thereby he created the ideal type of comedy, the comedy, as we say, of character, the comedy which trembles on the edge of tragedy and pathos, like all the real things of life where tears follow hard on laughter. To us, because we live after the event, it may seem an easy achievement. Perhaps Menander may have done something of the same kind in the later Attic comedy. Indeed, without any manner of doubt, so far as we can discover from recently unearthed evidences of his art, this is what Menander did. But for us in a modern world it is the great achievement of Molière, marking a notable advance on Shakespeare's comedies and illustrating the evolution of comedy from the grotesquely humorous or the fantastically humorous to the humour of real characters, the humour of life itself. And if we want to see why it was a great discovery, we need only observe how the later comedians follow in Molière's footsteps. Here precisely is the comedy which Sheridan wrote in *The School for Scandal ;* here is the comedy of Dumas and Augier. Here, too, is the comedy of Ibsen.

With regard to the first of the trio which I have mentioned, *Tartuffe*, we can easily understand why its appearance should so long have been delayed. The story of *Tartuffe* is well known. There is an ordinary bourgeois family, consisting of Orgon, the father, who has married a second wife, Elmire—a charming character—and who has a daughter, Mariane, affianced to Valere. We have besides Orgon's old mother, Madame Pernelle—a rather difficult person to get on with—and a very outspoken critic in the shape of Dorine, half a maid and half a companion, with a very established position in the family, for she speaks out her opinion on most subjects before she is even asked. Into this family is introduced a character, Tartuffe, an ostentatiously religious man who exercises a wonderful influence on Orgon, and whose appearance is carefully prepared for in the first two acts before he is shown us in the third. Tartuffe is an unctuously religious hypocrite, who, though he never unburdens himself in that kind of soliloquy which Shakespeare employed in explaining to us Iago, is abundantly revealed in his true colours by the skilful management of the dramatist. Tartuffe gains a complete ascendancy. Orgon is all for giving him his daughter, Mariane, in marriage ; he even makes him a deed of gift of his possessions. Tartuffe, however, does not want the daughter; he is attracted by the young wife, Elmire, and it is only when Orgon discovers Tartuffe making love to his wife that he realises what a hypocrite he has nursed in the bosom of the family. Then, when he is exposed, Tartuffe becomes truculent, makes much of the deed of gift, and claims Orgon's house. It requires the actual intervention of the King to put matters right, and finally to send Tartuffe about his business. That is the story, and though Molière makes us laugh at everybody, laugh at

Orgon, at Madame Pernelle, at Dorine, and above all at
Tartuffe himself, it is easy to see with what serious elements
he is dealing. Molière himself, of course, like most dramatists, like Shakespeare above all, disliked Puritans and
loathed hypocrisy in all its forms. But the court was
very religious, and the ecclesiastics of the time could not
be expected to welcome such an exposure of religious
affectation. Moreover, there is always one difficulty in
putting a religious hypocrite on the stage. You have to
put in his mouth expressions and sentiments which are
precisely those used by the really devout. In his case they
are not sincere, but the expressions are the same, and naturally give offence when attributed to worthless personages.
Molière was not specially a religious man; he was trained
in the schools of Rabelais and Montaigne. He was not anti-
religious, but he probably did not care for professions of
piety, and in *Tartuffe* he revenged himself on those ecclesiastical critics, as well as dramatic critics, who had found
fault with his *École des Femmes*. The King seems always
to have been on his side, but he had to proceed with
caution, and thus it came about that for five years Molière's
masterpiece was banned. He had created, however, a
character destined to be immortal. Tartuffe lives as the
very emblem and type of the sanctimonious, and whenever
or wherever the play is performed its essential humanity is
recognised. Being something real, and independent of
period or race, Tartuffe is an actor-proof part, like Hamlet.
About the time when discussions took place as to the
possibility of the play being performed, the Italian
comedians brought out a piece called *Scaramouche Ermite*.
According to a well-known story, the King is said to have
asked Condé why those who were so scandalised by
Molière's play did not object to this Scaramouche. Condé
answered : " The reason is that Scaramouche shows up
religion and Heaven, as to which these gentlemen care
nothing. Molière's comedy shows *them* up, and this they
will not permit."
    Perhaps it is unnecessary to say very much about the
other two great creations of Molière, although each has
its own special points of interest. *The Misanthrope* is in
many ways a rather puzzling play. The main character,
Alceste, whom Molière insists upon our calling a misanthrope—though we might very possibly have chosen
another title—is not especially a comic character. Indeed,

he has certain elements which make him ultra-serious. Molière devised him for his own acting, just as he portrayed Célimène for the acting of his wife, and, inasmuch as Parisian audiences would not stand Molière in anything but comic parts, it is quite obvious that we are intended to laugh, even though we have to laugh thoughtfully, at Alceste's extravagance. There was always a spice of tragedy in Molière, a certain strain of melancholy, despite his mirth-provoking qualities. As a matter of fact, however, the figure of a man who loudly protests against the fashionable hypocrisies of the day; who, although he is in love with Célimène, is continually upbraiding her for her frivolity and worldly character, reminds us of figures like Dr. Stockmann in Ibsen's *The Enemy of the People*, or even Timon of Athens, as Shakespeare drew him—figures cynical, morose, unfriendly, or perhaps we should say, uncompromising men, who refuse to accept the world's legitimate as well as illegitimate compromises. Observe that the somewhat morose traits of Alceste are preserved up to the last. He proposes to Célimène, after one of the usual disputes, that she should prove the reality of her repentance by going to live with him on a desert island. This, naturally, the high-spirited lady refuses to do, and the play ends with the amiable efforts of some of the hero's friends to try to bring about a better reconciliation. There are two other remarks which have to be made about *The Misanthrope*. One is that, as compared with *Tartuffe*, Molière is dealing with the higher levels of society in the later play, and with the bourgeois society in the earlier. Part of his object is to expose the hollow insincerities of the fashionable world in the time of Louis XIV. And so even his most delightful heroine, Célimène, is shown us as being infected, as it were, with some of the evil humours of society, so that she will sacrifice her best friends for a witticism, and give a satirical version of their characters in just the same way as Lady Teazle did later, in Sheridan's comedy, *The School for Scandal*. The other point to remark is that there is no real story in *The Misanthrope*. There is very little action, and we remain at the end pretty well in the same position as we were when we began. This is probably the reason why *The Misanthrope*—though all the more intelligent critics hailed it as a masterpiece—did not enjoy much success in Parisian representations. *Tartuffe* was a solidly built comedy, with a story which advanced from the beginning to the end. *The Misanthrope* consists of a series of episodes, with practically no story. If Parisian audiences found the play dull, there is really something to be said for them. For once Molière allowed his psychological instincts and his philosophy to overpower his intuitions as a dramatist. Dramas can contain any amount of philosophy and psychology, but they must be subordinate to the story which is to be unfolded before our eyes. Let us once be interested in the action and we can get all the more interest out of the characters, because they are deeply devised. But the reverse of this proposition is not true. If we can imagine Hamlet without the plot of Hamlet, we should get much the same thing as Molière put before his spectators in *The Misanthrope.* Here we are at the very secret of all drama, which is one of the most democratic of the arts, and can never be the choice possession of a coterie, however distinguished. In *Tartuffe* Molière wrapped his psychology in a powerful story; therefore, at once he gained a popular appeal. In Alceste he left his philosophy, such as it was, naked and unadorned, and therefore failed to please the average playgoer. Perhaps we ought to add that there is a great deal of Molière himself in the character of Alceste, and perhaps something, too, of his relations with his wife, Armande, in the controversies between Alceste and Célimène. Molière, too, was a jealous man. Molière felt bitterly the fact that his wife was a worldly woman. But we must not press a consideration of this kind too far. Various suggestions the dramatist can take from his own experience or that of others, but he is, first and foremost, a dramatist, and he must not be identified with any of his creations.

I have left myself but little space to discuss that which some competent critics have held to be absolutely the best of Molière's comedies, *Les Femmes Savantes.* The theme is, perhaps, not so important as either that which meets us in *Tartuffe* or that which underlies the character of *The Misanthrope.* But the *Femmes Savantes* is an exceedingly well-made play, and as the incidents are brisk, the characters interesting, and the dialogue lively and animated, we get a result of comedy at its best—humour slightly exaggerated, with a sound and serious lesson at its core. Molière had touched upon the question of learned ladies before in his *Précieuses Ridicules.* Their affectation and their absurd efforts to purify the language had passed under his satiric pen. But the class of learned ladies did not tend to diminish in Molière's time, or rather the point which struck the dramatist was not that a learned lady, as such, was a drawback to the State, but that all pretenders, whether male or female, were equally obnoxious. At the back of Molière's mind, and indeed tolerably patent in the general construction of the play, is undoubtedly the idea that women who set up to be learned are destructive of the integrity of that family life of which Molière was so keen an advocate. Not that his play is in any sense intended to be didactic, but the general form and construction and the arrangement of the characters suggest on which side Molière's own sympathies are to be found. And I believe that women, as a rule, especially the so-called feminists, do not appreciate Molière. Perhaps they have never forgiven him his *Précieuses Ridicules* and his *Femmes Savantes*.

Les Femmes Savantes is, in truth, an excellent comedy, a comedy in which the plot is determined by the characters of the play, and in which we move throughout on an ascending scale of interest. There is one curious feature about it that, although in this, almost more than in his other plays, Molière shows his complete independence of other stories and plots—for in his highest comedies he is always most original—we yet discover one character who is, without any doubt whatsoever, a copy from a living contemporary. Trissotin was certainly a caricature of the Abbé Cotin. Cotin had had a serious quarrel with Ménage, in much the same way as in the play Trissotin has a quarrel with Vadius. It is very unlike Molière thus to vent his spleen against a personage who was well known in Paris, whatever provocation he may have received. Perhaps he did it at the instigation of his friend Boileau. Perhaps what offended him in the Abbé Cotin was an absurd literary affectation which had no real roots in knowledge. To us at the present day it does not matter who the original of Molière's portrait was, because Trissotin is the type of pedantic prig familiar in all ages, and certainly not without example in our own country and century. Happily, there is no reason to think that Molière copied living originals for his women. I believe it has been suggested that Philaminte and Bélise are intended as caricatures of Madame de Sévigné and Madame de Lafayette. There is no justification for such a view, for the two women to whom we have referred were really cultured and educated. But what cannot be too often insisted on is that, though it may be of some interest to know how Molière's play stands related to the personages and events of his time, all these adventitious sources of interest fall away for us when we recognise that in *Les Femmes Savantes*, as well as in *Tartuffe* and *The Misanthrope*, Molière has given us the highest type of comedy, cultured, humorous, agreeable, witty, full of good sense, full of worldly wisdom; above all, a comedy of character, involving personalities as truly living for us as they were for Frenchmen of the seventeenth century.

REALISTIC DRAMA

I

THE modern English stage has developed mainly along the lines of realism. At the present moment it would be safe to say that the drama which is most alive, the drama which means most, both as an intellectual and as an artistic product, is that which is classed as Realistic. It is, relatively speaking, a modern tendency. At all events, during the first half of the nineteenth century a more artificial, fantastic, and romantic species of drama prevailed, which might, for purposes of comparison, be put under the head of dramatic idealism.

Let me attempt first of all to define these terms, Idealism and Realism. A dramatist, we will suppose, is asking himself how he shall treat human characters, and he discovers that there are at least three possible ways. He can say, in the first place, " I will paint human beings as I think they *ought* to be." In other words, he is applying, however unconsciously, a sort of ethical test to the men and women whose actions he is about to describe. He believes that it is his duty (in order, we will say, to help ordinary suffering and erring humanity) to paint certain ideals of conduct and behaviour, good and bad alike— heroes that are ideal heroes, villains that are ideal villains, heroines that are virtuous and in distress, comic men who, despite a lamentable tendency to idiotic witticisms, have a heart of gold—and all the other heterogeneous items in a romantic conception of existence.

We can imagine, however, a dramatist with a very different ideal before him. He says, " My business as an artist is to paint men as I think they really are," not very good, not very bad, average creatures, sometimes with good intentions, often with bad performance, meaning well and doing ill, struggling with various besetting temptations and struggling also perhaps with a heritage derived

M   161

from earlier generations—above all, never heroes and never heroines, nor even thorough-going villains, not beautifully white nor preternaturally black, but (as one might phrase it) of a piebald variety. This species of dramatist works from a scientific point of view. His mode of procedure, and also such inspiration as he possesses, is mainly experimental, based on what he has discovered—or thinks he has discovered—about humanity and its place in the world. If the first class of dramatist I am trying to describe is radiantly optimistic, the second is generally preternaturally sad, inclined to despair, teaching us that this world is not altogether a comfortable place, and that human beings are not especially agreeable to live with.

It is conceivable, however, that apart from these two classes of dramatists there yet is room for a third, a man who is neither a preacher nor a pessimist; not inspired with a moral idea nor yet inspired with a scientific idea, but a sheer artist, inspired by a purely artistic idea. He is aware that all art is an imaginative exercise, and that however he describes his *dramatis personœ* he can only do it from a personal point of view. He is not quite sure that, however scientific may be his procedure, he can ever paint men and women precisely as they are—he can only paint them as they appear to his æsthetic perceptions. He does not desire to draw any moral. He desires, it is true, to be guided by experience; but he does not give us the dry bones of scientific data. Being an artist he uses his selective capacity both as to his incidents and his characters. The latter he often makes typical rather than individual; but they will represent the inner verity of man, and not the mere external appearance. He has made the discovery, in other words, that you do not get rid of romance by calling yourself an Experimentalist or a Realist. He knows that men turn to art just because they do not want to live perpetually in a sombre, and actual, world. The world of art is something other than the world of reality, and as a dramatic artist he must make allowance for this fact.

Now here are three different types of dramatist, and, fortunately for our purpose, we can give them names. When drama, as we understand the term, began with the Greeks, that extraordinary race developed most of the types which are discoverable in the work of later men. The earliest dramatist was Æschylus, a profoundly moral and

didactic playwright who painted men and women as he
thought they ought to be, because he held it to be his
business to justify the ways of God to humanity. That is
the keynote of his *Agamemnon* and his *Prometheus Vinctus*,
of most of the work which has come down to us. A great
man and a real dramatist, and still more a seer, a prophet,
a teacher. The third of the Greek dramatists was
Euripides, who tried to draw men and women as he thought
they were. I should imagine that he, like many modern
men, revolted from the lofty conception of humanity as
idealised by Æschylus. He had no particular moral
lessons to teach, and did not want to justify the ways of
God to man. On the contrary, one of his aims was to
justify the ways of men to gods, to show how unjust the
gods were, how arbitrary, how poverty-stricken in idea.
His men, as we see, were real men as viewed by a man of
experience, his women—to the astonishment of his generation—were real women, and his general aspect was more
or less pessimistic. It is a poorish sort of world, he seems
to say, in which we have got to struggle, and strive, and
fail, and yet make the best of it, being content that now and
again, although we cannot cure the evils, we can at least
help the sufferers with a little ordinary compassion and
sympathy.

I have purposely omitted the second of the dramatists
in Greece. Sophocles, as distinct from his compeers, was,
as it seems to me, neither a moralist nor a realist, but an
artist through and through, impersonal and remote—an
artist in fibre, whose drama gives us the absolutely Greek
point of view, a little idealised here and there no doubt.
He will not extenuate, he certainly will not set down anything in malice; but he will draw real Greek types, and
yet leave room for imagination and fancy, and provide
some sustenance for the romantic instincts.

Here is an exemplification in history of the three kinds
of dramatist I have described. A man can paint human
beings as he thinks they ought to be, a man can paint
them as he thinks they are. The first is what we ordinarily recognise as an Idealist; the second is, undoubtedly,
a Realist. If modern examples are required, there are
many to choose from. Tolstoy, for instance—and especially in a play like *Resurrection*—is an Idealist and a
preacher. The French dramatist Brieux in nearly the
whole of his work is a persistent moralist, believing, as

he does, that it is the function of drama to attack the evils of the age, witness *Les Trois Filles de M. Dupont, Les Avariés,* and his last play, *La Femme Seule.* In his treatment, however, of these evils he is a sheer realist. Perhaps Mr. George Bernard Shaw might not altogether appreciate the society in which he finds himself, but he undoubtedly is in some aspects an idealist and a preacher. His method may be the method of realism, but he is intensely didactic, always running a tilt against the follies and hypocrisies of the age. One need only cite such pieces as *The Showing Up of Blanco Posnet, The Doctor's Dilemma, Major Barbara,* and for sheer undiluted idealism, *Captain Brassbound's Conversion.* The realistic school, as such, I shall have further opportunities of portraying. But the third species of dramatist of whom I have spoken, the man who is artist first and throughout, who exercises his faculty of selection, as every artist should, who is never a didactic moralist, any more than he is a photographer, who does not paint, so to speak, the wrinkles and the pimples, but gives you the general meaning of the face— the Sophoclean type in short—is one for whom there is not as yet a name—except the good old name of dramatic artist. Is there, however, no modern example? Yes, assuredly. There is Shakespeare himself. He is full of romance, he has over and over again the touch of the idealist, and yet no man will tell you more about human nature and more freely give you live, vivid, and freshly-drawn types. He is quite impersonal. He never preaches ostentatiously a moral. He tells you how things happen and lets you draw your own conclusion. His object is to show you how the world reveals itself to an artist—a very high and serious artist who, with the intuition of genius, understands and knows.

Now drama follows the general movements of thought in the world, although it seems to follow them somewhat slowly. This is a point which must be elucidated if drama is to be considered as a serious art, an art in the highest sense of the term, as a part of the human equipment, as much native to man as religion. We can see that up to a given time in the nineteenth century modern drama, though it may have in appearance aimed high, was quite artificial and unreal. Then about the middle and towards the close of the nineteenth century it gradually became imbued with a spirit of realism which, with few exceptions, has continued up to the present period. And what is the external history of the period thus summarily indicated? We know that the great feature of the nineteenth century, from 1850 onwards, was the extraordinary progress of science and the interpretation of nature. Everywhere it was discovered that by keeping close to the sphere of reality, by seeking to understand nature, we were able to make large progress, not only in knowledge, but also in the practical conveniences and utilities of life. If science won successes in the intellectual sphere, they were rapidly adapted to the uses of mankind, and the conquest over nature meant not only definite mental acquisition but a larger material comfort. Thus the keynote of the time was naturalism in thought, and utilitarianism in morals and social life.

It was little wonder, then, that art should, in its turn, be realistic. The other arts—painting, literature, music—can carry on their spheres of activity more or less in independence of the spirit of the Age: although they, too, when we look deeper, are subject in more ways than one to large contemporary influences. But the art of drama—a social art—must necessarily keep very close to the stages of evolution in social life and ethical thought. This is, of course, the meaning of Shakespeare's famous definition of acting and the actor as giving "the age and body of the time—its form and pressure." In the earlier portions of the nineteenth century drama might strive to be poetic, emotional; but when the reign of science began it was bound to lose some of its idealistic character and to accommodate itself to the prevalent conceptions which were, of course, realistic. In the beginnings of the present century, however, we note, here and there, signs of reaction. Even professors of science are beginning to be discontented with their most magnificent victories. When all nature has yielded up her secrets there still remain the indefeasible claims of the human soul. From materialism, as such, recent years are beginning to proclaim a revolt.

But, surely, there is no question which is the correct view, at all events to us children of the nineteenth century? The problem appears to be settled. We are only concerned with reality; metaphysical idealism is pure talk and word-spinning. Let us think of all that this scientific movement has accomplished. Man acquired a new and infinitely better knowledge of nature's workings, and thus was able by technical skill, acquired in a practical school, to make all sorts of improvements directly affecting human existence, which in consequence became wonderfully enriched, accelerated, strengthened. Social problems now became of prominent interest, existing conditions of life had to be improved. The object of man was to secure universal happiness for his fellow-men. Labour was organised, the proper distribution of wealth became one of the tasks incumbent on man; life was to be made more happy. Surely, in view of all that the nineteenth century has done, the older idealistic views are but vague mists destined to disappear before the light of the sun. From this point of view realism can be our only gospel.

Unfortunately, the matter is not so easy as it seems. Idealism has certainly taken some strange shapes, shapes which we now acknowledge to be of not much value. If, for instance, the idealistic drama of the nineteenth century is represented only, let us say, by Sheridan Knowles's *Virginius,* or by Bulwer Lytton's *The Lady of Lyons* and *Richelieu,* or, for the matter of that, by Victor Hugo's *Cromwell,* then, indeed, it seems a very unreal, purely artificial, quite valueless thing, totally unconnected with life as we know it, and quite righteously doomed to perish. But Idealism is a much subtler thing than this, intimately connected with the nature of all art. We speak of the triumphs of realism. Well, has the materialism of the nineteenth century triumphed all along the line? Has the whole life of man become transformed into the material conditions which surround him? Is a man a mere instrument for doing work? Why, this work itself has turned out not to be the gloriously unselfish thing, full of altruistic aims, which was to benefit the whole of humanity.[1] What does work mean to the majority of our contemporaries? It means a bitter struggle for existence, a struggle between individuals, classes, and peoples, and the passions which the struggle has aroused show how every day the field of conflict is becoming wider. Is it so true, we begin to ask ourselves, that mere work absorbs the whole man? Work never develops more than a portion of human faculty; the more specialised the work, the smaller the portion. If life is no more than contact with environment, it is a singularly bare and poverty-stricken thing. Is it not clear that behind the work are sensitive beings, craving

[1] Written before the War.

for something more than the work can give them, demanding from their work some personal compensation, even though the work itself may lose ? Does not the continual striving after some definite material result or success breed a certain weariness and distaste, and afflict us with the shadow of some vaguely recognised pessimism ? What is the cause of this deep-seated uneasiness ? In quite simple language we can give the answer. If work no longer satisfies us, it is because it leaves the soul homeless. If the nineteenth century, which more than any other period enlarged the whole aspect of life and improved human conditions, instead of closing with a proud and jubilant note ended rather with a dissatisfied and querulous wail, there must have been some error in the type of life dominating the whole epoch. What is the error ? Realism tried to get rid of the spirit of man, to prove it to be a purely derivative thing. It sought to eliminate the soul, and the soul refuses to be eliminated. The emphatic denial of the soul in its independent activity merely rouses the soul to further life, rouses it to carry on with whomsoever it. recognises as its God those immortal dialogues which are the staple of all Mystical literature. And so the twentieth century began with a reaction, and examples are easily furnished. After Utilitarianism, the characteristic philosophy of the nineteenth century, arose Pragmatism, which in some of its aspects is the Ultima Thule, the last expression, of the naturalistic practical movement. But Pragmatism would now seem to have spent its force, and men read Bergson. So, too, in Art ; wearied with Realism we turn to Symbolism and Mysticism : and the curiously suggestive, symbolic theatre of Maeterlinck is studied, even in the midst of the triumphs of the school of Ibsen.

But the question will naturally be asked : Has all this anything to do with drama ? Well, let us take the matter in detail. Modern drama in England has run through three or four distinct phases. There is the kind of drama with which, let us say, Macready had to concern himself, succeeded by a very bad and infertile period in which the chief productions were either adaptations from the French or else burlesque, many of which again had a French ancestry. No touch or breath of reality came across English drama till about 1860, or rather, to be accurate, till November 14th, 1865, when a piece entitled *Society* was played at

the Prince of Wales's Theatre, having as its author Tom
Robertson. From that time onwards, through various
illustrious names, the English drama has steadily advanced
in a direction which we usually call naturalism or realism.
Concurrently with this movement you will find that adaptations from Paris began to be rare. The native drama
has found its feet. The largest foreign influence is that
of Ibsen. None of our writers have been quite the same
since they made acquaintance with the Norwegian dramatist. A different quality has come into their work.

If such be in outline the history of modern drama, you
will now observe that it fits tolerably into the scheme I
have propounded. There was a time when every philosopher called himself an idealist, and sometimes idealism
was exceedingly vague, shadowy, and unprofitable. Then,
concurrently with the birth of vigorous and triumphant
science, philosophy itself turned to realism. It was the
latter half of the nineteenth century which witnessed the
slow and hesitating growth on the English stage of dramas
of realism. The only question is whether we have not
got to the end of the realistic tendency at the present time.
Some of our most popular writers, it is true, boast that
they have banished romance. But romance always returns.
It is like nature which you can expel with a pitchfork,
" *tamen usque recurret.*" The lesson which modern realistic
drama teaches is singularly hard, barren, unsatisfying. In
what mood does the spectator come away from *Hindle
Wakes, The Eldest Son, The New Sin, Rutherford and Son,*
and *The Younger Generation?* Does not the something
within him—no matter its name, soul or spirit—feel
starved? Has life nothing but the sordid struggles which
some of these dramatists paint? Can anything more depressing be conceived than the dramas of Mr. Galsworthy
—*Justice, Strife, The Eldest Son?* After a tragedy by
Shakespeare—even after a world-ruin like *King Lear*—
I know not how it is, but the spirit is uplifted, alert,
passionately believing in the reality of moral ideals. Does
any one ever have such a feeling after a modern realistic
drama? It is possible, therefore, that a reaction may be
slowly organising itself against some of the forms of realism
which have invaded our theatre. Perhaps even the war
may usher in a better, newer, more fruitful kind of idealism, which assuredly must be built up on experience and
veritable data, but which shall find room within its scheme

for unconquerable romance, for imagination, for fancy, for faith, for love—in short, for the human soul.

It was undoubtedly an uninspiring and difficult task which Macready had before him when he attempted to carry out his artistic mission. Macready, without question, had certain instincts which we should class as modern and realistic, but the material with which he had to deal, and his contemporary authors, defeated most of his efforts. He had, without doubt, his limitations, although no one who has even cursorily perused his recently published Diaries can question the fact that he had, in an almost tragic degree, the temperament of a sensitive and self-castigating artist. Now what was the kind of work by English authors which he found ready to his hand? I will take only two instances—Sheridan Knowles and Lytton Bulwer. James Sheridan Knowles, an Irish schoolmaster, who had also been an actor, whose father was first cousin to Richard Brinsley Sheridan, brought to Macready a tragedy called *Virginius*, widely proclaimed as a return to truth and to nature as against existing artificialities of the times. *Virginius* is an admirable example of the ordinary bourgeois drama, a bourgeois drama applied, unfortunately, to Roman tragedy. Every one knows, of course, the story of the soldier Virginius, who killed his daughter rather than she should fall into the hands of Appius. When Shakespeare dealt with Roman plays, he made, it is true, his characters Englishmen, but he made them of heroic mould. Brutus and Julius Cæsar, Mark Antony, and the rest, are certainly not commonplace, even though one can hardly describe them as accurately drawn in accordance with their Latin types. But of all the characters of Sheridan Knowles's play, it can safely be said that they are just mediocre, bourgeois, commonplace Englishmen and Englishwomen of the times. Virginius, for instance, is an excellent father of the middle class, whom we could imagine going down to his City office every day and returning to the suburbs in the evening. Virginia, the lovely heroine, is a simpering schoolgirl—a virtuous idiot. If this is what a return to nature meant, it must be confessed that it is a kind of nature that we do not want perpetuated.[1] Douglas Jerrold was in reality

[1] Cf. *Le Théâtre Anglais*, by A. Filon (chaps. 1 and 2), to whose admirable study of dramatic history I am much indebted.

a better dramatist than Sheridan Knowles, and the first act of his *Rent Day*, which was played in 1832, is a striking piece of work. But Jerrold, though he had undoubtedly considerable originality of his own, had to bow to the public taste of the time. He wrote *Black-eyed Susan*, perhaps his greatest success, undoubtedly also his worst play. The hero is, of course, that kind of seaman beloved of melodrama, compact of virtue and noble sentiments; and the heroine, though she is born from the lower ranks, can express the most exalted sentiments in a flowing and slightly academic style. The whole piece is a mass of unlikelihoods and absurdities: a very characteristic instance, as it seems to me, of that somewhat gross and common idealism of the crowd which likes to be transported when it goes into a theatre into another region where goodness is always rewarded, vice always punished, and " the man who lifts his hand against a woman " is reprobated by the howls of the gallery gods.

There came a time when Macready, face to face with failure, felt that he must try to retrieve his fortunes in America. He wrote to young Browning. "Make a play for me," he said, " and prevent me from going to America." The play was written. It was *Strafford*. It had, I think, four representations, but the unhappy Macready was not prevented from going to America. Still, a number of men of intelligence felt it their duty to come to the help of the distressed Macready. John Forster busied himself in the matter with characteristic energy; Leigh Hunt wrote a tragedy. But, above all, Lytton Bulwer composed three pieces, all of which enjoyed a distinguished celebrity at the time, and were played, undoubtedly, to full houses. These three pieces are *The Lady of Lyons*, *Richelieu*, and *Money*, and it would be difficult to say which of them is furthest removed from that kind of reality to which the stage should aspire. We ought to speak, I suppose, with a certain respect of the name of Bulwer, because he was an exceedingly prolific writer, a noted novelist, poet, politician, orator, as well as a dramatist. His novels were enough to make him famous. Every one knows something about *The Last Days of Pompeii*, or *Rienzi*, or *Ernest Maltravers*, or *The Caxtons*, or *Kenelm Chillingly*. As a dramatist he represented a sort of amalgam of different authors, without having any very precise characteristics of his own. For instance, he had some touches of Byron, as much, at all events, as a man of the world ought to have without giving offence to English respectability. He also copied Victor Hugo to a large extent—or, shall we say, was inspired by Victor Hugo? No one would pretend that his poetry was of the highest order, any more than that his historical romances were in any sense true. But he possessed a kind of windy rhetoric which pleased his generation, and he seemed to be a great figure in the annals of his time. *The Lady of Lyons* is still played, I believe, sometimes in America; it is not so very many years ago since it was played in London by Mr. Coghlan and Mrs. Langtry, and by Mr. Kyrle Bellew and Mrs. Brown-Potter.

Of all species of dramatic composition, melodrama, which has to be accepted literally and is adorned with the veneer of literature, is perhaps absolutely the worst. Every one likes melodrama. It has a frank charm, an undeniable glamour. But it must not attempt to be either literal or literary. In *The Lady of Lyons* we have great purple patches of poetry covering the bare places in an unreal melodramatic plot. None of the characters have any peculiar reality about them—they all ring false. Madame Deschapelles comes from the Palais Royal. Pauline, the heroine, can change her character in the course of the play, and pass from haughtiness to humility, from a stupid arrogance to an equally foolish submission, without turning a hair. And the worst element in the piece is the hero, Claud Melnotte, who is simply a villain if we take him seriously, certainly a charlatan and a cheat. Being nothing more than a simple peasant, he passes himself off as a prince, and marries under a false name a well-dowered young lady. And he talks throughout the play as though he were a model of the highest virtue ! The once-famous play *Richelieu* is in no sense better than *The Lady of Lyons*. No one for a moment would imagine that *Richelieu* is any closer to actual history than, let us say, Victor Hugo's *Cromwell*. It is all false rhetoric, as well as false history. As the French critic M. Filon once said, " It is a sort of plaster Hugo, daubed over with bad Alexander Dumas." And what shall we say of *Money*, which has had a distinguished stage history and been played by very distinguished actors and actresses ? If any one wants to understand how the native English drama has grown within recent years, how it has come to be something worth talking about, worthy of being put

side by side with the dramatic literature of France and
Germany, let him take the next opportunity he can find—
it may be difficult to find an opportunity—of seeing Bulwer
Lytton's *Money*.   It is all as dull and insincere and unreal
as any drama can be; the characters are not related to
life as we know it.   The piece is full of theatricality in the
worst sense of that word.   The hero is a prig, the heroine
a lady of extraordinary refinements and such abounding
conscience that she kills our sympathy in laughter.   These
were some of the pieces which stood for the English drama
in the first half of the nineteenth century.   They represent
a form of idealism which was bound to be shattered at the
first contact with truth.   Directly it came to be understood that the stage, instead of dealing with imaginative
fiction, should attempt, in however humble a fashion, to
represent actual life, all such pieces as *Virginius, Black-eyed
Susan, The Lady of Lyons, Richelieu, Money,* were swept
into that limbo of oblivion from which there is no return.
And the same thing would be true also of the burlesques
which Henry James Byron poured forth with so prodigal a
hand.   Some of Tom Taylor's pieces, such as *The Ticket-
of-Leave Man* and *Still Waters Run Deep*, still survive;
while Dion Boucicault struck out a new and interesting
variety of melodrama by his Irish pieces, such as *Colleen
Bawn, Arrah-na-pogue,* and *The Shaughraun.*   But realism,
as we understand it, made its first, shy appearance only
with Tom Robertson, after 1860.

In dating the tendency to realism from the first production of the Robertsonian comedy, I am quite aware
that I shall not have the sympathy of many critics.   As
we look back from our present point of vantage, it no
doubt seems obvious that Robertson's plays were anything
but realistic, in the sense in which we understand the term,
but in many respects extremely artificial.   It was in
reference to this doubtless that Matthew Arnold said that
English drama, floating uneasily between heaven and
earth, was " neither idealistic nor realistic, but purely
fantastic."   But here we must distinguish a little.   In
tracing the history of any movement, we must carefully
keep apart the spirit which animates it from some of its
admitted effects and results.   It may be true that some of
the plays, such as *Ours* and *School*, were utterly fantastic
in character and in structure.   But the thing which
Robertson was aiming at, the half-realised scope of his

enterprise, these are the points which ought to interest us. The truth is that we have here, almost for the first time, an effort on the part of modern English drama to achieve some originality of its own. Up to this date, for all practical purposes, the English stage was, as I have said, in entire subservience to the French stage. Adaptations of French plays, dramas, comedies, farces, even melodramas, were recognised to be the legitimate avocation of the dramatic writers in our own country. At all events, Robertson shook off this foreign bondage. He tried to do something that belonged to himself alone, and for that we owe him more gratitude than we sometimes are inclined to acknowledge.

There is also another consideration. Realism is, of course, as we have seen, a vague term. At all events, we can have a Realism in externals, as well as a Realism in internal spirit. Do not let us despise the former : it may be the beginning of better things. When the Bancrofts commenced their historic enterprise in the Prince of Wales's Theatre, they at all events gave us Realism in externals. The rooms that we saw on the stage were real rooms properly carpeted and boxed in, a ceiling was provided, together with appropriate furniture, such as could be found in any West-end drawing-room. This, indeed, was part of the crusade which the Bancroft management was undertaking. By making their little theatre a nest of something like luxury, by being careful in the plays they produced to imitate the tone, accent, the manners, the costume of the upper classes and the upper middle classes, these reformers of the theatre were initiating an economic revolution—the beginnings of a reconciliation between society and the stage. Earlier in the nineteenth century managers were always complaining that the wealthy classes conld not possibly be tempted to enter the doors of a theatre. But the Bancrofts managed to succeed where others had failed. The price of the stalls was raised to half a guinea, a daring stroke of policy which had its significant results in the fact that these stalls were always full. Society saw something which it really could recognise as part of its own daily life, and to its own surprise found itself coming to an obscure street close to the Tottenham Court Road, where it never had found itself before. This little theatre, in fact, built in a slum, became the rendezvous of aristocracy, and from this time forward it will be found that young men and young women of good position and good birth began to seek a career upon the boards. The style of acting suited them, it was so natural and easy, so devoid of all emotional excess, so quiet, so restrained—in a word, so gentlemanly, so ladylike. But because all this, though Realism of a kind, was only a superficial Realism, the drama was not yet considered something in which the intellectual classes could find interest. Society might be reconciled to the stage, but there was still the divorce between the acted drama and the deeper thoughts of students of life. That reconciliation had yet to come.

Probably there was no more curious or exciting an evening than the *première* of *Society*, produced on the 14th of November, 1865. *Society* is by no means a good play, nor is it characteristically Robertsonian, except in one point—Robertson's knowledge of Bohemian life. Those who were interested in the production of the play were especially afraid of the third act, in which was represented the "Owl's Roost," a more or less faithful transcript of the manners and habits of Bohemians and their clubs. For would not these same Bohemians resent such a delineation on the stage? Would they not think that Robertson had been unfaithful to his old friends and his own traditions of good fellowship? Therefore it was rather an anxious little company which commenced the performance of *Society;* and Marie Wilton, as she then was—Lady Bancroft as she is now named—mainly responsible for the venture, is always supposed to have occupied the final minute before the curtain went up in nailing with her own hands some little piece of stage decoration which had gone awry. But the result exceeded all anticipations. The tender little scenes of lovemaking in a London square, which occupied the second act, seemed pleasantly to suggest that romance was still possible under the plane-trees, and in the midst of the fogs of our Metropolis. But it was the much-dreaded third act which made the success of the play, especially the celebrated incident of the five shillings loan. A young man going to some evening social function finds himself devoid of the necessary wherewithal to pay his cab. He asks the first Bohemian friend he meets to lend him five shillings. "My dear fellow, I have not got it; but I can easily borrow it for you." And then we see a series of attempted borrowings, each man asking his neighbour in a laughable progress of generous inclination and of admitted impecuniosity. At last some one discovers the two necessary half-crowns, and then in inverse order the precious cab fare travels from hand to hand back to the original borrower. It is supposed to have been a real incident, and perhaps was recognised as all the more laughable on that account. There is no doubt that the Bohemians, at all events, were real, for they probably all had prototypes. As to the other characters, however, they were purely fantastic. Lady Ptarmigant takes the arm of old Mr. Chodd without hesitation, although he is what we should now call a " bounder " of the first water. Lord Ptarmigant—a character which John Hare rendered illustrious—had nothing to say and had only a single trick —he dragged his chair with him wherever he went, sat down, fell asleep at once, and most of the company tumbled over his outstretched legs. Marie Wilton (Lady Bancroft) was charming, as she always was, because Robertson amongst other gifts had remarkable skill in devising characters which would just suit her inimitable *espièglerie,* her sparkling personality. And Mr. Bancroft brought upon the stage a new type of languid Englishman. Sothern, in his " Lord Dundreary," had represented an English aristocrat as an absolutely brainless idiot. When the aristocrat appeared on the boards he was generally made into a caricature of fatuous imbecility. But Mr. Bancroft—as he was then called—put before the eyes of his audience a presentable, as well as a real, specimen of a man of breeding, a little haughty and disdainful, full of absurd airs, but by no means a fool, and always good-hearted. Of course, the most notorious example of his skill was Hawtree in *Caste,* whose appearance under the humble roof of the Eccles family is so irresistibly comic. He is so entirely a fish out of water, and yet so affably and pleasantly at home —a gentleman, in short, who is full of native kindliness. Through all this series of plays, *Society, Ours, Caste, School* —to take the best-known representatives of the Robertsonian comedy—the characters assigned to Bancroft and his wife never varied in general form, although in unessential details they may have varied. But if we look at them as a whole we are bound to confess that these comedies, full of easy grace and pleasantry, admirably written, endowed with a certain freshness of their own, were yet rightly named of " the milk-and-water school " and " the teacup-and-saucer type," more than a little fantastic and artificial.

For some twenty years after the Robertsonian drama had run its course, nothing critical or important in the direction of what we have called Realism is to be noted. Even after Robertson there was an undiminished flow of adaptations from the French. All the leading dramatists were occupied in this curiously ignoble and servile task. It was considered the *right* thing to do; at all events, from the managerial standpoint it was considered the *safe* thing to do. The French dramatists, from Scribe onwards, including Dumas *fils*, Augier, Sardou, and the rest, were held as the original patentees of a correct kind of drama. They had inherited the tradition of the " *pièce bien faite*," from Scribe, although gradually they were breaking from it. At any rate, they were models and examples, and the English theatres were in haste to borrow from them wholesale. Remember, for instance, that Mr. Sydney Grundy— who ought to have been, and afterwards proved himself to be, an original dramatist—was largely occupied with adaptations from the French, and we shall understand how the lesser fry thought it no unworthy task to transplant into alien conditions French drama, which, for the most part, was ill-suited for any such crossing of the Channel. Almost the one exception was the extremely successful adaptation of Sardou's *Dora*, under the title *Diplomacy*, which was not long ago revived with great success in London. It is clear, of course, that in this respect English drama was in leading-strings, and it was not until a reaction came, not until it was discovered that plays could be written on English subjects, full of English ideas which would bring money into the managerial till, that any change for the better could come about. In this noble duty of establishing a modern English stage there are three names especially prominent, although their work was essentially different : the names of Henry Arthur Jones, Sydney Grundy, and Arthur Pinero. If I were dealing with the rise of the modern English drama, I should have to say a good deal both of Grundy and of Arthur Jones. But the subject I am considering is the growth of Realism, a more special point that we must now look at again with, perhaps, an attempt at a clearer elucidation of its object and aims.

The dramatist whom we call realistic, in the first place,

accepts the conditions of the time in which he works and the country which is the scene of his labours. He begins, that is to say, with the principle that England has its own way of life and action, a way of its own, not by any means the same as that of other nations. That principle, of course, cuts at the root of all foreign adaptation. Most of the French dramas are racy of the French soil. The Parisian drawing-room is not the same as the London drawing-room; the characters move and talk in different fashion.

From that we advance to another principle. Each age has its own particular problems. The journalist and historian deal with these day after day. They mark the rise of a certain tendency, the gradual development of a new state of thought and feeling, the influence of novel ideas as they affect the settled conditions of English life. Take only a simple example. There is, and has been, in England a distinct school which we call the school of Puritanism, which has set itself with a remarkable determination, sometimes from the highest motives, but other times apparently through sheer blind prejudice, against art and all its manifestations, including, of course, dramatic art. Now, here is a state of things which you certainly cannot find in Paris and France. It is indigenous with us. As soon as a dramatist begins to think it his proper duty to put on the stage actual conditions of life as it is lived by the men and women around him, he is confronted by the Puritanical objection to many of those features which illustrate the artistic career. The dramatist, we will suppose, is not inclined to take the censures of the Puritans lying down; he strikes blow for blow. Thus you get a drama like Henry Arthur Jones's *Saints and Sinners* (1884) —a serious study of provincial life as dominated by narrow evangelicalism and the fury of the zealot. The two church-wardens in the play, who are called by characteristic names, Hoggard and Prabble, represent that kind of religiosity which is only an organised hypocrisy. For if the Puritans charged art and drama with suggested infractions of the moral code, the dramatist retorts by charging the Puritans with caring for the letter of the law and forgetting its spirit, with tithing mint and anise and cummin, and overlooking the simple obligations of charity and forgiveness. But we must not be diverted by taking the instance of Mr. Henry Arthur Jones, because he has never been a Realist, and never pretended for a moment that Realism

N

should be an ideal at which the dramatic writer ought to aim. I only refer to the play as an illustration of how the modern English drama, if it is to be vital, must deal with actual conditions of English life.

The Realist then, as such, advances to a third principle. He has already acknowledged that drama must be English and that it must have as its subject the contemporary problems of its time. But there is something else besides. The characters of his play must not be idealised or exaggerated, or transformed in any fashion by his imagination or fancy, but must be put before us exactly as psychological analysis reveals them. Men, we discover, work not from a single motive, but from complex motives. Their duties are performed, not always owing to a sense of moral obligation, but often because they happen to coincide with self-interest. Man is three-quarters mean and only one quarter, and very occasionally, noble. Woman is not an angelic figure to be placed on a pedestal and worshipped in a sacred niche with an aureole round her head. Still less is she the purely domestic drudge, but a human creature exactly on the same level as man, acting, as he does, from conflicting motives which she hardly understands, occasionally doing things right, as he does, more often doing things wrong, as he does, with particular temptations of her own which she finds it difficult to resist.

Now directly we begin to study humanity with the aid of scientific analysis, we have to take stock of these things, to say farewell to the older conceptions of drama which made the hero or heroine prosper in the end because he or she was good, and made the villain suffer in the last act because he was bad. Further, the romantic aspects of life tend, as a consequence of this analysis, to disappear. Romance is certainly not the daily food of human beings, and it is the everyday bread of humanity which we are concerned with. Thus a mortal blow is struck at the romantic drama, say, of Victor Hugo or of Bulwer Lytton, until at last we get, in the case of Mr. George Bernard Shaw, a distinct and determined attack against all romance, as being worthless, even if it exists, and unessential to the dramatist because it does not exist. Watch the single love scene in Mr. Shaw's *John Bull's Other Island*, and you will see how carefully the author has divested it of any touch of romantic glamour or poetic grace.

A further consequence of this realistic way of regarding

character is that we learn not to be afraid to call things by their right names. The older dramatist lived in a world of his own, where certain ugly facts were glossed over or forgotten, or, at all events, not emphasised. But the modern realistic playwriter, believing that such reticence is foolish and wrong, will give you the ugly facts with just their ugly names without shame. And from this point of view there is no question that Mr. Shaw's *Widowers' Houses*, produced in December, 1892, was a very remarkable instance of a modern realistic play, including also a didactic element which is never far absent from the work of Mr. Shaw. *Mrs. Warren's Profession* is, of course, another illustrative example.

Reviewing some of the features to which I have called attention, we discover at once that an exceedingly important and comprehensive influence came from the work of Henrik Ibsen, whose social dramas, produced in London, were received with undisguised hostility from 1890 onwards, but also profoundly altered the conception of drama in the minds of many English dramatists. And a date of no little significance as a prophecy of things to come is the 24th of April, 1889, when John Hare opened the new Garrick Theatre with *The Profligate*, by Pinero. It was a prophecy, I say, of things to come, because *The Profligate* as a play is in many respects an unripe piece of work, full of immaturity, if we look back to it from the later work of the same author. Nevertheless, it marks in its aims and objects, and also to some extent in its achievement, a very notable advance on anything which had been seen hitherto—an advance, I venture to think, in the direction of Realism which was consummated a good deal later, on the 27th of May, 1893, when George Alexander produced *The Second Mrs. Tanqueray* at the St. James's Theatre.

REALISTIC DRAMA

II

It was suggested at the end of the last paper that the production of *The Profligate* at the Garrick Theatre in 1889 was a significant event, and, indeed, was prophetic of the much more important occasion—the production of *The Second Mrs. Tanqueray* in May, 1893. I shall be concerned in the present article with the progress of Realism in Drama, and with some of those pieces of Sir Arthur Pinero which were conceived and executed in a realistic vein. Those which are convenient for my purpose in this respect are *The Profligate, The Second Mrs. Tanqueray, The Benefit of the Doubt, the Notorious Mrs. Ebbsmith,* and *Iris.* These are all realistic plays in the sense which has been already defined. The dramatist writing about his own country and his own times desires to paint not flattering portraits but veracious likenesses. He does not want to ignore the ordinary conditions, the salient characteristics of the era in which he lives. He believes it to be his business to look steadily at the social fabric, to observe the different elements of which it is composed, to note the peculiar perils which surround and enfeeble its health, and to play the part, not indeed of a reformer, for that would be too didactic an aim for an artist—or, at all events, for some artists—but of a keen, quick-witted, and occasionally sympathetic observer. And in similar fashion with regard to the personages of this drama, the playwright will seek to draw men and women, not as viewed through the spectacles of a fantastic imagination, but in their habit as they live. If he does this with a certain remorselessness, he is a Realist.

Now it is exactly this remorselessness of his which gets him into trouble with a number of different sections of our world. He is unflinching in his portrayal, and men do not like unflinching portrait-painters. They want the picture touched up by some indulgent and benevolent

180

philanthropist. The realist refuses to play with what he deems to be the truth. At the time when the younger Dumas was writing extremely interesting though not altogether persuasive prefaces to his plays, and was particularly occupied with some of the destructive activities of modern woman—a subject which, as we are aware, attracted him strongly—he made some remarks about the things we ought to laugh at and the things we ought not to laugh at. " It is our common habit in France," he wrote, " to laugh at serious things." We may, indeed, extend his observation and say that in England it is often our habit—especially in musical comedies—to laugh at serious things. But, according to Dumas, the only right attitude is to laugh at things which are not serious, and which have no pretension to be serious. When we are face to face with a grave social danger, it is a very curious sort of wisdom which dismisses such subjects with a laugh. There is, of course, a touch of pedantry in an observation like this, and there was certainly a good deal of pedantry in Dumas' didactic attitude. Nevertheless, there is solid truth beneath, which is very applicable to our modern audiences in England.

If we go back a certain number of years, to the time, for instance, when *The Profligate* was produced, or to the time when Ibsen's plays were first represented in our capital, we find that the common attitude of average people was one of shocked resentment. " The problem play " was looked at with open abhorrence, as though it were an accursed thing, revolutionary and immoral. Indeed, every serious effort made by the realist to represent life in plain, undisguised fashion was regarded, and is still regarded in many quarters, as savouring of impiety. Those who adopt such an attitude have certainly one justification. They point out that the playhouse is open to a very mixed public, of very different ages, and that it is wrong, or at all events highly injudicious to put on the stage problem plays which might be an offence to the youthful and immature. There is a further point also, which is somewhat open to controversy, but which is advanced by those who desire to keep serious discussion about life and morals away from the boards. There is all the difference, we are told, between what is read on the printed page and what is enacted before our eyes by living characters. The second is supposed to make a far deeper impression than the first, and therefore the enacted scene, if in any sense it is unpleasant, is likely to do more mischief in proportion to its vivid and lively character. It is difficult to dogmatise on a point like this, because it depends largely upon the individual whether a stronger impression is created by a story or a play. But the other point of objection proceeds on an assumption which no lover of drama can possibly concede. It assumes that a play is a mere entertainment, possessed of no serious dignity in itself, but only a sheer matter of amusement. In other words, it assumes that dramatic art is not art at all, because, directly we think of it, no art, whether painting, or sculpture, or literature, can be regulated in accordance with the age or immaturity of the public to whom it is presented. You do not ask your painter to remember that a child may look at his picture, nor do you ask your Hardys and Merediths to remember that their pages may be perused by young and sensitive persons.

The fact is that a good deal of ambiguity surrounds the use of such words as " the immoral," as applied to stage plays and the theatre. The very same critics who object to the problem play appear to have no objection when similar subjects are treated with easy wit and from a comical standpoint by the writers of musical comedy. What is it which should strictly be called " the immoral " ? Immorality consists, obviously, in putting people wrong about the relations of virtue and vice. It consists in adorning vice with seductive colours, in hiding the ugliness of the corrupt, in adopting little affectations of worldliness or wit in the effort to screen from the public gaze the real misery of a decadent civilisation. Or, again, when we have to treat with the actual conditions which obtain in this world of ours, it is plainly immoral to ignore the law of cause and effect. To pretend, for instance, that vice has no consequences, that everything can be put right, that plenary forgiveness waits on repentance and remorse, is immoral. It is possible for human creatures to forgive, and in some rare cases it is even possible for them to forget. But Nature never forgives, and no tears can wipe out the social effects of crime. To confuse the public on points like these, to present them with a false theory, is, indeed, an immoral thing. But how can it be called immoral to see some danger ahead and warn people of the enormous importance of avoiding it? How can it be immoral to observe men and women on the brink of a precipice, and to try to pull them back? The man who engages on a task like this cannot be called immoral, even though he may have to use very plain and ugly terms in acquitting himself of his disagreeable task.

This, I take it, is the defence of realism; its justification in the face of its numerous critics. There may be things to be said on the other side. Sometimes the realist may be like the satirist, and some satirists appear to have a predilection for ugly things. But that hardly touches the main centre of realism as we find it in drama. Its chief quality is to be absolutely fearless and ruthless in the exposure of all that is harmful, rotten, degrading, just as equally it should be its clear duty to set forth all that is helpful, stimulating, salutary. If realists are fonder of the first duty than the second, their excuse is that there is much necessary spade-work to be done in removing the evil before we can even hope to see the good. Besides, it is a melancholy fact that the good is, from the dramatic standpoint, not rarely the uninteresting. The true apology of the realist, however, is to be found in his passionate desire for truth—truth at all costs, his equally passionate hatred of all hypocrisy and sham, his zeal to anchor himself on solid facts and to refuse to care whether he gives pain or discomfort to men and women who would rather live in a fool's paradise. The best part of the influence of Ibsen on the modern drama is to be found in his clear promulgation of the necessity for truth. This point we shall have an opportunity of observing presently.

In April, 1889, when *The Profligate* was produced, Ibsen's influence on English dramatists had not yet begun. Indeed, clear traces of its influence are only discoverable in 1895, when *The Notorious Mrs. Ebbsmith* was seen on the boards. But the impulse to veracity, the resolute desire to study human nature, and especially to discover the effects on that human nature of a certain course of conduct more or less deliberately and recklessly pursued—these are the signs which prove to us that Pinero's *The Profligate* was in truth a drama of realism. The real change can hardly be better seen than in the treatment of the principal character. That a human being is to a very large extent a slave of his habits is adequately recognised in the play. In other words, we see the first beginnings of the doctrine of determinism. If a man acts from motives, and if the motives are in their turn automatically suggested by a type of conduct deliberately pursued through several years, then in the case of human action we get as much certainty of sequence between cause and effect as we do in external nature. Given the antecedents, the consequents will follow. Given the motives supplied by the past life, and a man's action is inevitable. Or, to put the matter in a concrete case where its immediate pertinence is easily seen, given a vicious career, then the ordinary and habitual conduct of the man at each successive episode or incident in his life will be vicious. I lay stress on the point because here is the commencement of a scientific psychology quite as much as an illustration of realism on the stage.

Dunstan Renshaw is a profligate—not, observe, merely an ordinary " man of the world," as we call it, but one who has done definite acts which stamp his nature, especially in his relations with Janet Preece. Dunstan Renshaw falls in love with Leslie Brudenell, and in the first moments of emotional excitement and expansion he declares to his friend that the companionship of a pure woman is a revelation to him. " She seemed," he tells Murray, " to take me by the hand and to lead me out of darkness into the light." All his high-flown language is perfectly explicable in a man who had, apparently, lived on his nerves and who was capable of intense moments of feeling. But what does not follow—what, indeed, is in the highest sense improbable —is that any radical change in character can be thus effected. Let us even suppose that such a sudden conversion were possible—which is granting a good deal more than the scientific psychologist would allow—there is always the terrible past, which is never buried but is always starting into fresh and vivid reality. How can a man like Dunstan Renshaw, merely because he marries a pure woman, wipe out his past? The past has " overtaken him," he says in one excited utterance. " You know what my existence has been; I am in deadly fear; I dread the visit of a stranger or the sight of strange handwriting, and in my sleep I dream that I am muttering into Leslie's ear the truth against myself."

Of course, his past sins find him out, as his friend Murray had prophesied. The whole pitiful history of Janet Preece comes to the light, and looks all the uglier because by the use of the long arm of coincidence Leslie's brother Wilfrid has loved Janet. Ah, you say, but the woman can forgive :

Leslie is a good woman! It is true that she can forgive, but she can hardly forget; and, even if she did, how does this help Dunstan Renshaw, who finds it impossible to forget? In other words, the past cannot be obliterated by a stroke of the pen, and it is the intimate and deadly quality of all sins that they leave permanent traces on the man and woman who have committed them.

> " And having tasted stolen honey
> You can't buy innocence for money."

We can understand how new a thing in English drama was this ruthless treatment of a grave problem, when we discover that owing to the solicitations of John Hare, the only true, as well as artistic, end of this play was changed. John Hare was guided by the popular prejudice in favour of a happy ending, and he therefore besought the dramatist to soften down the terrible conclusion into something wholly unreal and artificial, which should send the spectators away in a happier frame of mind. Well, it is an old-established prejudice in theatrical audiences to desire happy endings. Even Aristotle recognised the fact. But such exhibitions of human weakness do not alter the stern facts of life; they only proclaim aloud the hopeless divergence between popular art and an art based on psychology and science. There are some problems that cannot be solved by tears or forgiveness. What sort of married life was possible for Dunstan Renshaw and Leslie? The dramatist cut the Gordian knot by making the hero kill himself, for in no other fashion probably can a dramatist bring home to those who see his plays the dreadful consequence of certain crimes. But if we want to see what is the result of marriages of this kind, we cannot do better than turn to one of the works of the Norwegian dramatist, Ibsen. *Ghosts* is not a pleasant play, but it conveys a tremendous moral. In the course of the story we discover that Mrs. Alving's husband is a profligate of a type absolutely comparable with Dunstan Renshaw. For various reasons, including social and external decency, she determines to make the best of it and go on living with the man as if he were a sort of saint instead of a blackguard. Conventional morality requires that a wife should go on living with her husband whatever he may be guilty of—such is the moral of Pastor Manders. But it is exactly this worship of humbug and pretence which the true moralist reprobates in the severest terms. Ibsen's *Ghosts* is generally considered as a sort of sequel to Ibsen's *Doll's House*—it is equally a sequel to Pinero's *The Profligate*. Why Nora is justified in running away from her home is because in certain conditions life becomes impossible for a married pair. Why Dunstan Renshaw commits suicide is because certain sins are never forgiven or forgotten. If we choose to disregard these realities the next generation will suffer. " The fathers have eaten sour grapes, and the children's teeth are set on edge." The son of the profligate Councillor Alving ends by being a helpless idiot, crying for the sunshine.

It does not follow, of course, that *The Profligate* is in itself a good play, or even a good example of dramatic realism. It is worth while looking at this point for a moment, because it will throw light on our subject from another quarter. What are the obvious defects of *The Profligate ?* We notice a certain crudeness in the composition and construction. If you look at the opening scene of *The Second Mrs. Tanqueray* you will find one of the most admirable examples that Sir Arthur Pinero has ever given us of what is technically called " exposition." The dinner party given by Aubrey Tanqueray to his friends reveals in the most natural way in the world the story in which we are to be interested, and the clever manner in which Paula is herself introduced at the end of the first act gives us a very necessary sight of the heroine who is to play so fatal a part in Aubrey Tanqueray's destiny. *The Profligate* commences with a conversation between Hugh Murray, Renshaw's friend, and Lord Dangars, which is by no means so happy. Moreover, in carrying out the intrigue there is a decided lack of naturalness, or rather of inevitableness. Every play of the sort must invoke the aid of coincidence, because in presenting a little picture, foreshortened and concentrated, of a complete and rounded-off story, the playwright must be permitted to use all the expedients which we recognise to be of the nature of accidents. But the use of coincidence in *The Profligate* goes beyond all bounds. It is necessary, of course, that Leslie, wife of Dunstan Renshaw, should come face to face with Janet Preece, who has been her husband's victim. But the mechanism which produces this result is decidedly arbitrary, if not far-fetched. Hazard and accident play an overwhelming part. Accident brings Janet to Paddington Station at the same time as Leslie and her brother; accident decides that Leslie's school friend, Miss Stonehay, should take Janet as a travelling companion; accident, once more, brings the Stonehay family precisely to the environs of Florence, and to the villa in which the Renshaws are living; and finally, there is not so much nature as artifice in the arrangement by which Janet stays with Leslie at the villa instead of going away as she naturally would—through feelings of sheer delicacy. There is another side on which *The Profligate* is open to criticism. The danger of all realistic plays is that they are apt to tumble unaware into melodrama. I mean by melodrama an exaggeration in the drawing of character, the sacrifice of a good deal of probability in order to accentuate the situation, and a noticeable want of connection between the motives and acts of the personages involved. The character of Dunstan Renshaw shows many signs of exaggeration. His *raison d'être* in the piece is to represent a profligate and a seducer, and a man who has lived the particular life that he is supposed to have lived, and who, even on the eve of his marriage, indulges in a stupid carouse, is hardly capable of those finer shades of feeling, of remorse and self-chastisement, which he betrays towards the end of the play. So, too, Leslie's evolution is decidedly abrupt from the innocence of the earlier stage to the knowledge of life after one month's *tête-à-tête* with her husband.

How different is the masterly treatment which we come across in *The Second Mrs. Tanqueray !* We understand the situation from the very beginning. The characters are not exaggerated, and we see them developing before our eyes on lines which we recognise as essentially probable and true. The personality of Aubrey Tanqueray may be a little obscure here and there, but Paula is an admirable creation, whose conduct throughout is what we might have expected of a woman in such circumstances and subject to such temptations; while, as in the case of Greek tragedy, we are dimly aware from the first scene to the last of a Fate hanging over all the characters and dooming them to their eventual ruin. There is, it is true, one coincidence which may strike some observers as strange. It is the accident which brings back Ardale, the accepted lover of Ellean, into the presence of the heroine, with whom he had such close relations in the past. Nevertheless here, as it seems to me, the coincidence is not in any sense surprising or unnatural,

given the past circumstances of Paula's life and her numerous adventures before she became Mrs. Tanqueray. It is
because of its fine theatrical execution, because it gives
us living figures whose dispositions and character inevitably
work up to the *dénouement*, and because it does not slide
over into melodrama, that *The Second Mrs. Tanqueray* is,
so far as I can judge, one of the masterpieces of the modern
English stage.

For what is, or ought to be, the supreme excellence of a
play which purports to deal with real events and real characters, true to the country in which they live and explicable
on proper psychological grounds ? I think the great test
is this. Do we look upon the enacted drama as a mere
spectacle, or do we find ourselves part of it ? Are we merely
sitting as spectators in a theatre divided from the stage by
the footlights, living our own lives while the people on the
boards live theirs ? Or are we transported in very deed
into the enacted scene, as though it were part of the life
which for the time we ourselves are leading ? A great play,
which greatly deals with supreme issues, has the power to
make us forget that we are in a theatre at all, or that
there is any distinction between us and the actors. In
other words, we live in the play, and do not merely look at
it. But how rarely do we undergo an experience like this !
Assuredly, it is impossible in plays of romance ; it is equally
impossible in melodramas or farces. But the supreme
virtue of a drama of realism is that now and again it has
this strange power of transporting us out of ourselves. The
audience becomes a part of the play. Every one, perhaps,
will have his own instances to give of an experience of this
kind : for myself I felt it when I first saw *The Second Mrs.
Tanqueray*, and again, to take quite a modern instance,
when I saw *Hindle Wakes*.

This seems a fit opportunity for saying something of the
predominant influence of Ibsen. I have called it predominant because it seems a mere matter of fact that since
the vogue of the Norwegian dramatist most of the play-
writers of England have either altered their methods or
their style. But it is necessary to look at the matter a
little closer, because the influence which a man exerts on
the literature of another country is a somewhat intangible
thing, and we are only too apt to go wrong as to its range
and quality. The main influence of Ibsen has, undoubtedly,

been in the direction of realism, defined in the sense in which I have all along tried to use it. Realism means above all else a devotion to the bare and explicit truth of human life and human character, and the avoidance of all romantic or poetic devices for obscuring the main issues. No sooner had Ibsen begun to compose his social dramas than he found himself immersed in a task—evidently congenial to him—of tearing down the social conventions, exposing the social hypocrisies which disguise the face of reality and truth. Nearly every one of his social plays is an exposure of humbug of some sort. Now it is the case of some ship-owner, who recklessly sends a rotten old hulk to sea for reasons purely commercial; and now it is the more intimate relationship between men and women in the married state, which seems to the dramatist to require careful analysis and elucidation. Or, again, it is the fetish of mundane respectability at which Ibsen will gird. He will show us a Pastor Manders trying to persuade Mrs. Alving to go on living with her profligate husband for the sake of external decency; or else will paint for us the character of a sincere enthusiast for the truth who wishes to purify a town's water supply, together with all the fatal consequences in his case, the loss of personal prestige, the accusations of treachery, the desertion of all his friends. These are the various themes which Ibsen takes up in *The Pillars of Society*, in *A Doll's House*, in *Ghosts*, and in *An Enemy of the People*. And then, by a sudden change of outlook, in order to prove that he cares more for truth than for theory, Ibsen writes his strange play *The Wild Duck*, the whole purport of which is to show that a fanatical devotion to truth may cause just as much injury as the studious and calculated suppression of truth. 'What is wrong with society is the reign of conventional ethics, supported by such interested apostles of things as they are as clergymen and business men. There are many dark corners which ought to be looked into in this matter. Nevertheless, like everything else, truth is a difficult goddess to worship, and the intoxicated fanatic who devotes himself to her cause will often do her graver harm than even the conventional liar. Such seems to be the lesson of *The Wild Duck*, albeit that it is a play which has always caused a certain searching of heart among the disciples of Ibsen. But the general impulse of striving to attain to the exact and veritable fact remains as one of the chief heritages which

Ibsen communicated to the dramatic world, and it is easy to see in this respect how great has been his influence amongst modern playwrights.

I pass to another point—the question of dramatic construction. Ibsen is a master of dramatic craftsmanship. He certainly learnt some lessons in the school of Scribe in Paris, but he applied and transformed the *pièce bien faite* in his own fashion, so that, externally at all events, an Ibsen play seems to differ *toto cælo* from the ordinary pieces produced on the French stage. In some respects Ibsen has an almost classical severity and restraint of form. His *Ghosts* is, technically, like a Greek tragedy, so sure is the progression of its incidents, so close is the interaction between cause and effect. *A Doll's House* might possibly commend itself to Euripides, although, of course, the Greek dramatist would have solved the problem in his usual fashion by introducing some god or goddess to cut the Gordian knot. A method of which Ibsen was especially fond in his plays was what has been called the retrospective method. You start your plot on the very eve of a *dénouement*, as close as you can to the tragic issue. Then you make your characters expound the past in a series of animated dialogues, so that when the conclusion is reached you have become thoroughly acquainted with the personages who bring it about.[1] Ibsen shows a wonderful skill in the fashion in which he makes the personages of the drama reveal their past actions and also themselves, to which we may add the obvious fact that his conversations themselves are conducted with a sense of actuality which makes them extraordinarily vivid. You can read a play by Ibsen with almost as much pleasurable interest as you can witness it on the stage, because there is not only something easy and natural in the sentences put into the mouths of the various characters, but there is also a distinct economy of effect. The sentences themselves have weight and importance because they so clearly lead up to the issue.

The only thing which interferes with this triumphant actuality is Ibsen's increasing tendency as he grew to his later years to use symbols and images, sometimes of a very vague and elusive character. The symbol of the Wild Duck is comparatively easy, for it very fairly indicates both the character and the fate of the girl heroine, Hedwig. In

---

[1] Mr. Bernard Shaw uses this method in *Mrs. Warren's Profession*.

The Lady from the Sea we have advanced a step further in the symbolic direction. After all, the Wild Duck was a mere symbol, subordinate to the plot itself, but in *The Lady from the Sea* the idea of the play itself is wholly symbolic. The problem of married life is not discussed as it had been, for instance, in *A Doll's House*, but is merged in a sort of allegory suggestive of the romance of love. Plays like *Rosmersholm* and *Hedda Gabler* belong to the earlier type, but when we come to *The Master Builder* and *Little Eyolf*, and especially to the last, *When We Dead Awaken*, symbolism is once more in full swing; and, indeed, in *When We Dead Awaken* it represents, or perhaps disguises, a definite weakening in dramatic power. According to the French critic, M. Filon, however, it is just this symbolism or allegorical element in Ibsen which makes him congenial to Anglo-Saxon and Teutonic tastes, while it renders it much more difficult for Parisian audiences and the Latin races to understand him. There is, undoubtedly, a strong strain of mysticism in all Northern peoples, Teutonic, Scandinavian, and Anglo-Saxon, but in the representations of Ibsen's plays in England I have never been able to detect that Ibsen owes such popularity as he has gained to his mystical elements. As a matter of fact, he never has been popular in the widest sense in England, and certainly the performance of plays like *A Master Builder* and *Little Eyolf* has not enabled English spectators to welcome Ibsen as akin to them in essence and spirit. Obviously, too, the symbolic tendency interferes in no slight measure with the realistic tendency which belongs to the best work of Ibsen. Symbolism may be valuable inasmuch as it suggests that realism is by no means the last word in dramatic art, but it is not a phase in the great Norwegian's work which has lent itself to much successful imitation on the part of his followers and admirers.

There is another aspect of Ibsen's work, however, which deserves attention, especially as connected with modern movements in social and intellectual life.[1] I refer to the extraordinary prominence which he has given to women in his dramas, and especially to women as representing the individualistic idea as against State action or collectivism. Ibsen, undoubtedly, thought, as most of his social dramas

---

[1] Cf. *Henrik Ibsen. A Critical Study*, by R. Ellis Roberts (Martin Secker), a book of no little value to the student of drama.

prove, that all State action, as such, whether exercised through a compact majority or through police or other agencies, is entirely harmful and crippling because it puts chains upon the individual. As against society the individual is always right. Now, who are the great individualists? Women, undoubtedly, who not only attack problems in their own fashion, but instinctively resist the pressure of laws imposed upon them, as it seems to their intelligence, in an entirely arbitrary manner. Hence the importance of women in Ibsen's plays, and hence, too, the idea, for which, indeed, there is a good deal to be said, that Ibsen was the great feminist writer, doing more for the cause of women both as poet and artist than any thinker had done before him. It is not quite certain, however, whether the Norwegian dramatist really liked this identification of his views with those of the ordinary feminist platform. He certainly did not keenly support any women's movements, and, apparently, he was annoyed that his play *A Doll's House* should have been interpreted as a tract for feminism. But it remains true that to women he assigned all the virtues the possession of which he denied to men. The love of truth, a clear perception of what is reasonable, a fine dose of enthusiasm, immense energy, all these things are attributed to women in his plays, whereas, on the contrary, the men exhibit the mean vices—stupidity, selfishness, sometimes cowardice, sometimes also rascality and a reckless greed. There are exceptions, of course. Hedda Gabler is a woman entirely devoid of conscience, while Dr. Stockmann is a fine example of the well-meaning moralist who pursues his love of truth even though society be shattered. So, too, Dr. Wangel is a husband entirely praiseworthy, but I know of hardly any other husband in the Ibsenite drama of whom the same thing can be said. The women, I say, have all the virtues, or, at all events, all the virtues from the point of view of the Norwegian dramatist. Many examples occur. There is Nora, for instance, in *A Doll's House*, who cannot endure a married life which is not founded on respect for individual duties, as against her husband Torvald, who only desires to hush up scandal. Or there is Rebecca in *Rosmersholm*, a far finer character than the unhappy Rosmer, much braver and more resolute in her determination to save her soul through love. Or in *The Master Builder*, while Solness seems only inspired by the single idea that somehow or other he must keep back the advancing tide of the younger generation, Hilda is inspired by a much more healthy ambition in trying to restore to Solness his earlier dreams. Or, once more, in the last of the Ibsen plays, *When We Dead Awaken*, it is Irene who has truth and right on her side, as against the egotist Rubek, who only desires to make use of human personalities in the selfish pursuit of art for art's sake.

As we review these and many other instances we see that to Ibsen woman is not only the born anarchist, but that she is also justified in her anarchical views. The world is poisoned because every one is contented with outworn social and ethical conventions. Women refuse to be blinded by the dust of these antique superstitions; they are on the side of freedom, independence, self-realisation, the only ideals at which human life ought to aim, the only ideals which Ibsen, at all events, chooses to glorify. Of course, Ibsen was very one-sided in views of this kind. The progress of humanity depends on two movements which must go on side by side. One is the impulse towards change; the other is the steady drag towards stability. To prevent a given social state from petrification there must be constant revolts, a continuous series of fresh and lively efforts to strike out new paths. But in order that a social state may exist at all, the newer impulses must be harmonised with the older structure. Order is as necessary for the world as progress. Ibsen's ideal of self-realisation, if carried to its logical results, means the destruction of stability for the sake of a few hare-brained individuals. Nor yet is self-realisation to be distinguished in the last resort from a greedy and assertive selfishness.

In his influence on the world of drama, however, Ibsen's fondness not only for drawing women but for endowing them with energetic qualities has played no small part in the evolution of feminist ideas. In all modern realistic work whether you observe it in the plays of Pinero or of George Bernard Shaw, the woman has attained a prominence and importance far removed from the older dramatic conception of women either as a toy or as a goddess or an idol to be worshipped in a shrine. None of us in this modern generation are likely to forget either Mr. Shaw's Candida or the same dramatist's Ann Whitefield. The first is to me, I confess, a somewhat enigmatic personage. You will remember what Candida, the excellent wife of an excellent clergyman, dared to do in the play bearing her name.

o

She knows that she is loved by her clergyman husband; she is also aware that she is the object of a fantastic adoration on the part of a young poet, Eugene Marchbanks. She daringly puts lover and husband to the test, and says that whoever is the weaker and needs her most will have her for the future. She plays this cruel game, although she knows that her stupid common-place self-opinionated husband—who, by the way, is a very successful clergyman —adores her, and that her namby-pamby sentimental febrile lover puts her on a pinnacle as being much too great for her commonplace surroundings. Of course, the dramatist gets out of his difficulty by explaining to us that the Rev. James Morell was in reality the weaker man who needed Candida most of all, and so all comes right in the end. But whether we are for this reason to forgive the wife, or whether she is acting as all women act in similar circumstances, are questions which the mere man finds it difficult to answer. Mr. Shaw's heroines are not always pleasant people, with the exception, of course, of Lady Cecily Waynflete in *Captain Brassbound's Conversion.* Some of them are of the hard huntress type, like Ann Whitefield in *Man and Superman,* who runs down her quarry with magnificent persistence and success. Barbara is a subtle conception, subtle and interesting, but her creator does not improve her character as the play proceeds. To compare the women of Mr. Shaw with the women of Ibsen would be an interesting topic, but one for which, unfortunately, I have no space.

The women of Sir Arthur Pinero are very carefully drawn, and in this perhaps, once again, we can see the influence, consciously or unconsciously, exercised by Ibsen. I have already referred to Leslie Brudenell in *The Profligate,* and to Paula in *The Second Mrs. Tanqueray.* I have yet to deal with the heroine of *The Benefit of the Doubt,* with *The Notorious Mrs. Ebbsmith,* and with *Iris.* With regard to Agnes Ebbsmith, interesting character as she undoubtedly is, there is perhaps less to be said because the play in which she appears is not so carefully wrought, or at all events is not so successful as the others of which mention has been made. Still, the character of Agnes Ebbsmith raises several most curious problems which are worth studying, quite apart from the success or want of success of the play called by her name. There is a strange tragedy about the woman. She is full of independence and spirit,

and without any doubt she wanted to be the companion,
friend, and fellow-worker of Lucas Cleeve, with whom she
had elected to live. Perhaps Lucas Cleeve himself thought
at one time that life was possible both for him and for
Agnes on the high platonic plane of companionship and
camaraderie. But because Lucas is a half-baked creature,
or rather because he is merely the ordinary man, *l'homme
moyen sensuel,* the experiment is a failure. Agnes is forced,
deliberately, to appeal to his senses and lower nature in
order to fortify his constancy.

I turn to *The Benefit of the Doubt* and to *Iris.* Both the
heroines of these plays are, from an ordinary masculine
standpoint, neither sincere nor praiseworthy. Yet, on
the contrary, thanks to Pinero's art, we are only too
ready to forgive them both. We make excuses for them;
we say that circumstances were too strong, that their
positions were unendurable, that their sins ought to be
forgiven. Here is Theo Fraser in *The Benefit of the Doubt.*
She is married to a hard, dour Scotsman, Fraser of Locheen,
who will wear kilts at the dinner table, and insists on
having his deplorable bagpipes played on every occasion.
Well, it is not fair to a sensitive woman, on whose nerves
these things act with terrible force. So she flies for refuge
to Jack Allingham, and there is a scandal, an action for
divorce, and the judge gives her the benefit of the doubt.
Now, mark what ensued. Fraser, not being an absolute
ass, says that they must go abroad in order to get over the
malevolence of spiteful tongues. He wants to hush up
scandal like Torvald in *A Doll's House.* Theo resolutely
refuses to do anything of the kind, and says, on the contrary, that the situation must be faced, and that they must
remain in town. She may have been right in principle,
but the sequel proves that she was wrong in fact. Upset
by her husband's arguments, she goes once more to Jack
Allingham in a half-fainting condition; she drinks cham-
pagne on an empty stomach, and, not to put too fine a
point on it, she gets intoxicated. In this condition she
implores Jack Allingham to run away with her. Not a
nice woman this, and yet, upon my soul, the dramatist
makes us forgive her! Apparently he forgives her himself,
for he lets her fall into the hands of the wife of a worthy
bishop, who is going to spread her immaculate reputation
over Theo's peccadilloes and gradually restore her in the
public credit. I am always wondering why this fine play,

The Benefit of the Doubt, has never been revived. I suppose we must wait until the National Theatre is established before we can hope to see it again. The first and second acts are masterpieces.

But let us continue with *Iris.* Iris Bellamy, according to her own account, is more sinned against than sinning. She is left a widow at a very early age, with a certain fortune, which she is to resign if she marries again. Round her are at least three men—Croker Harrington (who perhaps does not count, for he is a faithful, dog-like creature); Laurence Trenwith, an impecunious young man, with whom she is sincerely in love; and the Mephistopheles of the piece, Frederick Maldonado, a hard, wealthy, masterful financier. Now, Iris cannot be straight with any of these. She cannot make up her mind to live in poverty abroad with Laurence Trenwith. Poor Croker hardly enters into her calculations. Suddenly she is herself confronted with poverty, owing to the ill-doings of a rascally attorney; and this is Maldonado's chance. He leaves a cheque-book with her, and she makes use of it. He prepares a beautifully furnished flat for her, leaving the key with her, and eventually she drifts into accepting it. Then Trenwith returns, and she tells him the whole story, expecting him to forgive her. Immensely hurt at his refusal to have anything to do with her, both hurt and surprised, she is left to Maldonado's mercy : and because he has discovered the intrigue between Iris and Trenwith, she is finally driven out into the streets. You will say that she is punished, and terribly punished. It is quite true. The point is that we are genuinely sorry for her. And yet could there be a more worthless woman ? Was she wicked, or merely weak ? We really cannot say. Perhaps she was what Paula was originally before she commenced her career as a courtesan. But the case stands as it does with Sophy Fullgarney in *The Gay Lord Quex,* whom the hero very justly describes as a cat which scratches the hand that tries to pet it. Yet Sophy Fullgarney becomes in the sequel a quite estimable character, although she is a mean, despicable spy. And Iris, too, lives in our memory, although she is quite non-moral, perhaps even basely immoral. Need I add the instance of Paula Tanqueray ? Did she ever love Aubrey Tanqueray ? I think not. I think she only cared for comfort, for the satisfaction of living in a proper home, of being respected as a legitimate wife. She betrays her husband at every point. Capriciousness is the least of her vices. She asks her disreputable friends to stay with her. Even if she had won the love of her step-daughter, Ellean, it is doubtful if she would have known what to do with it. And yet—and yet—we are more than a little inclined to forgive Paula Tanqueray, although she had absolutely ruined a good man, and brought positive agony to his daughter. " There is a soul of goodness in things evil "; that is the dramatist's lesson. Or perhaps it is only an illustration of the famous text, " To know all is to pardon all." Pinero has made us understand his women, and though our judgment and our common sense rebel, we are sympathetically interested in them, and inclined to grant them plenary absolution.

We have yet to see how the progress of realism in drama has manifested itself among our latest contemporary writers, and especially among such dramatists as Mr. George Bernard Shaw—who is in some respects perhaps too fantastic to be called a realist—Mr. St. John Hankin, Mr. Granville Barker, Mr. Arnold Bennett, Mr. Galsworthy, and Mr. Stanley Houghton. I hope in a subsequent essay to find an opportunity of dealing with some of the most modern developments. In the present instance it seemed worth while to spend some little time over a period, which means more perhaps to the middle-aged man than it does to the more youthful of our contemporaries, and especially over the work of Sir Arthur Pinero, whom this present age, a little fickle and oblivious of what has been done in the past, has begun somewhat ungratefully to disparage.

But before I end, I must go back to a point which was alluded to in my first paper, and which indeed is suggested by movements that are going on all round us, both in literary and dramatic art. We have been living under the tyranny of realism for some years past, and in some respects I think the dominion of realistic modes of thought has become an obsession. If I confine myself to what realism means in drama, I should say that its tendency is to lead us straight to pessimism, to that characteristically sombre and gloomy pessimism which has invaded foreign literatures even more than our own, and of which the Russian literature affords us admirable specimens. Why should realism lead to pessimism? The answer is quite simple, and also instructive. The realistic treatment of human character lays stress on the individual, his rights, his claims, his sorrows, his passions, all that he demands of life and all that life seems to deny him. Now, despite the teaching of Ibsen, the individual is not always right as against society, nor does ultimate wisdom reside with the minority as against the majority. The individual by himself is a weak and feeble thing, and the enumeration of his particular grievances distorts the proper perspective of human existence in general and depreciates the average health and sanity of the social state. Reflecting on his personal woes, the individual naturally becomes a pessimist; or, if we may put it in another way, selfishness, a narrow absorbing egotism, is the root of all evil. At all events our realists, both in literature and in drama, exhaust themselves in denouncing the injustice and the hopelessness of human life, because they persist in taking the standpoint of the acutely sensitive individual instead of regarding such matters from an objective or world standpoint.

One of the best ways of trying to discover the tendencies of a particular movement amongst ourselves is to see what is happening in foreign literatures. The Russian literature is very apt for this purpose, and, as we are aware, modern Russian literature has been not incorrectly described as " pessimism devoid of humour." I will not take such well-known writers as Tolstoy, Gorky, Dostoieffsky. I will only mention one of the modern novelists, Artzybascheff. A recent novel, entitled *At the Utmost Limit*, has no other theme than to portray the black night, the utter and irremediable senselessness of all earthly existence, and to suggest suicide as the only panacea for human ill. Nevertheless, what is happening even in Russia, the home of pessimism?[1] There is a school of younger writers who, in reaction from this state of things, might almost be described as optimists. Something of the same sort has been happening among ourselves.

There are only two ways of waking from the nightmare of realism when pushed to its extreme of egotistic mania. One is the way of symbolism, the way of dreams. You may tell yourself that the only means to discover the mystery of the universe, and to reconcile the contradictions and disorders of life, is to shut your eyes to the ordinary world and throw the reins on the neck of imagination and fancy, living in the mystic's paradise, finding an ideal happiness in

---

[1] Written before the Russian Revolution.

a world within the four walls of human consciousness.   That is what Maeterlinck does in some of his plays.   Many hints of the same kind of thing are to be found in Ibsen, who, as his life progressed, grew to be more and more fond of symbols.   In a certain fashion also the Celtic mode of thought of Yeats and other writers of the Irish school affords another illustration.   Mysticism then is one of the modes of reaction, which come easy to some dreaming minds, a mysticism which may be ascetic or may be sensuous, but which is at all events wholly imaginative.   I am not sure that it is the more hopeful or the more effective path to lead us out of our swamp of despair.

There is another way.   You may choose not to ignore the evils of life, but you may study them, just as the physician and the surgeon study all the morbid growths of mental and corporeal life.   By a close study of the dreadful foe you may in the end master the secret of his destructive power, and, perchance, you may come upon this discovery, that the evils of life do not flow from the nature of things, but from human blindness, from human selfishness, from precisely that lack of cohesion amongst the various members of the human family which alone can raise them to higher levels of culture and happiness.   If men were more sensitive to each other's feelings, if they could understand one another better, they would cease to deplore their own sufferings and find that life in the larger sense, a corporate life of consenting human individualities, contains within itself potentialities of real happiness.   *La joie de vivre,* which is extinguished by narrow egotism, may burst out afresh in altruistic aims, in the efforts of a community to purge itself of its maladies, in its resolute concerted striving towards an exalted goal.   Quite elementary and simple things like pity, and affection, and love, supply us with materials, not for wailing and misery, but for a rich contentment and a serene peace.   And so from the realism of dreadful facts we get to the idealism of simple emotions, the discovery that man is not by nature depraved, but by nature good and filled with the joy of life, finding in love and human service the satisfaction alike of his heart and his head.   Perhaps before that morrow dawns man must needs pass through the valley of the shadow of doubt and despair.   But he may win the happy secret at last, and, if I may judge once more from the tendencies of Russian literature, and from the work especially of the young writer Alexis

Remizoff, it is thus that we may find the path towards our future deliverance. We shall not be untrue to life; we shall not close our eyes to the existence of evil; but having once grappled with the malady of pessimistic selfishness we shall discover how the idealism of simple things can, as though by magic, make us healthful and sane.

REALISTIC DRAMA

III

WHY do we speak of a " new " school of dramatists ? And in what sense do they exhibit novelty, as compared with their predecessors ? Many of the conditions for the production of drama are, we know, fixed and constant—the conditions, for instance, which are involved in the presentation of a concentrated story or episode, carried out by living personages, moving and talking before us. The dramatist cannot *explain* to his audience, he can only *illustrate ;* he reveals character not by description but by action and dialogue : he has only a short time to produce his effect, and therefore he must hit hard and hit early. All these things we know, for they constitute the difference between writing novels and writing plays. But there are other conditions—or perhaps we ought to call them traditions or prejudices—which are inessential, variable, dependent on mere custom and fashion. If a man ignores such as these, which his precedessor respected and of which very likely he made a fetish, then on this ground he might be called a " new " dramatist. There are, for instance, the prejudice for a happy ending, the use of soliloquies and asides, the necessity for " situations " at the end of each act, the idea that you must not introduce fresh personages in the last act, but gradually allow the course of your story to strip off the unessential characters and leave you towards the close with just the two or three vital characters who matter. These are all temporary and accidental fashions, so to speak, and a play is not necessarily better because it retains them, or worse because it chooses to ignore them. Even Scribe's sedulous care for a *pièce bien faite* has now become an outworn game—at all events, with some of the moderns. Dramatic construction, though still considered a counsel of perfection, is not recognised among our contemporaries as absolutely necessary to dramatic salvation.

But there are much more subtle differences than these

between the newer and the older school. It is a question of temper, a question of manner, a question of preferred subjects. The attitude towards the world has changed, the attitude, in especial, towards moral problems and social questions. Those doubters and agnostics who in the 'sixties and 'seventies were sealed of the tribe of Matthew Arnold and Arthur Clough were more than a little sad about their obstinate questionings. Their scepticism was not audacious : it was diffident, humble, melancholy. They were very sorry that they could not agree with the orthodox—it was their misfortune, not their fault. They ought to be condoled with, not reprobated. The more modern attitude is not so much daring as incurious. Why should we bluster and say with John Stuart Mill—" and if such a Being condemn me to Hell, to Hell I will go " ? Really there is no reason for any fuss. All the fighting is over and done with. We need not brandish our sceptical steel in the face of opponents whose opportunities for offensive attack are so strictly limited. Therefore the new school neither strives nor cries because it is persuaded that belief or unbelief is mainly a matter of temperament or of ancestry, for which the individual cannot be held responsible. If he is born a religious mystic, he will write poetry like Miss Evelyn Underhill or Mr. Francis Thompson; and if his nature is to be an agnostic, he will compose poems like Mr. Thomas Hardy. Things are what they are and they will be what they will be. Why should we allow ourselves to be disturbed ?

One result of this temper or attitude is that all the ethical and social problems which our fathers fondly and foolishly thought to be solved are regarded by their sons as entirely open questions. There are no moral laws of the absolute character which Kant delineated : there are a set of conventions, some of them of considerable authority, but many of them merely transitory and more or less accidental, depending on time and place and associations. Did you think that it was wrong for a girl to run away from her home ? On the contrary, it may be a sign of a fine independence, as in the case of Janet de Mullins in Mr. Hankin's play, *The Last of the De Mullins*. Did you suppose that when a prodigal returned to his home, he came back in a chastened and repentant state of mind, having sown his tares and very grateful that there was a home to welcome him ? Oh no ! He comes—as in *The Return of the Prodigal*, also by Mr. Hankin—to make what terms he can with his outraged father and secure for himself a further period of indolent wastefulness at the paternal expense. Did you imagine that a woman naturally preferred wedlock to a looser bond of connection, in order, among other things, that her child should be legitimate? You are wrong. The man she chose for her lover might not suit her for a husband, as in the case of the heroines of *Hindle Wakes* and Mr. Galsworthy's *The Eldest Son*. Indeed, when the instinct for maternity is very strong, a woman will not care who may be the father of her child. Let him fulfil his temporary function, and she will fulfil her lasting one. On this point read again Janet's views in the very illustrative play already referred to, Mr. Hankin's *The Last of the De Mullins*. The classic instance is in Maxime Formont's novel *Le Semeur* (translated as *The Child of Chance*); but also some suggestion of the same spirit is found in Mr. Bernard Shaw's *Man and Superman*. I am not concerned, of course, to pass any ethical criticism on these things; I merely note them as remarkable signs and evidences of a modern temper.

And this naturally leads me to consider the kind of subjects with which the new dramatist prefers to deal. The great phenomenon of our time is the Emergence of Woman, and it obviously affords a splendid opportunity for the dramatist. One of the most constant qualities in all dramatic work is the implied antithesis between the human being and some great force, or forces, with which he is in conflict. These forces may be envisaged either as a great impersonal fate or necessity; or as the heritage of a particular kind of character bequeathed from generation to generation; or, once more, as the great mass of social prejudice and convention, accumulated through many ages. The individual feels himself cribbed, cabined, and confined by these forces which seem to be outside himself —or, at all events, outside his own instinctive impulses— and the course of the struggle in which he engages to free himself from restraints and live his own life is of the essence of drama. Men have been all along more or less in revolt, and in the struggle have proved themselves either heroes or villains. But it is a more delicate and interesting thing when woman dons her armour and goes into opposition, because her revolt touches, in a very immediate fashion, sacred institutions like home and family. Ibsen was one of the earliest to understand the significance of this woman movement, and because he regarded woman as the born anarchist his plays gave a powerful incentive to feminism and set the example for many dramatists. A characteristic example also is to be found in Sudermann's play *Heimat*, which we know as *Magda*. In this the heroine turns her back on her home, and seeks an independent career outside. On her return she has some very bitter things to say of the conditions which made her home life so intolerable to her, as—for that is the assumption— they would to any other girl of spirit. Within recent years we have seen, of course, several examples of plays based on this insurgence of womanhood, many of them written by female authors.

It would, in consequence, hardly be too much to say that the nineteenth-century frame of mind was built up on ideas with which the more modern mood is glaringly at variance. A woman's life, so the older notion ran, should be more or less a secluded life; her girlhood should be under the tutelage of her father and her mother; her marriage should not so much emancipate her as put her under another guardianship. Having accepted her husband, she was bound to make the best of him, whatever his mental or moral deficiencies. For marriage was an institution intended to protect the woman, and keep her in a safe position, free from the soul-harassing competition of ordinary commercial and professional life. One of the drawbacks of this theory was found to be the large predominance of women, and the consequent impossibility of their all finding a home. Hence, when the daughter began to revolt, she was able to plead in self-defence that, although she was apparently educated for matrimony, matrimony was not likely to come in her way. It was not mere wilfulness, therefore, but rather a duty that she should look out for herself and take her own chances in the rough and tumble of things. But when once a revolt begins you never know to what it may lead. As a matter of fact, the revolt of the daughter was mixed up with a much larger revolt of women as such, whether daughter, wife, or mistress. What is the value of laws which enjoin domestic privacy on the female? Apparently they were made by man for his own convenience, and they have no other sanction except the tyrannical verdict of the male. Thus marriage is one of the institutions first assailed.

Why should a wife go on living with a husband whom she despises? Why should marriage unions last through the whole life? Why should not the instinct of motherhood be treated quite separately from the usual environment of a legal husband and a recognised home? Remember that woman is the born anarchist, because in certain senses she is more of an independent individual than the average male. Men are more or less alike: women are often, perhaps always, diverse. And thus all so-called ethical laws, moral ordinances, social conventions, are put into the melting-pot and, as we have seen, women, as treated by the new dramatists, do many strange and unusual things in the pursuit of their ideal freedom. Ibsen, perhaps, started the business; Mr. Granville Barker, Mr. St. John Hankin, Miss Elizabeth Robins, Miss Netta Syrett, and many others, joined in the cry. The worst of it is that sometimes in their hot-headed enthusiasm the apostles of freedom get on a wrong scent.

Probably many of us have read Miss Elizabeth Robins' so-called novel, to which she gives as a title, *Where Are You Going To?* The point of the tract, for it is more of a tract than a story, was to support the agitation against the White Slave traffic, and a lurid tale was told of how two innocent girls living in the country were trapped on their arrival in town and taken to a house of ill-fame. But the story, as one read it, struck one not only as paradoxical, but also as a revival of a somewhat ancient legend. The average observer of life wondered whether such things could be. And it appeared, from an article in *The English Review*, that so impartial and unprejudiced a writer as Mrs. Billington-Greig set herself to investigate the available facts. The result of her exhaustive inquiry is that there is not, and apparently has not been in recent years, a single well-attested case in which a girl has been trapped into the White Slave traffic in this country against her will. Obviously, there are, of course, cases of seduction, and insidious advertisements are sometimes published enticing girls abroad; but the lurid accounts of compulsory detention and outrage appear to be entirely baseless. So, at least, Mrs. Billington-Greig thinks, and to a large extent proves, in her extremely careful study of the whole question. The true reformer must not be in such a violent hurry, or he may do damage to his own cause.

Personally, I hardly realised how great was the change that had come over, not only the topics with which the modern dramatist chooses to deal, but also the temper in which he approaches them, until I saw one of the performances of the Stage Society in November 1907. It was a performance of Mr. Granville Barker's play, *Waste.* It is true that it was a " prohibited " piece, but sometimes one can understand these matters better when one looks at extreme cases. Here, at all events, was a fine and serious piece of work, full of drama, keenly interested in psychological analysis, with the issues of the story carried out in a most unflinching and remorseless fashion. The very title gave one an indication of the plot. In a modern world there is a great deal of wastefulness. Women are sacrificed, children are sacrificed, above all men of light and leading are sacrificed. The hero is a politician of something more than mere cleverness, for Henry Trebell is a man who has become a considerable personage in the politics of his time, a statesman whom everybody imagines as a possible member of a Ministry of all the talents. Suppose that such a man in a moment of madness, in a moment which he describes as a " drunken fit," compromises a married woman with fatal effects. Is the whole of his political career to be blasted, not only to his own damage but his country's? That is one of the most serious and also the most obvious of the problems which Mr. Granville Barker put before us in *Waste.* Henry Trebell's special line of work is education, education such as every citizen ought to be able to command for himself and his children, education, not so much secular—with all the damaging associations of that term—as national, and neither religious nor irreligious. This is the sphere in which Mr. Trebell excels. He has the art of conciliating the High Church party; he has won over Lord Charles Cantelupe, who represents the ecclesiastical interest; he is equally happy, it appears, in his management of the Nonconformists and Dissenters, and he has his own scheme for dealing with ecclesiastical funds. Such a man is a valuable acquisition for any administration in our modern England, and when, after some dallying with the Liberal camp, he transfers his services to the Conservative ranks, the Earl of Horsham, the Tory Prime Minister, determines on the bold stroke of including him in his Cabinet.

And now we come to more delicate problems, concerned

with the relations between the sexes and the intricacies of a certain kind of masculine character. Henry Trebell is a man who, as his sister (a character, by the way, admirably played by Miss Henrietta Watson) describes him, has a certain scorn both of men and of women. It is a dangerous thing to look upon human beings of either sex from a standpoint of contempt. The man who does so is only too apt to regard his fellow creatures as puppets, to be used as his fancy dictates. Certainly Henry Trebell treated politicians with an easy negligence, and if he had confined himself to this ingenious and also reprehensible *rôle*, he might still have been hailed as the saviour of society. But he was not content with this. He must needs treat women as playthings also, as some bachelors have a temptation to do. And it is just here that the shadow of Nemesis is waiting for him. Mrs. O'Connell is a slight, inconsiderable, vivacious, empty-headed, attractive woman, with no settled principles, idle, vacuous, easily swayed by any masterful spirit whom she encounters. Trebell, who thinks no more about her than he does about others of her sex, engages lightly and thoughtlessly in an intrigue. That is in July; and in the second act, which takes place in October, we find him confronted with the consequences. Truly the results are dreadful enough, for Mrs. O'Connell has been childless hitherto, much to the sorrow of her husband, and she will not face the prospect of the appalling scandal that is hanging over her. In the third act we find that she is already dead, dead under such suspicious circumstances that an inquest is to be held, although we of the audience know well enough that she had put herself into the hands of a worthless doctor, and that Trebell is technically guiltless of her death. But the issue is not only fatal to Mrs. O'Connell, but to the man with whom she had so heedlessly associated herself. In the first place, what is Lord Horsham to do ? He is forming his Cabinet, and his intention was to include Trebell in its ranks. If such a scandal gets known, can his Administration survive ? In an extremely clever conference at Lord Horsham's house, we find the Prime Minister himself, surrounded by Lord Charles Cantelupe, Mr. Russell Blackborough, George Farrant, and others, debating the matter backwards and forwards. Justin O'Connell, the husband, decides—for reasons of his own—to hold his tongue. But there are many other considerations involved, and the final decision arrived at by Lord Horsham is to write a letter to Trebell and tell him that in the circumstances his services will be dispensed with. Political failure is thus the first of Trebell's punishments. It is not the only one. By a strange reaction from his former position of cynicism, he suddenly discovers within himself an immense contempt for the woman who could destroy his child, an immense desire to " express himself " (the phrase is not mine, but is put into the mouth of one of the characters) in the offspring which should inherit his genius and his aspirations. This is the most terrible penalty of all, and it is the direct consequence of, or reaction from, his own sceptical scorn of the customary motives which weigh with men, the usual passions which control their hearts. And so in an impressive last act we have the suicide of the hero, the final culmination of a great life greatly thrown away. His country is deprived of all the useful services that he might have rendered. That is one form of waste. And to this we have to add the destruction of human life— three lives, man, woman, and child—because of a deliberate violation of human and ethical laws.

It is unnecessary to pass any comment on a play of this kind, except so far as it indicates and illustrates certain well-defined modern tendencies. The main point to observe is the underlying assumption—that there is no sphere of human action, no kind of subject with which art cannot claim to deal. It is rather a large assumption because art is not necessarily nature, and least of all is it a mere copy of nature. The business of the artist is to select, whether in painting or writing or fashioning figures out of marble. In each case he enjoys the free exercise of his creative powers, which include discrimination and therefore also rejection. In his play of *Waste* Mr. Granville Barker interprets this theory in his own fashion. Art may deal with anything it chooses—even abortion. Dramatic art may take up any subject, even the most repellent one, so far as it can be shown to concern the interests of humanity. Even if we granted the assumption, which, of course, some people are not prepared to do, we should have to consider a necessary corollary. The artist is to be allowed the privilege of treating any subject he chooses on one very serious condition, namely, that he can lift up his subject into the sphere of art, or, in other words, that his treatment of his subject should be in the best sense of the word artistic. If art claims every province of human life as its own, it must justify this claim by the manner in which it deals with its theme. The case stands here just as it does with plagiarism—a man is permitted to borrow from preceding writers if he can justify his theft, as, for instance, Shakespeare could, by the use to which he puts it. But does Mr. Granville Barker justify his choice of subject by his treatment? Certainly there can be no more important problem than the extent to which a man of public importance is to be condoned, or condemned, on the score of his private immorality. But Mr. Barker chooses so to paint his hero as to make him unsympathetic—in fact, a very exceptional type of man, with a distinct vein of brutality. Most men who have made fools of themselves with women are still endowed with sufficient chivalry of nature to be sorry for the woman, to have some pity and tenderness towards her, however light and frivolous she may be. Henry Trebell has no such feelings towards Mrs. O'Connell. His scene with her in the second act is absolutely appalling in its coarse brutality, a horrid episode of something which, to the woman, at all events, must appear as the extreme of masculine callousness. One could imagine even a theme like this illustrated in far different fashion, and, possibly, made more powerful because the man was a better specimen of his sex and the woman a more intelligent one of hers. But in this matter Mr. Barker is only too docile a pupil of his master Mr. Bernard Shaw. There must be no romance in the relations between the sexes, no sentimentalism, no generous emotion. Perhaps this was the more accentuated in the actual production of *Waste* because Mr. Barker himself played the part of the hero, which was originally designed for Mr. Norman McKinnel. In Mr. McKinnel we should have had the brutality of a really strong man. In Mr. Barker's case we had the callousness of a man to whom it never seemed natural to be either brutal or coarse. Mrs. O'Connell was very cleverly played, but the more truly feminine the actress was, the greater grew our indignation at the treatment to which Mrs. O'Connell was exposed by Henry Trebell.

It is strange how the casting of a play can affect its æsthetic values and the balance of its characters. An apt illustration is afforded in the case of Mr. Galsworthy's *The Eldest Son*. The scene is laid in a country house

P

presided over by a sporting squire of the old school, who possesses a large family of sons and daughters and an admirably devoted wife. Unfortunately, the eldest son enters upon an intrigue with a lady's maid, who is the daughter of the gamekeeper. The usual result follows. The girl has to reveal to the young man that she is expecting to be a mother, and the whole *esclandre* comes out. What is to be done? The squire, who is bent on forcing a young under-keeper to make reparation to a village girl whom he has wronged, shrinks from the same problem when it is presented in the form of his heir and his wife's lady's maid. Happily for all concerned, the gamekeeper, who has some family pride, refuses to let his daughter marry her lover on the very proper ground that the match would be un-suitable, and by no means likely to lead to happiness. The whole point of the play clearly is that in the case of obvious *mésalliances* there is no real " honour " involved in the performance of a contract which is not to the advantage of either party. You cannot compensate a girl's loss of virtue by offering her a marriage more ruinous than the original bad act. Therefore the head-keeper is quite justified in refusing to see that two wrongs make a right. But somehow in the play itself this estimable moral came out very strangely and paradoxically. What we saw before our eyes was a very pretty and charming girl (the part of the lady's maid was played by Miss Cathleen Nesbitt) who was much too good for her young man, and seemed much more distinguished than all the gentlefolks put together. The eldest son would indeed have been a lucky fellow to get so nice a wife, even if they had both of them to go to Canada; while by the side of this brilliant young heroine the squire's wife, sons, and daughter un-mistakably paled their ineffectual fires ! The ladies ought, one may suppose, to have exhibited their superior social station, if the dramatist's story was to come out right, whereas it was the servant who won hands down. That is the worst of having a sympathetic part played by a clever actress—unless, indeed, one may suspect Mr. Gals-worthy of the cynical suggestion that in matters of " honour " and so forth, the so-called upper classes are inferior to their gamekeepers and ladies' maids. *The Eldest Son*, however, is not so good a play as *Hindle Wakes*, with which in a certain fashion it can be compared. For in *Hindle Wakes* our sympathies are intended to be wholly enlisted on the side of the spirited girl, the mill-hand.

Having enjoyed her week-end " lark," she sees clearly enough that marriage is a very different affair from an episodical amour—amongst other reasons because, as one of the characters remarks in one of Mr. Hankin's pieces, " it lasts so long." She therefore does not have to depend on her father to make up her mind for her. She refuses point-blank to have anything further to do with the son of her employer. And seeing the young man and the sort of home-life which he enjoys, we honour her for her decision. *Hindle Wakes*, moreover, was admirably cast. It was enacted by men and women who knew the kind of life they were depicting, and were therefore able to convey a real thrill of actual vitality to the audience. And Miss Edyth Goodall's performance as the heroine was a very fine one.

No one, however, would select *The Eldest Son* as a typical play of Mr. Galsworthy. I imagine that most people who desire to get a true appreciation of the dramatist's position in the modern world would turn rather to pieces like *Strife* and *Justice*. Here emerges one of the chief characteristics of Mr. Galsworthy, so far as I am able to observe, a tendency which can only be described as pessimistic. Life does not appear to him to be a pleasant affair, though that very largely may be due to the arrangements we make for living it. Modern society is hampered by several outworn conventions, legal enactments, and perhaps also creeds, and the point which strikes the dramatist is the exceeding hardship which is often involved for the individual. Or again. We find ourselves in a critical time with the two forces of capitalism and labour ranged against one another in continuous and deadly combat. Sometimes the victory sways in one direction, sometimes in another. But here again, just because the forces are evenly balanced, it is the individual who suffers— most of all perhaps in his domestic relations. And what are we to say of the outcome of the struggle when it remains so uncertain, when the tragedy of conflicting aims and purposes ends, from the point of view of the social observer, in a farce of wasted efforts, of hopeless endeavour, of absolute sterility ? That, I take it, is the lesson (the word may be pardoned) of the play called *Strife*, which closes with a touch of real cynicism, a cynicism which may be detected in *The Silver Box*, but which comes out very strongly in the later play. The Secretary of the Employers turning, just before the final curtain, to a Trades Union official, says in an excited tone, " Do you know, sir, these terms (of compromise) are the very same we drew up together, you and I, and put to both sides before the fight began? All this—all this—and—and what for?" Harness, the Trades Union official, replies in a slow, grim voice, " There's where the fun comes in ! " I can hardly imagine any remark more flippantly cynical, expressive as it is of the whole dreary inutility and hopelessness of a conflict which at the close leaves the two contending parties as they were before the fight began. That is, of course, the peculiarity of a play conceived in the modern fashion, as ending in an *impasse* or a note of interrogation. But it also explains why such a drama can never be popular in the best sense of the term, and must belong to the intellectual drama of a clique rather than to the nation at large.

It is worth while to enlarge on this point. *Strife* was undoubtedly a very fine play, admirably acted by such artists as Mr. Norman McKinnel and Mr. J. Fisher White, and entirely worthy of the reproduction which it subsequently enjoyed at the Comedy Theatre. Nevertheless, the attitude of most people who have seen the piece is distinctly cold and negative. They are glad they have seen it once, they have found a real interest in the story, but they rarely want to see it again. It would seem that *Strife* does not belong to that category of work which enlists on its side all sorts and conditions of men. What is the story? Briefly, it is a long combat between John Anthony, Chairman of the Trenartha Tin Plate Works, and David Roberts, a representative of the workmen. Each side is presented with absolute neutrality and fairness. John Anthony is a hard, dour capitalist, who has built up his industry with infinite pains. He has come to his own conclusions as to the conditions under which it can be run successfully. No more concessions must be made to the workmen; the more they get, the more they will desire. A stand must be made some time if the capitalist class is to be preserved; otherwise the proletariat will ride roughshod over individual property. On the other hand, David Roberts, equally clear-sighted, discovers that the present conditions do not admit of a proper living wage for the labourer. He, too, asseverates that a stand must be made once for all, and he encourages the other members of the workmen's Committee to prolong the strike, even though they see their own kith and kin starving around them. In his own case he has to go through the unutterable anguish of seeing his wife die—die of starvation caused by his obstinacy or his firmness, whatever point of view you adopt. But the struggle has other issues besides the death of a woman. Gradually the moderate men on both sides are led to the conclusion—a conclusion dear to all Englishmen—that there must be a compromise. Some of his friends desert John Anthony; a good many of his fellow-workmen desert David Roberts. And so we arrive at the final scene in which the Chairman of the Tin Plate Works is upset by his own Committee, and the chief spokesman of the employés is betrayed by his friends. It is a fine scene, for the two principal antagonists have a sincere respect for one another. " So they have done us both down, Mr. Anthony ? " says Robert; and Anthony replies, " Both broken men, my friend Roberts." The extreme partisans being thus got rid of, the compromise is carried through, and the Secretary discovers, as we have seen, that the actual terms for the cessation of war are identical with those suggested many weeks previously, " A woman dead; and the two best men broken ! " such is the general summary as enunciated by Harness.

Now if we want to see why such a play cannot unreservedly appeal to an audience, I am afraid the answer must be that it holds the balance too evenly. The people who throng a theatre have certain peculiarities of their own, amongst which is to be found the idea that they must not be confused as to the side on which their interest and sympathy are to be bestowed. In general terms we express the principle as a dislike of being hoodwinked, an eager wish to " know all about it," a ready determination to take sides if only the spectators are shown which side they ought to take. Of course, this is not a very estimable characteristic of an audience. Doubtless the intellectual thing is to study very carefully what is to be said on both sides. It is not only in the theatre, however, that the democracy shows these qualities or feelings. Is a philosophic statesman ever popular ? Is it a good characteristic in a leader of a party that he is able so thoroughly to understand the opposite faction as to give their standpoint as clearly as his own ? The career of Mr. Balfour, as compared with that of Mr. Gladstone, is sufficient to prove how important it is for a party leader to ignore all that can be said for his opponents and to advance his own cause with ruthless pertinacity. Much the same thing happens in a theatre. You take, for instance, a play like that of Robert Browning on Strafford. Pym and Strafford are

left at the close confronting each other, and each has
a very good account to give of himself and of his own
aims. It is six to one and half-a-dozen to the other. A
thoroughly careful and intellectual balance is preserved.
Strafford was not a successful play, and perhaps one of the
chief reasons was the very fact of this intellectual equipoise.
A far inferior craftsman, Mr. Wills, writing a play on
Charles I, and having at his finger-tips theatrical technique,
did not hesitate to blacken the character of Cromwell
just in the same proportion as he exalted the character
of the Stuart monarch. When Shakespeare had to deal
with the struggle between Richard III and Henry Tudor,
he did not leave us in any doubt as to the proper direction
of our sympathies. The result may have been, probably
was, exceedingly unfair to Richard Crookback, whom
many subsequent historians have tried to whitewash and
with no little success. But Shakespeare had the instinct
of the theatre, and he knew that it would be ruinous for
his play if he allowed his audience to wonder which was
the hero and which was the villain. It is no good protesting that this is a popular infirmity which ought to be
sternly resisted and corrected. It belongs to the whole
attitude of the populace towards politics, religion, and
life. You must not keep your audience in the dark as to
some necessary fact in the intrigue which is being dissected
before their very eyes. Nor yet must you allow your
audience to vacillate in its interests and sympathies.
There can be no question, if we look back over its past
history, that drama is the most democratic of the arts,
and that when it was at its best, during the Elizabethan
period, it involved an appeal to every class and section
of the community. Purely intellectual drama, written
for superior persons, may have every merit, but sometimes
it perilously resembles the so-called literary play, not meant
for popular production but only designed for perusal in
an armchair. What would have happened to an Elizabethan audience if they had come out of their wooden
theatre wondering which of the two, Edmund or Edgar,
was right in *King Lear*, or whether there was not a good
deal to be said on behalf of Iago in his duel with Othello?
A psychological analysis which proves that there is no
such thing as heroes and villains, that we are all more or
less alike, that we have no right to judge, may be both
philosophic and true. But it does not help the theatre as
such, nor yet in the larger sense of the word does it help

theatrical art, because an artist must select, and, by the mere fact of selecting, becomes a partisan.

We touch a deeper note in Mr. Galsworthy's *Justice*, or rather we are involved in utter and blank despair. Never was so cruel a play written. Hardly any piece that I am aware of is so drenched in an atmosphere of inspissated gloom. The author, of course, is anxious to show us what a ghastly thing solitary confinement in prison is, how ruinous it is to the individual, how hopelessly unjust and unfair. He would hardly affirm that it is so in all cases, and therefore we have to understand that it is in his special case—the case of a sensitive, highly strung junior clerk in a solicitor's office. Naturally, therefore, the dramatist is forced to cog his dice because he has taken an exceptional case and has to treat it exceptionally. Not for one moment does Mr. Galsworthy relent in his treatment of the story. Falder, who forges a cheque for a woman's sake, is doomed from the moment of his sin to remorseless punishment. I still remember with a shudder, when the play was performed at the Duke of York's Theatre, the horrible picture of Mr. Dennis Eadie as Falder, pacing backwards and forwards in his cell like a hunted animal, and finally being driven to bang at his door in hopeless impotence. Even when he is at last released, and it looks for a moment as if there might be some chance for him, fate dogs his footsteps and he throws himself down the stone stairs in a vain effort to escape the tyranny of " Justice." One wonders whether such things are going on all round one, and winces at the bare possibility. There is only one figure in the appalling drama which one remembers with a faint sense of gratitude. It is the senior clerk, Cokeson, a simple, kindly, religious man, with a touch of Dickens characterisation about him, who serves to redeem our hopes in humanity. When Zola's *L'Assommoir* was turned into didactic melodrama and produced in English form under the title of *Drink*, we thought it a horrible piece, made if anything more horrible by the admirable acting of Mr. Charles Warner as Coupeau. But *Justice* is far sterner stuff, cruel, relentless, soul-shaking. Such themes should be treated in a pamphlet, unless we are all to become sterile and ineffective pessimists, through sheer despair of our fellow-creatures.

Cynicism and pessimism—these are the " notes " which are never far away from modern realistic drama. If we look at the dramatic works of Mr. St. John Hankin, which in themselves require and deserve a careful study, we shall observe that the development of the story is nearly always conceived in a vein of cynicism. Mr. Hankin has many dramatic qualities. He has an admirable sense, for instance, of appropriate dialogue, almost as good as that which Ibsen possesses in some of his most characteristic pieces. The scenes between the elder and younger brother in *The Return of the Prodigal* are excellently written, with no surplusage, terse, brilliant, and to the point. Nevertheless, it is in the vein of cynicism that Mr. Hankin pursues his dramatic themes, and when all is said and done, cynicism is the fume of petty hearts. Take the play to which allusion has just been made, *The Return of the Prodigal*. What is its main point? It shows us the wastrel, Eustace Jackson, returning to his father's home by means of a conscious artifice in order to provoke sympathy, getting the best of everything by means of the persistent obstinacy of thoroughgoing idleness, and finally obtaining from his father a pension of £250 a year as one of the conditions of leaving him alone. Listen to these sentences :—

Mr. Jackson (*grumbling*) : " What I can't see is why I should allow you this money. Here's Henry, who's perfectly satisfactory, and has never caused me a moment's anxiety. I don't give him money. Whereas you, who have never caused me anything else, expect me to keep you for the remainder of your life."

Such is the father's perfectly reasonable attitude, but the elder son unexpectedly sides with Eustace.

" Father, I think you had better do as he says. If you gave him a thousand pounds he'd only lose it. Better make him an allowance. Then you can always stop it if he does not behave himself. It is a shameless proposal, as you say, but it's practical."

So it is on this promise of £250 a year that the bargain is settled which keeps Eustace from want and enables him to continue his career of inefficient passivity. If that is not a cynical *dénouement*, it is difficult to say what is. But there is much the same cynicism in *The Charity that began at Home*, in *The Cassilis Engagement*, and in *The Last of the De Mullins*. Fortunately, there is a good deal besides which we can heartily commend, for in the last-mentioned play Janet de Mullins is really a fine character, though we could have wished that she had not been quite so defiantly impertinent and so cocksure of herself.

The Silver Box, the earliest of Mr. Galsworthy's plays, is in certain respects comparable with Mr. Hankin's *The Return of the Prodigal*. The particular prodigal in Mr. Galsworthy's play is a young Jack Barthwick, who stumbles into his father's house late at night with a bag and purse which do not belong to him, but are the property of some light-o'-love whom he has picked up in the streets. A ne'er-do-well called Jones comes in with him, and when the young man falls to sleep on the sofa, decamps, not only with the purse, but with a silver box conveniently found at his elbow. Jones is the husband of Mrs. Jones, who is charwoman in the Barthwicks' house. Now, without any doubt, the original culprit is young Jack Barthwick, but it is the Joneses, husband and wife, who have to stand the racket and bear all the blame. Mrs. Jones loses her job, although, poor woman, she has nothing to do with the whole affair, and Jones gets one month with hard labour. Once more, notice carefully the conclusion. This is Jones's comment : " Call this justice ? What about 'im ? 'E got drunk, 'E took the purse, but it's his money got him off,"—which, parenthetically, is quite true. While Mrs. Jones turns to Barthwick with a humble gesture and with the appealing words, " Oh, Sir ! " the magistrate closes the affair : " We will now adjourn for lunch." This is the kind of cynicism which, clearly, appeals to Mr. Galsworthy, for in the more intense and vivid form it is to be found both in *Strife* and in *Justice*.

In Mr. Galsworthy's case also, as well as in Mr. Hankin, there are other and sounder elements. Let me not forget that Mr. Galsworthy wrote *The Little Dream* and *The Pigeon*. He calls the latter a piece fantasy. It is the most delightful of his plays to read. If it did not come out quite so well on the stage—at all events it had but little success when produced at the Royalty Theatre—the cause probably lay in the casting of some of the characters, especially, perhaps, the eccentric Frenchman, Ferrand. But it is a charming piece of work just because it is touched with a tender idealism, the idealism of simple emotions. And perhaps it is not altogether an inept commentary on the modern realistic drama that two most successful plays have been Mr. Arnold Bennett's *The Great Adventure* and *Milestones*, which, though they may have the realistic manner, no one would call realistic dramas.

EUGÈNE BRIEUX, MORALIST

ONE of the outstanding theatrical successes of the year 1917 in London was gained by M. Brieux. Not only was his much-discussed play *Les Avariés* (*Damaged Goods*), acted for several months, but his other and far better play, *The Three Daughters of M. Dupont*, enjoyed an almost equal prosperity. When we consider the kind of entertainment prevalent in the Metropolis at most of the theatres, Brieux's success seems curious and remarkable. There is no question that theatrical managers discovered during the greater part of 1917 that the lighter forms of dramatic work were far more likely to please and attract than any of those pieces which might be called problem plays or even formal romantic comedies. It would be by no means unjust to say that farces, musical comedies, and revues represent three-fourths of the dramatic fare recently offered in London theatres. Naturally there have been exceptions, but the fact that the majority of the spectators are soldiers, returning from the Front to enjoy a brief holiday, necessitated, in the view of those responsible for theatrical production, the cheerful, good-natured, laughable play with no pretension to reality, a frank make-believe, in order to turn gloomy thoughts away from too serious a pre-occupation with the war. To find, therefore, in the midst of frivolous programmes of this kind a play like Brieux's *Damaged Goods*, winning not only a modicum of prosperity but actually constituting one of the great successes, might evoke a certain amount of surprise. While all around consisted of the light flummery of music and dance, or else the stereotyped surprises of American " crook " stories, there was witnessed a piece written by an earnest moralist, very outspoken, quite reckless of the ordinary conventions, and with a daring frankness of tone and language which held the attention of numerous audiences, not only in London itself, but in the provinces. We may, of course, give a different explanation of this seeming paradox. We may assert that the element of prurient curiosity, the idea that something rather tremendous, and certainly scandalous, was going to be witnessed on the boards—and the discovery that the actual production of the play involved a striking change of mental

and moral attitude on the part of the licensing authorities
—had something to do with the financial prosperity of a
strong, sincere, and unconventional piece of work. No
doubt it is true that some of those who crowded into the
St. Martin's Theatre were not animated by the highest
and most ethical of motives. Nevertheless, there must
have been many who accepted this piece of Brieux, as
the author intended it to be accepted, as a fearless study
of an exceedingly difficult problem, with the insistent
moral that society for its own sake must recognise and
take precaution against a hidden evil which was poisoning
its very roots.

In the same way, though in a less degree, *The Three
Daughters of M. Dupont* received a welcome from the
thoughtful people who knew that the dramatist was
touching large and difficult questions. The play, it is
true, is very different from *Les Avariés*. In the latter
case the dramatist presses his moral with unrelenting force.
Unless the legislature will do something to check the
progress of disease, the whole of human society will suffer.
But in the former case the dramatist's touch is more
uncertain. Has he any moral? There is one certainly,
which suggests that the natural function of a wife is to be
the mother of children, and that if she is denied this privilege her position in the household is shorn of its true value
and meaning. But there is a cynicism about the close
of the play not always to be found in the work of Brieux.
There is no question that Julie, the daughter who is unhappily married, accepts her lot with a certain amount
of newly learnt philosophy because she sees that it is
capable of alleviation. She intends to do as others have
done, and if she gets on badly with her husband—well,
there is a chance with other admirers. The world is too
big, the dramatist seems to say, for any given individual
to struggle against. Society is too securely founded on
its hypocrisies and conventions to be overthrown by any
iconoclast, however earnest and sincere.

In this respect the play is a little like *La Foi*, in which
Brieux's apparent object is to prove that mankind must
have their religious delusions, and that without them life
for the majority of mankind would be intolerable. You
may destroy the false idols as often as you please, but
there always remains the permanent instinct of the human
mind to worship something, it hardly cares what; while
in the majority of cases if you uproot a faith you find in

its successor, or successors, a variety of degrading superstitions. *La Foi* was translated under the title *False
Gods*, produced at His Majesty's Theatre, and had a considerable run, much to the surprise of those who, perhaps
with small superficial knowledge of Brieux, understood
that he was a sort of dramatic Don Quixote tilting at
windmills.   In the play in question we are clearly expected to have every sympathy with the young reformer
who wishes to abolish degrading superstitions and prevent
the common people from believing in a lie.   The scene is
laid in Upper Egypt, where every year the sacrifice of a
virgin is made to the goddess Isis.   A young and earnest
rationalist called Satni, engaged to the maiden who has
been designated for the sacrifice, inaugurates a great
movement amongst the people with a view to abolishing
the doctrines which had hitherto been accepted from the
priests.   Pharaoh gives orders that Satni and his followers
should be removed out of the way; the High Priest has
a more subtle method of dealing with him.   He takes him
to the Temple and shows him how the miracles are worked.
The great statue of Isis is made to bend her head to signify
her satisfaction with the sacrifices offered to her, and after
that miracle has taken place many wonderful cures amongst
the populace are reported.   Satni, when he sees the
wretchedness of the people, their hopes of some alleviation in their lot, their instinctive faith in the unseen, himself draws the lever which moves the statue, having made
the pregnant discovery that it is better for the people to
have some faith than to have none at all.   The truth of a
religion, in other words, does not matter so much.   What
does matter is the satisfaction, consolation, appeasement
of the human mind, always craving for something beyond
itself.   It would seem that Brieux on some earlier occasion had been to Lourdes, and having himself watched the
touching credulity of the worshippers and their immense
elation at the prospect of cures of long-seated ailments,
came to a conclusion, which he afterwards put into the
mouth of his reformer, Satni.   He adopted, in this matter,
a position somewhat different from that taken up by Renan
in *The Priest of Nemi*.   Renan is quite aware that a good
deal of harm can be done by the abolition of old superstitions, but on the other hand he is convinced that reform
will triumph, and that an attitude of mind more in accordance with the demands of logic and reason is infinitely
preferable to a blind and uncertain faith.   It is not quite

certain how far Brieux would go with Renan in his desire
for reform.   Certainly his play *La Foi* leaves us with the
impression that religion is useful for the common people,
a doctrine also held by Voltaire.   Humanity needs its
crutches, and their value must not be despised.[1]

I believe the first play of Brieux produced in London
was *Les Bienfaiteurs*.   That was succeeded by *Maternité*
and *Les Hannetons,* both done by the Stage Society, and
False Gods, which, as already stated, saw the light at His
Majesty's Theatre.   The Stage Society also produced *Les
Trois Filles,* with Miss Ethel Irving in the cast.   It is clear,
then, that Brieux has gone some way in the conquest of
London.   But it is not easy to understand what Mr.
Bernard Shaw means in his Preface to " Three Plays of
Brieux " when he declares that London found out Brieux
before Paris did.   According to Mr. Shaw, Paris is " easily
the most prejudiced, old-fashioned, obsolete-minded city
in the west of Europe." [2]   She did not know what a dramatic
treasure she had in Brieux until England pointed it out.
So far as I can discover this is very far from the truth of
the matter.   Some of the best critics in Paris, like Lemaître,
Faguet, René, Doumic, and even to some extent Sarcey,
had given a great deal of praise to Brieux's early plays,
and had very little hesitation in proclaiming him a dramatist who counts.   To single out Brieux from the majority
of dramatists of France, as though he were engaged in a
work belonging to himself alone, and quite unlike that of
others, is a mistake which could only be made by those
who are not familiar with the modern products of drama
and novel in France.   Nearly all the themes developed by
Brieux find their echoes in other writers.   I need only
mention men like Hervieu, Bataille, Bordeaux, Bazin,
Margueritte and others to prove that Brieux's voice was
not that of one crying in the wilderness, but that he had
many collaborators in the work of criticism and reform.
One of Hervieu's best-known plays, *Le Dédale,* has almost
precisely the same plot as Brieux's *Le Berceau.*

One reason why some French critics have looked as-
kance at Brieux is, that they have been offended by his
lack of style.   A well-known critic once began an article
on the novels of Georges Ohnet by asking pardon of
his readers because he was not going to deal, as he

---

[1] Euripides' *Bacchœ* suggests the same moral and awakens the same
surprise that a professed rationalist should defend superstition.

[2] *Three Plays of Brieux.*   Preface by Bernard Shaw, p. xxviii.

usually did, with literature, but with Ohnet. Nevertheless, Georges Ohnet had a reputation of his own, and he, too, enjoyed a triumph in London when *The Ironmaster* was produced by the Kendals. Ohnet could write novels which were not strictly literature—a phenomenon common enough, by the way, in our own country. But that did not prevent him from becoming a force of some kind, a sentimental and melodramatic force, perhaps, but still by no means devoid of a real influence. Brieux, too, is hardly to be reckoned amongst those who write literature; he has none of the fine reticence, the purged and polished style, the exquisite tact, the punctilious self-control of the literary artist. Nevertheless, he is a dramatist whose plays, through sheer force of strong individuality, have won their place in contemporary drama. It may be interesting and worth while to ask why Brieux has obtained so strong a hold on the contemporary world, and why his contributions to the general total of what men and critics think and say represent so valuable and important a body of work.

Eugène Brieux began writing plays at an early age, but it was not till he was over thirty that the particular quality of his dramatic art was revealed. If we look at the list of pieces produced during the last quarter of a century we shall find that they are nearly all didactic and are aimed at some weakness, wrong, or iniquity of the social system.[1]

[1] Brieux's plays are usually divided into three periods, the first including the earlier and less mature pieces, the second period representing the storm and stress of the intolerant reformer, while the third and last period shows the dramatist in a milder, and possibly even in an optimistic mood.

BRIEUX, BORN 1858.

First Period.			Third Period.		
Ménages d'Artistes	. . .	1890	*Les Remplaçantes*	. . .	1901
Blanchette	. . . .	1892	*Les Avariés*	. . . .	1901
M. de Réboval	. . . .	—	*La Petite Amie*	. . . .	1902
La Couvée	. . . .	1893	*Maternité*	. . . .	1903
L'Engrenage	. . . .	1894			
Les Bienfaiteurs	. . . .	1896	Third Period.		
L'Évasion	. . . .	1896	*La Deserteuse*	. . . .	1904
			Les Hannetons	. . . .	1906
Second Period.			*La Française*	. . . .	1907
Les Trois Filles de M. Dupont		1897	*Simone*	. . . . .	1908
Résultat des Courses	. . .	1898	*Suzette*	. . . . .	1909
Le Berceau	. . . .	1898	*La Foi*	. . . . .	1909
La Robe Rouge	. . . .	1900	*La Femme Seule*	. . . .	1913
			Le Bourgeois aux Champs	.	1914

Twenty-two serious plays and six or eight lighter pieces. I take the list from *Brieux and Contemporary French Society* (Putnam), a careful and valuable study by W. H. Scheifley, to which I am much indebted.

Euripides, the Greek dramatist, who accepted as his mission the task of revealing to Greek audiences human nature as it is, not as it might be, converted many of his dramas into an appeal against the injustice of the gods of the Greek Pantheon—especially Athene, Apollo and Artemis. Brieux does not impeach Providence; he is not concerned with the rule of the Divine powers, and therefore does not take it as his business, except incidentally and inferentially, to base his criticism on the supposed delinquencies of Heaven. Like Rousseau, he attacks directly the social system. Whatever men and women might or might not be naturally and originally, at all events they are imprisoned, mainly by their own acts, in an organisation which represses some of their better instincts, exaggerates here and there evil tendencies, and makes them the slaves of institutions radically bad and harmful. A very brief review of some of his plays will prove this point. *Blanchette*, produced in 1892, pointed out the evil results of education on girls of the working classes. *L'Engrenage*, 1894, was a tirade against corruption in politics. *Les Bienfaiteurs*, 1896, pointed out the glaring defects of fashionable charity, the frivolity of those who handled such artificial modes of doing good to fellow-creatures, and the harm produced by allowing selfish individuals to give indiscriminate alms instead of making charity a settled policy. Then came *L'Évasion*, in 1896, which satirised too submissive a belief in the doctrine of heredity. In this play Brieux was tilting not so much against science itself, as against the way in which it is interpreted in loose talk by those who have not really studied the subject. Human beings can easily torture themselves by a one-sided application of even well-based scientific principles. A year later was produced *Les Trois Filles de M. Dupont*, to which I have already referred and to which I shall have occasion to return. *La Robe Rouge*, 1900, revealed the injustices of the law. *Les Avariés*, which saw the light in 1901, was forbidden by the Censor, on account mainly of its medical details. Later plays included *Maternité, La Foi*, and a brilliant comedy of arresting power, entitled *Les Hannetons*. This brief enumeration is sufficient to show with what seriousness of purpose Brieux adopted the *rôle* of dramatic and ethical teacher. Mr. Bernard Shaw has stated that " what we want as the basis of our plays and novels is not romance but a really scientific natural history." In many respects the sentence describes the programme of Brieux. In his efforts at didactic moralising he takes up the work of Zola, with equal power and, perhaps, with greater intelligence. As a playwright he may be said to be the disciple of Ibsen, though he is manifestly deficient in that power of construction, and that remorseless analytic psychology which distinguish the great Norwegian dramatist. As an interpreter of life, Brieux is, above all, a critic occupied with the wounds and sores of suffering humanity. He is called a realist because he aims straight at abuses and is not afraid of strong and clear language. With the ordinary artificialities of the stage he has nothing to do. He does not believe in the necessity for a happy ending; he does not always believe in the necessity for an ending at all. He will take a chapter of human life, reveal its rottenness, probe its dangers, and define as accurately as he can the effects on the men and women concerned in his study. He is especially concerned with the future welfare of children.[1] Romance, however, is far from his intention, for to him romance is largely deception, hypocrisy, a refusal to look straight at the problems of life, an evasion of the main issue.

Compare all this with the ordinary attitude. We go to see plays for many reasons; Brieux practically asks us to accept at his hands only one great mission of the dramatist. Dramatic art is often described as an entertainment, something that is to heighten our spirits, to interest and to amuse us, to make us laugh so that we may be saved from all temptation to tears. Brieux does not indulge us in any of these ways. Romance is as much falsehood and deception to him as it is to Mr. Bernard Shaw, mainly because the romantic play or the romantic drama involves the career of heroes and heroines who are unreal, exaggerated, one-sided portraits to which little corresponds in our actual experience. But interpretation—another of the great objects with which the dramatist is concerned— Brieux fully acknowledges as his aim, an interpretation, be it remembered, based not so much on appreciation as on criticism. In order to interpret, the dramatist must analyse human character as well as human institutions. Indeed, it is by the behaviour of the human beings in the play under a given system that the spectator discovers

---

[1] Eight of his plays deal with the interests of the rising generation. The future of the child, of course, enters largely into the question of divorce.

how deficient and obstructive the prevailing system is. It is open, however, for us to remark that you can get quite as false ideas of human nature by studying defects as you can by exaggerating merits. The vice of all didacticism is that the *dramatis personæ* are invented to subserve a particular ethical purpose. They do not exist in and for themselves; they exist because the exigencies of the dramatic framework require them to be of a particular character. In many of Brieux's plays, and especially, perhaps, in *Les Avariés*, we fail to become interested in his characters because they are so obviously puppets used to enforce a moral. *Les Avariés*, however, is an extreme case, and even in this avowed tract, or social manifesto, the character of the doctor, as we saw when the play was recently produced in London, belongs to a powerful human type. He carries out the usual tasks of the " raisonneur " on a high ethical plane, and his image persists in the mind, not merely because he enforces a particular moral, but because as enacted by Mr. Fisher White he was human and true. And sometimes, too, the dramatist forgets the intensely serious procedure of the play, as, for instance, in the third act, where, in the midst of dreary discussions, he introduces the extremely vivid portrait of a courtesan, fresh and original and accurately observed. She also points a moral, it is true. But meanwhile she lives.

To me, I confess, Eugène Brieux is especially interesting, not merely because he reveals some of the defects which inevitably attach to edifying and didactic drama, but because he is subject to influences and impressions coming from various sources which do not always coincide with his didactic aims. As I understand him, he is a man of considerable force of character, largely self-taught, who, as he develops, takes up one subject after another, carries it to an excess, and does not trouble his head as to whether or no the total outcome is so far a consistent whole as to be described under a specific formula. Some critics have pointed out inconsistencies in Brieux. That is inevitable in every moralist, for when he attacks any particular phase of the social order he is so engrossed with his subject that he does not realise how each part of that social order is dependent on the others, and how extremely difficult, if not impossible, is the work of piecemeal reform. I mentioned just now the play which is called *L'Evasion*.

Q

Here our author is protesting against that superstitious reverence with which some of us are apt to surround the dicta of science. The dramatist portrays the character of a doctor, narrow-minded, a victim of his own phrases and hypotheses, who believes so intensely in his doctrine of heredity as to employ it alike in the physical, the social, and the moral sphere. Because certain physical tendencies are passed on from father to son, it is assumed that all tendencies are so transmitted. A man who has a drunken father is certainly tempted to be a drunkard, but it does not follow that a tendency to madness or a suicidal tendency is similarly developed. Two young people, one of whom had a father who has committed suicide, while the girl is illegitimate and the daughter of an immoral woman, are in love with one another and are prepared to marry. The doctor intervenes and points out the fatality of this course. The girl, when she has become a wife, will go wrong; the young man will reveal a certain propensity to destroy himself. But all this the dramatist declares is a superstition of science, and people who cultivate their will and who have faith can conquer the supposed fatality. Such is the main teaching of *L'Évasion*, but obviously such teaching does not accord with that scientific background which was declared just now to be the characteristic of Brieux's dramaturgy. It might be conceded, of course, that a scientific hypothesis is not necessarily a scientific truth. But the man who is going to reform an unreal romantic and sentimental drama by providing a scientific background is hardly at liberty to diffuse so much scepticism about science. His business, one would suppose, would be rather to show what truth exists in the doctrine of atavism and heredity rather than to demonstrate its falsity.

Or take another instance. In one of his plays, as we have seen, Brieux points out how miserable is the condition of a wife who is not allowed to become a mother owing to the selfishness of her husband. That is part of the lesson of *The Three Daughters of M. Dupont*. But in another piece, *Maternité*, we are shown all the misery caused by a too prolific marriage—how deplorable is the case of a mother who is perpetually increasing the number of her children.[1]

[1] There was reported a short time ago a case which illustrates this point. Mrs. Moran Tubberclair, of Athlone, has given birth to her twenty-

Of course, inconsistencies of this kind can be defended on the ground suggested by Mr. Bernard Shaw. He affirms that a teacher is always afraid of his extreme disciples, and that for this reason he is careful to suggest the antithesis to his doctrines, if only to anticipate the follies of those who are so anxious to press a particular doctrine to an unreal extreme. But inconsistency, even so far as it can be proved against Brieux, only makes him in a sense a more interesting dramatist. He is, so to speak, learning every day; he adds fresh points to those accumulated before; he is inspired by new motives; he sees new visions; and, just as a particular point seizes his attention, he develops it without paying any particular regard to what he himself had advanced in previous work. The general tendency of his dramas is to dethrone romance and to substitute for it something more real and more scientific. Yet every now and then there appears the romantic impulse which makes his figures more human, and, as I think, in better correspondence with life as we find it. Many men have sought to abolish romance from dramatic art, but, as I understand it, romance is one of the indestructible elements of humanity. A man whose business it is to present a complete picture of humanity will never be able to get rid of one of its most constant elements.

From this point of view *The Three Daughters of M. Dupont* is a very significant piece of work. The author is here carrying out, not one design, but several, and I am not sure that he makes his whole picture quite plausible or persuasive. M. Dupont, who is not a successful man of business, has three daughters, two, Caroline and Angèle, by a first wife, and Julie by a second. Now one of the social injustices which Brieux is going to attack is the necessity of providing a *dot* for a daughter on pain of not

---

second child. Eleven of her children are under fourteen years of age. If we assume that the remaining eleven, the elder group, have much the same intervals between their respective births, we shall conclude that the oldest is about twenty-eight or thirty, and that the unhappy mother, from say eighteen onwards to forty-eight, has been producing a child every thirteen or fourteen months for the last thirty years ! That is the sort of thing which justifies Brieux's *Maternité*—a protest against the condemnation of women to perpetual childbirth. I take the paragraph from *The Globe* of 'December 29, 1917. Poor Mrs. Tubberclair was very obviously sacrificed on the altar of excessive fecundity !

getting her a husband. What follows, then, in a small bourgeois household when a daughter can only find a husband if she brings him a certain amount of money? Well, either the girl does not get married at all, or if she does get married is married unhappily, or altogether goes to the bad. That is to be exemplified in the play before us. Caroline becomes a *dévote*, Angèle commits an "indiscretion" and is banished from home to win her livelihood in ignoble fashion in Paris; Julie marries Antonin, the son of another bourgeois family, who is attracted by the promise of a *dot* with Julie, which in reality M. Dupont has no hopes of being able to furnish. Such appears to be the general scheme, but in working it out the author allows himself, I will not say changes of intention, but the influence of other considerations, adding, without doubt, to the general rich significance of the drama but with scant regard for the main contention. Julie marries Antonin, and, as they are complete strangers to one another, they do not find the path of matrimony especially easy or pleasant, There has been deceit and evasion on both sides. Dupont, as has been said, has promised a *dot* without being able to fulfil his promise. Antonin's parents have not revealed the fact that Antonin's uncle, from whom large expectations are suggested, is in reality a bankrupt. There is an equal amount of duplicity in the case of the young married pair. Each pretends to the other to be not what he or she is in reality, but something calculated to attract and to please. And when these pretensions are exploded the result is, of course, disillusion and exasperation. Julie and her husband "have it out" with one another. First of all the girl explains how much she has been deceived in matrimony. And then it is the turn of the young husband to point out that her conduct has been quite as mendacious as his own. And at this point we almost expect to find a kind of reconciliation based on these mutual avowals. The great point is, that the pair have begun to understand one another; and understanding might very well lead to tolerance, pardon, and perhaps, in the last resort, to love. In that case we should have comedy of the ordinary type, first, misunderstanding and unhappiness, and then, through many tribulations, peace.

Hereupon, however, the author bethinks himself of his mission as a moralist. Julie deplores the fact that she has

not been given a child. Antonin assures her that children did
not come within the scope of his conjugal ambition, that he
had not the slightest intention of founding a family. Then
Julie becomes a woman in revolt, a woman who is baulked
of her dearest and most natural desire—the wife prevented
from being a mother. A terrible scene of violence ensues,
in which all our sympathies are to be given to the unhappy
Julie and we are asked to reprobate the infamous conduct
of her husband. So far the lesson obviously is that a
marriage conducted on principles of this kind is an outrage, and the wife in such conditions no better than a
mistress. Is this all? By no means. We now revert
once more to the original plan, which was to exemplify
by means of the three daughters of M. Dupont the thesis
that in a middle-class family each possible career is a fraud
and equally ignoble. First of all Caroline is wounded in
her devotion. She has allowed herself to become enamoured
of a workman belonging to her father. He seemed to her
to be a genius, unjustly debarred from making the success
he deserved. Surreptitiously she gives this workman a
large sum of money left her by her aunt, only to discover
that he has a *ménage* of his own and three children.
Thereupon, in a fit of passion, she is prepared to sacrifice
her religion and, because she has found that men are
deceitful, to accuse Heaven of injustice. Julie, in her turn,
after her experience of matrimony, is keen for a divorce.
Then comes the turn of the sister in Paris, Angèle. Angèle
reasons with both her sisters and points out that her
particular solution of her difficulties was as fatal to her
peace of mind as were the careers of either Caroline or
Julie. And, finally, Madame Dupont is brought in to
explain to the daughters, and especially to Julie, that most
women are unhappy in matrimony and that the attitude
of revolt, however natural, is impossible in existing social
conditions. What is the result? It brings back all the
characters exactly to the position in which they started,
and leads to the cynical conclusion that you had better
leave society alone, and that you cannot reform it
but must accept such alleviations as may be possible.
Julie bethinks her that, though she may have been unhappy in marriage, she may well be less happy out of
marriage, and, despite all the nobleness of her sentiments in the furious scene with her husband, she relapses
finally into the conviction that if she does not care for

her husband she may adopt a lover for whom she does care.[1]

It is clear that we have passed through a good many different phases in this drama. Either Brieux has been so interested in his creations as to allow them to depart from the original plan traced for them, or else, like the ardent and generous moralist he is, he pursues one path after another without troubling his head about the logical consistency of his scheme. The sentimental comedy suddenly turns into an Ibsenite drama, full of passionate revolt, and then ends, if we must not say in a farce, at all events in the cynical suggestion of acquiescence in existing conditions as being on the whole the least likely to upset people. Marriage is an iniquity in certain conditions, but it has its alleviations. Most of the careers for the young women of the middle classes have their disadvantages. We must accept society as it is. To apply ideal principles is to ignore the complexity, the inter-dependence of social conditions. All this, let it be admitted, makes an extremely interesting play, and also, as I venture to think, shows Brieux in a more engaging light than as the severely scientific moralist who cares nothing for his characters so long as they fulfil the task assigned them—who only desires to finish his play like a problem in Euclid with the logical ultimatum, Q.E.D.

I come now to the consideration of that so-called realistic method which is especially illustrated in Brieux's *Les Avariés* and in Ibsen's *Ghosts*. Realism is, of course, an ambiguous word, because it involves one or two assumptions which are not always verifiable. There is no greater realism in describing details which most people would pass over as either unsavoury or unnecessary, than there is in other forms of dramatic or literary art which do not think it necessary to emphasise the sordid or the unclean. In the one case as in the other the artist is making use of that principle which is his by nature, the principle of selection. He uses the materials which are necessary for his purpose and he disregards the others. An artist painting a picture groups together various elements, not so much copying Nature as adapting Nature to his uses. A dramatist who would be called romantic proceeds in precisely the same fashion, throwing into high relief the figures of his hero

---

[1] Cf. Jules Lemaître's *Impressions de Théâtre*, 10th series, pp. 278 *et foll*,

and his heroine and emphasising the sentiments and emotions appropriate in such cases. But what we sometimes forget is that the so-called realist has a precisely similar method of working. He, too, is occupied with arranging a picture, and in order to bring out his scheme he emphasises certain points and allows others to recede into the background. He uses his characters, not like independent personages, but rather as vehicles for illustrating the purpose or lesson which he has in mind. From this point of view the realist is just as unreal as the romantic dramatist. Or to put the matter otherwise, he has the same justification which the artist claims for himself, selection being of the very essence of the artist's problem.

We must not, therefore, take it for granted that because Brieux wrote the play which in the English translation is called *Damaged Goods*, or because Ibsen wrote a play which is called *Ghosts*, they are necessarily nearer the ultimate truth of things than, let us say, Victor Hugo with his romantic drama. We call it realism when the materials are sordid, and we call it romantic when the materials are sentimental or emotional. But the artist is a free worker; he can manipulate as he desires. Even the man whom we might call the most thorough-going of realists probably has some dream or ideal which, tarnished as it may be, yet has in his eyes all the value of the beautiful. The artist is always the votary of the Beautiful, however he may construe it. The question of truth hardly enters into these considerations. The dream of the artist is always true of him, and true for all those who see eye to eye with him in his work.

To me, I confess, the whole question of what we vaguely call realism ought to be envisaged from another standpoint. If we look at the matter historically, knowing as we do that in the history of art progress is made by a series of spiral actions and reactions, we discover that romance pursued up to a certain point produces a feeling of satiety or unreality, and therefore naturally gives place to an opposite theory which calls itself logical and scientific. After Victor Hugo came Zola, Ibsen, and Brieux, just as in an earlier stage of the process of development the remoteness and frigidity of the classical drama gave place to Victor Hugo's romantic enthusiasm. The important thing, however, to notice is, that the different artistic attitudes correspond to different periods in the evolution of a nation or of humanity at large. Nothing is clearer than the fact that what we sometimes call the Victorian outlook, that is to say, the attitude towards men and things congenial to the nineteenth century, is in large measure superseded, and it is interesting and important for us to recognise how the generation which we may call Georgian reacts against its predecessor. It would have been impossible in the Victorian era to produce for the public plays like *Les Avariés* and *Ghosts*. Why? Because the theory of art was different: the temper of the public was different: the atmosphere was different. The appeal of the nineteenth century was to the heart: that of the twentieth century is to logical processes of the intellect. The office of drama is to popularise, as it were, scientific conceptions, to make use of scientific principles, to illustrate them in some imagined scheme, and thus to convert and metamorphose drama into a tract for the times.

In pursuit of this purpose there must be no concealment or evasion of the main issues. We must not hesitate to call a spade a spade. We must deal with matters, not particularly savoury, but necessary for purposes of instruction. The ills of humanity must be cured by a ruthless veracity. Young men and maidens must discover the things which are necessary to their salvation. The veil must be torn from all kinds of secret conventions, and the bare truth, wherever that can be ascertained, must be laid before audiences without reserve and without disguise. And if there be some grave and deep-seated malady which is afflicting humanity, the dramatist must not hesitate to probe the evil at its source and eradicate the poison, or, at all events, help to eradicate the poison, by plain and courageous truth-speaking. The romantic aims of art must be left alone for the present. Romance may be an indestructible element of humanity, but no particular emphasis need at present be laid upon it. We are occupied with sterner things. Hence, for a twentieth-century public, the dramatic artists who most nearly correspond to the needs and necessities of the time must be permitted frank speech and a resolute, almost apostolic fervour in elucidating social problems and laying bare social sores. And it is perhaps not altogether fanciful to find in the greater range granted to women in the modern world, an influence in the direction of plain speaking and the exposure of antique shams. Women desire to know the truth, in the fervent hope that the truth will set them free. Men are apt to be more sceptical—to echo Pilate's celebrated question.

But is the drama the proper vehicle for the inculcation of these moral truths, or for the preaching of reforms? To that question the answer of the modern world is explicit. Every platform is to be welcomed, every means made use of to get hold of the attention of the public, and because the stage is a popular institution and attracts popular audiences, it is to be utilised as fully and as unreservedly as any other mode of appeal. The stage, no doubt, has great advantages in this respect. It is better than the pamphlet, the tract, most kinds of propaganda literature, and other devices of the printed page. Print only appeals to the eye, but actors in movement on a stage appeal not only to the eye but to the ear. Moreover, it is maintained that the stage-appeal to the eye is of a more illustrative quality, more attractive, more persuasive, more seductive, than anything that can be got out of a book. Or shall we utilise the pulpit? But sermons are not so widely effective in their appeal as plays. They are directed to a smaller audience to begin with, while the audience itself is of a somewhat special kind and by no means representative of the public at large. Thus the modern world seems to have decided that, whatever may be the subjects ripe for discussion, the dramatist has quite as much qualification to deal with them as the politician, the social philosopher, or any one else. And the range of subjects is undoubtedly large. If we take any social structure which has been in existence for a good many years, we shall find a series of defects which become more obvious and patent as time goes on. Certain laws have lost their usefulness or become actually oppressive; certain customs, which no doubt had their justification in the past, have developed into veritable curses; power has been arrogated by a few tyrannical hands, as, for instance, the power of the parent over the child, the power of the judge over the criminal,[1] the power of money and of the Press over all.[2] When there are so many topics inviting discussion, why should the dramatist confine himself to mainly sexual interests? Why should the eternal " triangle " between husband, wife, and lover be the sole theme to be witnessed on the boards?

[1] Cf. Galsworthy's play, *Justice.*
[2] Cf. Arnold Bennett's play, *What the Public Wants.*

There are all sorts of vital problems dealing with education, government, public health, population, marriage, divorce, parental duties, religion. There is no lack of interest in these, and the modern world has decided that any and every subject shall be treated frankly and with sincerity.

That at least is clearly Brieux's view, and he has illustrated it in his practice. Thus the dramatist becomes in a proper sense a public servant. He cannot, of course, help his own idiosyncrasies. He has his own views, peculiar, it may be, to himself, or shared only by a relatively small section of society. His vision may be distorted by all kinds of prejudices. These may be disqualifications for his task, but they do not in the modern judgment affect the urgency of the task itself. It is the business of the dramatist also to see that the special didactic interest does not overpower every other dramatic factor, such as construction, analysis of character, artistic appeal. The older theory, that art exists merely for the sake of art, is discredited nowadays. In France, at all events, the view held by the serious dramatist has made numerous converts. Art is to have a distinctly moral aim, and Brieux in this is merely reflecting a vast amount of contemporary opinion in his own country as well as in England.

But there is another side of the question. I have tried to depict Brieux as a man with a distinct theory of dramatic art—to which apparently he does not always adhere—as a moralist, as an anxious and indefatigable reformer of abuses, and above all as a realist who desires to paint things as he sees them, and not to allow the play of fancy, imagination, or the instinctive love of romance to interfere with the work in hand. What I have *not* shown is Brieux as an artist, and that for the best possible reason, because it is precisely on the artistic side that Brieux is deficient. He is an artist sometimes in his management of scenes, or in his treatment of character. But that does not interfere with the main contention, that if and where he fails, he fails as an artist. The reason is plain. To him art is an instrument, a means to effect something, and art does not admit of being used in this fashion. It is an end in itself and cannot be subordinated to alien pressures. If Brieux were asked what, in his opinion, was the end of the dramatic art which he practised, he would, if he were consistent with his theory, say that it subserved ends of morality, that it could be used to enforce a moral, that it could instruct and edify humanity. But as I understand the matter, art can never run patiently under the yoke of something which is not art. Art has nothing specially to do with morality. The highest art is always moral, because it is in accordance with the great laws which govern the world, but that is an inseparable accident, no part of the essence of Art. To the query, " What is the end of Art? " there is, I think, only one answer. It is *delight*, in the widest and broadest sense of the term. It exists to make us feel more intensely the fervour, the joy, the exhilaration of life, it makes us see, it purges our eyes from their blindness, it opens to us new realms of beauty and truth. If you look at the practice of great artists, you cannot say off-hand what particular ends they subserve. But you can say of all artists worthy of the name, especially the great dramatic artists, like the Greek tragedians and Shakespeare, that they add to our delight, that they open our eyes, extend our field of vision, and make us understand all the vast and intricate interests of humanity and life.

Thus the great charge one has to bring against Dramatic Realism is, that while it is rarely artistic, it is not always real. Art can never be made scientific, and it only commits suicide when it attempts to base itself on a strictly scientific procedure. When one says that Art is re-presentation, one has said all that is necessary. Art is not presentation, that is the work of the photograph. It is re-presentation—that is, presentation bathed in the colours of the artist's personality, and suffused with his proper idiosyncrasy.

" OUR EURIPIDES, THE HUMAN "

EURIPIDES may be said to have founded the school of dramatic realism. He also gives us piquant hints as to the limits of realism as an interpretation of life. His position, his scope, his intention have been the subjects of much controversy—ranging from Aristotle's admiration, " the most tragic of poets," and Mrs. Browning's tribute to " Our Euripides, the human," down to the scorn of Walter Savage Landor and the vitriolic abuse of Algernon Charles Swinburne. On the whole the ancient world admired him much more than the modern world seems inclined to do. Schlegel's criticism of him in his *Theatre of the Greeks* is childish in its petulance and injustice. On the other hand, certain English scholars—Dr. Verrall and Professor Gilbert Murray, for instance, to mention only two names—are quite prepared to concede to him the very highest honours.

Let us ask ourselves first—What is it precisely that Euripides did? To that the reply in the broadest and simplest fashion is that he altered the dramatic formula, undermined the axioms and postulates of his predecessors, and challenged the prejudices, religious and ethical, of the more conservative of his fellow-citizens. If ever there was a man determined *épater les bourgeois*—to shock the respectability of the middle class—it was Euripides. It was nothing less than a revolution at which he aimed, a revolution of thought about things human and divine. He was a pupil of Anaxagoras, a daring physical philosopher who suffered for his temerity in calling the sun a molten mass of metal : he was a friend of Socrates who had to drink the cup of hemlock for introducing new gods. And he was a silent, uncommunicative, solitary man who loved birds and the sea, loved working in a cave at Salamis, but eschewed the companionship of his fellows; who pondered the deepest problems of life and suggested by means of his dramatic art the gravest doubts about the

divine denizens of Olympus. Remember, too that this
recluse, who was one of the first men to collect a library,
only won the first prize five times. And yet he wrote
poems so rememberable that Athenian captives in the
stone quarries of Syracuse gained their freedom by reciting
them to their captors and on their return to Athens sought
out the old man to thank him for their recovered liberty.
He did not write for the people, but for students; and
yet his dramas were so well known that Aristophanes
could be sure that his jeering allusions to the Euripidean
texts could be appreciated by a popular audience. Two
other facts about him may be recalled. He was forced
to leave Athens, where his notorious scepticism was bringing
him into trouble, and he then wrote in retirement for the
Macedonian court of Archelaus a drama on the new cult
of Dionysus, apparently full of reverence, which no one
has been able thoroughly to understand from that day to
this. Was he recanting his early scepticism? We do
not know.

The most succinct way of explaining what he did is
to say, as was said in ancient times, that he drew men
and women not as they ought to be, but as they are.
Now, whenever a dramatist elects to portray mankind as
it is, he creates a revolution and is sure to be called a
cynic. Unscientific artists—some artists—are a generous
folk, and they love to adorn the characters they draw
with all kinds of trappings and decorative clothes, sometimes disguising the real and essential elements in the
process. So when our reformer insists on taking off their
clothes and exhibits men and women in their nudity, all
kinds of unpleasant revelations come to light, and the
reformer is styled a morose satirist and eventually, perhaps, a dangerous atheist. So it happened in the times
of Euripides, as also it happened in the times of Balzac
and Zola and Ibsen. The world as depicted by Dickens
is very different from the world as it appeared to Thackeray. Humanity in the plays of Victor Hugo cuts a very
different figure from humanity in the plays of Dumas
fils, Augier, Hervieu, and Brieux. And when Æschylus
thundered his iambics and his dithyrambs he gave to
his heroes and heroines a stature as of the gods; while
Euripides was content to garb his dramatis personæ with
rags so that the bare bones of their humanity might be
visible to all spectators.

Let us take an example or two.   The Oresteian legend is
well known—how Agamemnon, returning from Troy, was
murdered by his wife Clytemnestra, and how Agamemnon's
children Orestes and Electra avenged the crime by killing
Clytemnestra and her paramour, Ægisthus.   *Electra* is the
title of one of Euripides' plays—one of the most original
in treatment, so original, indeed, that it has been found
shocking by various critics.   According to the earlier legends
Electra was a fine exponent of a blood-feud, a heroic
character, a king's daughter.   She came of a lineage of
heroes, and, indeed, exercised an inspiring influence over
her neurotic brother Orestes in the execution of the deed
of vengeance against Ægisthus.   Euripides with these
facts before him began by introducing a wholly novel
fact which he probably invented himself.   Because the
guilty pair at Argos desired to make themselves safe
against popular execration Electra was compelled to be
affianced to an ordinary yeoman, so that any children
born of her might have a plebeian taint and so be the
less likely to foment rebellion.   In the play, therefore,
Electra is seen clad in shabby clothes working at menial
tasks in order to keep up the humble home of her husband,
who, on his part, is portrayed as a plain and honest man
only too much exercised how to fulfil the onerous responsibility of being wedded to a king's daughter.   The
marriage was, of course, no marriage.   That at least we
might expect from the natural awe and reverence surrounding members of a royal house.   But the *mise en
scène* of the play—the humble home, the menial tasks,
the loyal, anxious peasant husband, all help the dramatist
in carrying out his conception on broad and simple lines
of human nature.   And how is Electra herself portrayed ?
You can imagine how a playwright of a sentimental turn
might paint the affair.   We should have great stress laid
upon the indignity of the heroine—a proud soul fretting
herself in obscurity and relative indigence bearing her
burden with no little difficulty and travail of her soul.
Touches like these, of course, are to be found in Euripides'
play—and I may remark in passing that the portraiture
of her husband shows Euripides' sympathy with honest
yeomen who are upright and loyal, respectful, and punctilious, assiduous in attention and yet possessing an
innate nobility of their own.   But Electra ?   She is
assuredly no heroine as Æschylus and Sophocles painted

her. She is just a woman placed in an unfortunate position, bearing about with her all the marks of a victim of
an unscrupulous tyranny. She is haunted by her past
experience, poisoned by it, embittered. Intolerant of
poverty, she is getting to middle age, unpopular amongst
her fellow-citizens, unkissed, unkind, unmated, as her
very name indicates, though faithful to the death, as her
brother testifies, never ceasing to remember the debt
she owes to her dead father. Observe particularly that
she is not made a sympathetic character. She is too
hard and intense. Like her mother, Clytemnestra, she
is soured by disappointment. Clytemnestra, it is true,
seems to be a prey to remorse and anxious to atone. Electra
has no weaknesses of that kind; it is her business to urge
on her brother, to fortify his fainting soul and drive him
resolutely to the great purpose of revenge. In this aspect,
therefore, it is clear that Euripides' play is a protest
against classical standards and canons.[1] The dramatist is
concerned to analyse character in a real human being, to
discover how any woman placed in such circumstances
would be likely to feel and act.

Or, take another instance of Euripides' realism. I am
choosing on purpose familiar plays, because they not
only illustrate the Euripidean method but deal with well-
known stories. Let us, then, glance for a moment at the
play called *Alcestis*, of which the heroine is a noble wife
who died for her husband's sake in order that he might
enjoy a few more years of his much-desired existence.
The ordinary conception of this husband, Admetus, was
that of a man who was the friend of the gods, whom
Apollo was supposed to befriend and to whom Hercules
might appeal as a host capable of regal hospitality. To
Admetus, therefore, as the friend of the gods was given
the option of avoiding death by procuring the death of
one of his kinsfolk. Alcestis filled the breach, and according to the current Greek conception nobly fulfilled the
proper feminine task of subserving masculine ambition.
How does Euripides treat this fable? He does full justice
to the character of the wife Alcestis, but he fastens his
criticism on that of the husband. What sort of man was
Admetus? The answer for a psychologist is not difficult.

[1] It is possible that Sophocles' *Electra* was produced after that of
Euripides and was intended to be an answer or antidote to a too realistic
portrait.

Admetus was one of the most thoroughly selfish men who ever lived, and one of the meanest. He allowed his wife to die for him, and he had a bitter controversy with his father, whom he charged with pusillanimity for not offering his life to save his son. Even in the midst of the funeral ceremonies, when Alcestis was being carried out for burial, Admetus had not the frank honesty to reveal to his visitor Hercules how inconvenient was his arrival at the house of mourning. He must keep up his reputation for hospitality. He had such a low notion of friendship that he was unable to take Hercules into his confidence. He forwarded with most indecent haste all the necessary preparations for the sepulchre. Not one jot or tittle of the criticisms which might be passed upon this recreant hero is omitted by Euripides. Hercules in single combat with death rescues Alcestis from her fate and brings her back again to her home. We feel how little sympathy Euripides has for this happy ending, and the suggestion has been advanced that the dramatist intended to hint that Alcestis never died at all but only went off into a swoon from which she was promptly awakened by Hercules. Be this, however, as it may, the student can have no doubt whatsoever as to the estimate of Admetus' personality. Treated as a real character, not as part of a heroic legend, he stands out in all his petty egotism, a man whom other men ought to despise, gaining at the close a reward which he did not deserve, and blessed with the possession of a wife whose shoe's latchet he was not worthy to unloose. I ought to add that the whole play is somewhat of a stumbling-block to critics just because it has a happy ending and because it exhibits here and there comic elements, like Hercules' drunkenness, which seem out of place in a tragedy. It may have taken the place of the Satyric play with which the ordinary trilogy of dramas usually ended. Or, indeed, *Alcestis* may be one of the earliest specimens in dramatic history of what we in modern times would call a comedy, with scenes of comic relief and a *dénouement* of happiness and mutual congratulation for every one concerned.

A good deal more is involved in this new reading of ancient characters than meets a superficial glance. It may seem to us to matter very little whether Electra was drawn as an ordinary woman or as an antique heroine; or whether the chief stress in the case of Admetus was

laid on his friendship with the gods or on the utter selfishness of his conduct. It matters psychologically, of course,
for only when the aureole is taken from the brow and the
festal garb is exchanged for homespun is the man to be
discovered in his human elements, as apart from a glorified
puppet or coloured saint in the cathedral window. But
in Euripides' case we have indications of a religious,
moral, and social revolution actually taking place before
his eyes and largely aided by Socrates, Anaxagoras,
politicians of the day and thinkers and poets like himself.
Aristophanes is always sighing for the good old days and
regretting the absence of warriors who fought at Marathon.
It is as though Wellington in his later years looked back
to the stout men-at-arms who fought that " damned
near-run thing " at Waterloo. Æschylus belonged in
heart and spirit to the Marathon-fighter days, when men
reverenced the gods, accepted the old legends as gospel,
and were decently respectful to their elders and betters.
In Euripides' time, however, a new generation had arisen
" which knew not Joseph "—dialecticians, sophists, pinch-
beck politicians, litigious busybodies, sceptics who doubted
about everything, atheists who believed in nothing—in
fact, the whole crew pictured by Aristophanes as belonging
to the new age of unsettlement and chaos. Euripides
himself was part of this new age, for he had studied the
new philosophy and wrestled in the spirit of the rationalist
with moral and religious problems. Æschylus was a
metaphysician whose task it was to reconcile men with
the ways of Heaven. Euripides was an analytic thinker
who tried in vain to reconcile the ways of Heaven with
doubting and inquiring men. To Æschylus the existence
and reality of gods were a postulate, an axiom. To
Euripides the existence of such things as pain and sorrow
and evil seemed to preclude the hypothesis of Divine
Providence. As a matter of fact Euripides with his
scepticism and Æschylus with his faith eventually arrived
at much the same conclusion, both accepting in the long
run a vague pantheistic creed with Zeus as the primal
source of all being. But the method of approach was
entirely different in the two cases, the later poet com-
mencing with man as his starting-point, and the earlier
with the gods as the foundation of his structure. Hence
the results also were entirely different, Æschylus drawing
heroes and heroines, and Euripides painting ordinary

R

men and women. Thus, if Clytemnestra in the *Agamemnon* is a magnificent figure of evil clothed in purple pomp, Clytemnestra in the *Electra* is an unhappy middle-aged woman, anxious to atone for her guilty past.

But Euripides with his new way of looking at things was confronted by a peculiar difficulty in constructing his plays. The traditional method, the method of Æschylus and Sophocles, was to exhibit the working of the gods in human affairs, showing how sin inevitably brought its punishment according to divine law. Moreover, the dramas themselves as enacted in Athens were produced under the ægis, as it were, of Apollo and Dionysius and Athena, and dedicated in a certain fashion to their glorification. How, then, was Euripides, with his scanty respect for Olympus and his distaste for superstition, to recommend his plays to Athenian audiences, the majority of whom were accustomed to a traditional method and were guided, no doubt, by pardonable prejudices ? His plan was an unhappy one, but we may admit that the dilemma was serious. Ancient and modern critics have alike fallen foul of his prologues and his epilogues, because they have little or no connection with his plot, being for the most part formal explanatory matter put into the mouth of a god or a goddess and dramatic devices of the nature of a *deus ex machina* to bring the play to a conclusion. The prologue is an index of events, the epilogue is a tag, summarily arresting further action. Both are otiose to the main thesis. What was Euripides to do ? If theatrical custom demanded the introduction of the gods and he had the misfortune not to believe in a Pantheon of magnified and non-natural beings guilty of every moral depravity, his only resource, as it seemed to him, was to pay lip-service to Apollo and Athena in a prologue, allow these conventional deities to end his play—which had got itself into such a tangle that it could only be ended abruptly—and throw all his interest and his dramatic skill into the portraiture of character and the representation of actual and real human creatures. In other words, the introduction of the gods was nothing but—the word is inevitable nowadays—a " camouflage," an elaborate piece of humbug to satisfy uneasy consciences while the more instructed spirits would know how to estimate it at its proper measure. On any other interpretation Euripides can only be considered a bad artist for trying to combine incompatibles and for being so clumsy in construction.[1] If he had a slightly satirical purpose, at all events we may admire his cleverness, even though we may in a savage mood call him a hypocrite.

Observe, however, that we have already thrown an interesting sidelight on dramatic realism. The drawback of all realism is that it sets the realistic artist at loggerheads with an average audience. The audience have their fixed prejudices and they do not like to be disturbed in their theatrical habits. They come to the theatre expecting the usual thing, and when they receive something else—something unpleasantly new and provocative—they are only too apt to believe that, having asked for bread, they have been presented with a stone. Some artists sacrifice their principles and allow themselves to bow down in the house of Rimmon. Others attempt a more or less uneasy compromise. Others, again, skilfully conceal their intention, as Euripides did, keeping their purpose up their sleeve, with a sly wink to those in the know. The modern problem is not, of course, the same as that which confronted Euripides, but it is of similar import. The average audience, the conservative and conventional theatre-goers, want a happy ending, as Aristotle long ago observed. They want their heroes and heroines to be obviously good people and their villains to be obviously bad people. They think that tragedy only applies to great persons, to kings and tyrants, or at the very least to dukes and earls. They believe in " situations," and desire a clear-cut ending to the play. And your thorough-going realist disappoints them in every particular. He will not give them happy endings if the plot demands a melancholy conclusion. He will not give them an ending at all, for humanity goes on and life does not admit of such convenient stopping-places. He will not make his characters all white or all black, for there is a soul of goodness in things evil and a seed of potential evil even in the good. Nor will he confine tragedy to courts and baronial halls, but sees tragic elements in cottages and acute drama in the relations of quite humble beings. He will bring down his curtain when he has had his say and will not disturb himself, however much you protest as to the absence of an artistic finish. And so realists are

[1] This is, of course, the view taken by Dr. Verrall in *Euripides, the Rationalist*.

abused until they can train their own audiences.   Perhaps
Euripides trained his.   Ibsen, after much furious altercation, undoubtedly succeeded in educating a school.

Among the various antagonisms in which realism stands
towards other schemes or theories of art one of the obvious
antithesis is between realism and romance.   This has a
particular historic significance which is best illustrated
from French literature.   Victor Hugo, in reaction from
the cold classical perfection of Corneille and Racine,
introduced romantic drama.   When the rage had passed
for bombastic heroes and melodramatic situations the
time had come for another reaction—realistic or naturalistic fiction, as in the novels of Zola; realistic drama, as
in the work of Brieux and some of his contemporaries.
Thus it became one of the dogmas of the new naturalistic
school to eschew romance on the ground of its artificiality
and its absurd unreality.   But, apart from this historical
justification, there is no intimate or essential reason why
realism should exclude romance.   Romance enters largely
into most of the tragedies and comedies of life, and so far
as we can see it is an integral part of that human sen-
sibility which adds colour to existence while it exposes us
to suffering.   If you shut out romance at the front door
it is very apt to return by the back door, and be the more
troublesome the more it is ignored.   There is no little
romance in Euripides—romance and sensitiveness and
sentiment—and he makes a strong appeal to our capacity
for tears.   *Sunt lacrymæ rerum* is as much his motto as
it is Virgil's.   This comes out especially in his treatment
of women in his plays.   He was much interested in women,
a thing which his contemporaries could not understand
and which they tried to explain by his unfortunate experience with two wives.   They said—Aristophanes at
least said—that he was doing harm to the cause of womanhood, and that women hated him.   But our modern
experience enables us to see more clearly.   We know how
often avowed feminists are accused of doing harm to the
very sex they try to defend.   Emancipated womanhood
is held by conservatives and reactionaries to be a wronged
womanhood.   But here Euripides is on modern lines.
Both he and Plato recognised that Greek society did
serious harm to women.   An imperfect ideal of woman is
a disease of which, perhaps more than anything else,
ancient civilisation perished.   Let us do honour to the

Greek philosopher and the Greek dramatist for a perspicacity denied to the men of their age—even to a man so highly intellectual as Pericles. Ἔρχεται τιμὰ γυναικείῳ γένει. "Honour comes to the race of women." [1] It preludes a triumph which was only to be realised centuries afterwards.

The play *Medea*, from which I have just given a quotation, is a veritable tragedy, but the treatment of the heroine is on the lines of romance. It is a very striking piece of work, belonging to Euripides' early years of authorship, and—perhaps because of its very originality—it only won a third prize. The professed and orthodox moral is that a marriage between a Greek (Jason) and a barbarian princess from Colchis (Medea) is no marriage. But to look for a moral at all in the case of a highly imaginative and artistic creation like this is a pedantic piece of supererogation. It is as though we took the play of *Romeo and Juliet* in our hands and solemnly declared that the lesson to be learnt from it was that " violent delights have violent ends." I forget whether Gervinus draws this moral, but he is quite capable of it, and I have little doubt that some of the academic editors of Euripides have duly extricated this gem of wisdom about foreign marriages from the play of *Medea*. The real interest lies in the wonderfully-drawn portrait of the heroine, while the whole story depicts the fading of a romance, the end of a riotous honeymoon of passion and battle. Jason leads his Argonauts to win the Golden Fleece past the Symplegades or clashing rocks to the shores of Colchis, and though, indeed, he wins the prize of his enterprise his chief conquest is the victory of the Princess Medea. Without her love he would have been powerless; with her aid he surmounts every peril. And she, poor, infatuated fool, with all her wild exuberance and barbarous frenzy, escapes with him only to discover that passion yields but a Dead Sea fruit and the end thereof is dust and ashes. Medea is a typical villainess—a savage, untamed animal. She is prodigal of her crimes : she deceives her father, poisons the dragon that keeps watch and ward over the treasure, stabs her brother Absyrtus, lures Pelias to his death, kills Creon and his daughter, and murders her children. She did it for love. Never did a woman so resolutely accept the maxim " All for love

[1] Eurip., *Med.*, 419.

and the world well lost." Euripides takes a character like this and transforms it into a wonderful presentment of a woman scorned. Medea becomes veritably human— I was almost going to say sympathetic—in the process. She is a Gorgon, a Fury, a Valkyrie, but you cannot for the life of you hate and condemn her. No wonder that the chorus, who ought to detest so fierce a representative of a barbarian race, take her side in the controversy and keep her fatal secrets. We cannot forgive her for murdering her children. And yet, and yet—when in a marvellous bit of stage-craft Euripides depicts her as suddenly bursting into tears over the children she is going to sacrifice—ὡς ἀρτιδακρύς εἰμι καὶ φόβου πλέα[1]—well, the tears are ready to start to our eyes. In his command of pathos Euripides is irresistible, and probably that is why Aristotle called him the most tragic of poets. Nor is Jason less admirable as a study. We feel that to him, a characteristic Hellene, woman's love is of little account, and that Medea in the midst of a Greek civilisation is frankly a bore. The love of his lifetime was not Medea or any other woman, but his stout ship *Argo*, a fallen timber from which is said to have ultimately killed him. And Medea goes up in a chariot of fire at the close, taking the bodies of her murdered children with her. She had indeed executed vengeance on all her foes, and in her barbaric fashion vindicated the right of womanhood.

I could go through many of these plays in similar fashion—especially *Iphigeneia in Taurica*, which again gives us a perfect study of a woman, hardened by exile and " wild with all regret," and as a play is a pure romance, happy ending and all. But something should be said about *The Trojan Women*, which, it will be remembered, was played some time ago at the Court Theatre, and quite recently produced at Manchester by Mr. Drinkwater, for it throws a sidelight on Euripides' relation to the current politics of his time and illustrates the nature of his humanity.

Despite all their brilliant culture the Athenians were not a humane people. Human, artistic, civilised, the Athenians were without any doubt, but not humane. Or perhaps they had grown sharp and cruel, as a selfish race inevitably tends to do when it grasps an empire and exploits it solely to its own advantage. At all events,

[1] Eurip., *Med.*, 903.

during the Peloponnesian War the Athenians committed
several cruel acts, which Thucydides notes with his usual
judicial coldness—the massacre of Melos, for instance,
the condemnation of the Mitylenians to a similar fate, the
resolution being rescinded next day—to say nothing of
the habitual ill-treatment of the slaves in the silver mines
of Laureion. Xenophon, too, tells us that during the
last stages of the war the Athenians cut off the right
hands of all the prisoners they took on Spartan vessels
so that they might row no more for the enemy. They
must have been hard and tyrannical, for the islanders in
the Ægean hated them and took the earliest opportunities
of revolting when the crash of the Sicilian disaster came.
The Melian affair was peculiarly horrible, for Melos did
not belong to the Athenian Confederacy and the population was Doric rather than Ionic. Yet the island was
ruthlessly taken by storm, the women and children sold
into captivity, and all the males put to the sword. Even
Thucydides was revolted by such a transaction. He does
not hesitate to put into the mouth of the Athenian envoys
in their arguments with the Melians sentiments which we
should now call those of *Realpolitik* and which we attribute
to the military camarilla at Berlin.

But Thucydides was not the only one to be shocked.
The Melian massacre happened in 416 B.C. In the next
year, 415, Euripides brought out his *Trojan Women,* a
most moving and pathetic drama which was only placed
second, the first prize being won by a certain Xenocles,
" whoever he may have been," as Ælian scornfully says
in his *Varia Historia.* He paints for us the scene of
desolation which followed on the capture of Troy, the
women given over as slaves to the Greek chieftains, the
little son of Hector, Astyanax, dragged away to be thrown
over the battlements, and the savage conqueror, Menelaus,
striding on the stage to carry off Helen as his prey. Euripides sets before us a close and penetrating study of what
happens when a beleaguered town falls into the hands of
its foes, a picture of ruin and agony—the other side, as
it were, of the glory of victory. It is hardly a drama : it
is an analytic presentment of a single scene, realistic in
detail, and poignantly true. There are four women in
the foreground : Hecuba, the mother, Cassandra, the
daughter, Andromache, Hector's widow, and Helen, the
cause of all the trouble and the curse of Troy. Each of

them has her story to tell. They were once queens and princesses; now they are to be the slave-concubines of their captors. Only Helen preserves her triumphant beauty, for she has a touch of the supernatural about her; she is a wanton, but divine. In the background are all the ruins of what once was Ilium, the coming to and fro of Talthybius, the Greek herald, and the insolent captains, the final crash of towers which marks the end of the story. All the portraits are vividly described and felt, and if Helen is marvellously studied, no less a triumph is Menelaus, torn between his brutal rage and his no less brutal passion for Paris's paramour. We do not know whether the Athenians took the moral for themselves. But we do know that when their final agony came upon them and Lysander was thundering at their gates, they remembered all that they had done to the Melians and other islanders, and trembled to think what would be done to them. Euripides' realism never stood him in better stead than when he, most tragic of the poets, portrayed the tragedy of fallen Troy.

Let me add a few remarks of a more general character. We have now seen what Dramatic Realism meant for Euripides. He was a realist because he painted men and women not in an artificial or etherealised fashion, but as they are—Cromwell, so to speak, with all his warts. How far it is possible for any artist to be so purely objective is a grave question, with which I do not at present deal. The artist, I may observe, cannot help or avoid his own idiosyncrasies — he cannot jump off his own shadow. Let that pass for the moment. Euripides is a realist because he will have little or nothing to do with the purple pomps and trappings of tragedy. Tragedy itself can be discovered in humble circumstances in the ordinary relations of human beings to one another. Therefore the gods and goddesses are figured by Euripides in a purely rationalistic way, suggesting that if they commit actions morally objectionable " the less gods they." The ancient myths, too, are very freely handled—Electra, for instance, being represented as engaged in menial tasks and as the wife of a common yeoman. On the other hand, Euripides' realism does not exclude a romantic and sentimental treatment. Indeed, he revels in sentiment, and Aristotle suggests that he was too fond of an enervating pathos.[1]

[1] Arist., *Poet.*, 26.

Realism, one would be inclined to say, must be made of sterner stuff.

And now that we have in some measure understood the poet's attitude, let us ask, Was he justified? To that I think our answer must be that artistically he was justified, for every artist has a right to his own attitude and point of view, and we can only judge or condemn him if we find that he is guilty of flagrant inconsistency. But we open a larger question if we ask whether he was justified as a moralist and a philosopher. A heavy responsibility rests on those who deal with the highest subjects of thought and attempt to solve ultimate problems of our life and destiny. One point is clear—that it is dangerous to apply a destructive criticism unless room is left for reconstruction on a higher plane. When Plato had shown that current moral notions were misleading and false he led the student to lofty conceptions in his system of Ideas, and especially to the Idea of Good, the apex of his philosophy, equivalent to God. What did Euripides do? He practically destroyed the whole of the legendary framework surrounding and supporting men's ordinary notions of good and evil, and showed them a world void of the Godhead. He laughed at the denizens of Olympus and brought them down from their celestial heights to the dusty thoroughfares where men chatter and bargain, dispute, and quarrel in everyday life. By depreciating heroic myths and heroic characters he did his best to banish a fixed external standard of morality so far as that standard existed for ordinary people. And so Good was analysed into mere convention and custom, while Truth was frittered away into individual opinion. That is why Euripides was held up by Aristophanes and others as a dangerous sophist.

But we must not leave matters thus, as though this were all. Euripides deserves better at our hands than to be called a sophist. A deeply thoughtful man, he was throughout struggling with the problems of Evil and the possibility of Divine government; and from time to time gave utterance to his doubts or his surmises in accordance with his prevalent mood. Like all of us in our own smaller degree, he varied in his opinion as different facets of the great mystery presented themselves to his gaze. Let us not forget two things : Euripides was a realist, but he was also a reformer. In the *Troades*, for instance, he wants to take the tinsel off military glory and to show what an awful thing war is. And if he is a sceptic, he, too, can rise to some mystical faith of Pantheism. For he puts in the mouth of Hecuba—also in this play—an appeal to the Highest God of all, the Supreme Intelligence, who corresponds to what Anaxagoras called Nous and Plato the Idea of Good.

SIR HERBERT TREE AND THE ENGLISH STAGE

An Open Letter to an American Friend

You ask me to give you some idea of Herbert Tree—what principles he stood for in art, what was his contribution to the English stage, what was the basis of his personal popularity. And I find it hard to give you satisfactory answers, for two reasons, one of which has to do with you and the other with myself. Let me take the latter first. I have been a friend of Tree for more than a quarter of a century—a rather intimate friend with whom he would discuss matters concerning which he would remain silent with others. He talked freely with me because he thought (and I hope he thought rightly) that I would understand him and sympathise with him. Therefore, now that he is dead, you may be sure that I shall instinctively take his part, and though I may suggest certain lines of criticism, I shall naturally be inclined to laudation rather than censure. I was fond of Tree, and because he had a real affectionateness of disposition—which sometimes he carefully disguised—companionship with him was always easy and pleasant, and to me delightful.

And now let me turn to your side of the question. I take it that judging Tree entirely from the outside, you have sometimes wondered why on this side of the Atlantic we thought so much of him. You were aware that his first visit to America some years ago was more or less of a failure, and that his idiosyncrasies struck people in that continent more forcibly than his positive qualities. On the occasion of his last visit you were minded to make exceptions and discover differences; you tolerated his Cardinal Wolsey, though the slow delivery of his speeches irritated you; you admired the sumptuous manner in which the play was set on the stage, though sometimes you thought that the frame was too ornate for the picture. When it came to Thackeray, you frankly rebelled. You considered his Colonel Newcome *not* the ideal of an English gentleman, but the laborious effort of an actor to look like it; it seemed to you that the pathos was wrong, the humour sometimes misplaced, the sentimentality too much in evidence. You never saw Tree in Dickens, did you? I ask because in *David Copperfield* Tree gave two performances, both of them admirable. He was both Dan'l Peggotty and Micawber, and of the two I think the Peggotty was the better. He was also a very vivid and picturesque Fagin. And the moral of my remark is that the pathos of Dickens, the humour of Dickens, the sentimentality of Dickens suited Tree's art better than the similar qualities (which exist in a very different form) in Thackeray. If Tree had been a reader of books—he emphatically was not—he might have understood Thackeray better. You cannot get at the author of " Vanity Fair " from the outside, or by any ingenious or brilliant *a priori* methods; you have got to live with him in prolonged intimacy; his books must be at your bedside; his curious, elusive spirit, half-preacher, half-cynic, must be your constant companion. With Dickens it is different. You can have a very good bowing acquaintance with Dickens and do him little or no injustice. His characters have the melodramatic tinge and strike one easily and forcibly. They are not pure creations of the Comic Spirit like some of the characters of Thackeray and Meredith. Farce, sheer, undiluted Farce, enters into them so largely that for stage purposes they suit admirably an actor with a frank liking for caricature.

And that reminds me that you have not seen—I do not think I am wrong—Tree's Falstaff or his Malvolio. You have missed a good deal, though perhaps you would have had the uneasy feeling that these, too, bordered on caricature. But did not Shakespeare intend them for caricature? I am thinking for the moment of Falstaff, in the *Merry Wives of Windsor*, not of the hero of Eastcheap. In the Historical plays Falstaff is far too prodigious a creature to be included in any of our usual categories. He is a world in himself. He has an overpowering humour and a most wistful pathos. He is Every-man, enlisted in a riotous conception of life and working to his doom with a blithe devil-may-care recklessness. Shakespeare never traced on his canvas a more wonderful being, so detestable and so lovable. But Falstaff in the *Merry Wives*, *is* a caricature, and Tree, who accepted him as such, gave a ripe, unctuous performance of an All-fatness, oozing out drink and a maudlin sentimentality at every pore, which was quite irresistible. Malvolio belongs to the same order of humanity, the fatuous egotist, the pedantic megalomaniac.

Tree was clearly doubtful whether average audiences would understand the conception, for he repeated Malvolio in the servants who formed his retinue and who, in their turn, caricatured the caricature. In the heyday of Malvolio's pompous idiocy Tree excelled; when it came to the poor pedant, bullied, imprisoned, and tortured, it was of course another matter. But has any one reconciled the earlier and the later Malvolio? Henry Ainley, who did so well in the part at the Savoy Theatre, found himself confronted with the same difficulty.

You will have gathered, of course, that versatility was Tree's chief characteristic, or, as some might say, his besetting sin. Versatile he undoubtedly was; he tried to show his skill in very different fields of dramatic work. He essayed tragic *rôles*—at one time he was very anxious to act King Lear, as a pendant or culmination to his Macbeth, his Othello, his Hamlet. He was a comedian either with or without a touch of melodrama; he made his name originally in farce, as those know who saw his *Private Secretary*. Versatility is undoubtedly a perilous gift; you know how a so-called versatile man is supposed to waste himself and his talents in many channels of activity—and to succeed in none. I have said a " so-called versatile man " because no man is really versatile : he only thinks he is, or is idly so reported by others. There is always one thing he does which is better than others, despite his many-sidedness; and if he is wise, he will discover what it is and cultivate it to the best of his ability. Tree liked to be considered many-sided; indeed, he resented any suggestion to the contrary, and for this reason, I suppose, wrote two books, though he ostentatiously declared that he was not a book-reader. His restless and unbounded activity was compelled to show itself in various fields; I do not think I ever came across any man who was more pertinaciously and assiduously alive. He was " a dragon for work," as they say, and had a greater range of vivid interests—literary, political, social, dramatic—than most of us can lay claim to. His quick alertness of spirit, his ready apprehension, his humour—which at times verged on the *macabre*—made him a most stimulating companion. He always saw objects from the less obvious standpoints and delighted in all that was unconventional and paradoxical. His wit was never mordant, nor was it always very pointed. And his epigrams were for the most part ebullitions of high spirits.

But if you ask me in what within his own proper sphere of work, the dramatic, Tree was best, I answer without hesitation. It was, as perhaps you might gather from what has just been said, in the representation of fantastic, eccentric, bizarre characters, characters with a twist in them which made them peculiar and original. Here a long list of successes testifies to the actor's easy mastery. I take some names, just as they occur—Svengali in *Trilby* first and foremost, a fascinating study; the hero and villain in *A Man's Shadow ;* Izard in *Business is Business ;* Captain Swift; Montjoye in *A Bunch of Violets ;* the spectacled Russian detective Demetrius in *The Red Lamp ;* Dr. Stockmann in *The Enemy of the People*—there is so long a list that I should weary you if I gave even a tithe of them. But let me add at least the curiously sympathetic impersonation of Caliban, a really remarkable effort of imagination in the sphere of animality, which was in its way quite as illuminating as Browning's *Caliban on Setebos.* To see Tree make up for his part was a privilege I often enjoyed. There in his dressing-room you saw the artist at work, the creative artist who adds touch after touch to complete the picture, until suddenly the whole conception bursts into significant life. When Tree had thoroughly got inside the skin of a character—which often took some time—he seemed to partake of a new and alien life. A singular illustration was Zakkuri in the *Darling of the Gods,* in which by degrees Tree gave us, I do not say a true, but an extraordinarily vivid and convincing, portrait of a Japanese statesman in all his horrible subtlety and coarseness. Another example was Izard in *Business is Business.* Tree was never a smoker in the true sense of the word, he only smoked for the sake of companionship, taking a modest fourpenny cigar, while he gave his guest Coronas. But in Izard he was perpetually smoking big and black-looking cigars. I asked him how he managed to stand it; he answered that, as it seemed natural to the character, he found it easy for himself. Off the stage he could not have done it; on the stage it was appropriate and therefore a piece of unconscious mimicry. Svengali smoked, I think, cigarettes or long Vevey fins. The Duke of Guisebery smoked, quite as to the manner born, a pipe—a luxury in which Tree, the individual, not the actor, never indulged.

You must forgive me for rambling on in this desultory fashion ; I want you to understand how, for those who knew him and liked him, Tree the man, over and above all the parts he assumed, gained his great personal ascendancy. It is Tree the man I remember now, and, doubtless, my appreciation of his personality colours all my judgment of his acting.   It is Tree the man who figures in my memory and perhaps his shade—if such things can vex those who have passed into the land of shadows—is inclined to rebuke me for writing about him.   For I recall an incident bearing on the point.   He asked me one night at supper at the Garrick what I had been writing.   I answered that I had been trying to write an obituary of my friend, H. D. Traill. " That must be an odious task," he said; " the more you like a man the less ought you to write about him."   I agreed, but remarked that journalism required such heavy sacrifices of feeling and affection; and that, anyway, it was better that an obituary notice should be written by a friend than by a merely critical observer.   This is my only defence now in taking up my pen.   In many ways I should have preferred to be silent.   To say nothing is the only becoming   attitude   for   friendship.   But   however   more congenial it may be to be silent and to remember, there are other considerations which are bound to be operative. " You are always a little cold when you write about me," Tree said to me once.   " Is not that natural ? " I replied. " You know the old adage about a cold hand and a warm heart."   " It is all very well to dissemble your love.   But why did you kick me downstairs ? " Tree quoted gaily. " But of course I understand," he added with his genial smile.   As a matter of fact, we never had even the slightest difference in all the twenty-seven years of companionship. With most men he had an open, genial manner which they found very attractive.   Even his occasional affectations —which no one laughed at more heartily than Tree himself, but which obviously he could not help—did not annoy them, because they foundthe amusing.   I am not sure however, whether women understood him as well as men —any more than the average woman can understand why to some of us Falstaff is as great a creation as Hamlet.

Yes, I know what you are thinking at this moment. You imagine that I shrink from the main issue and that I am toying with purely subsidiary points just because I find it difficult to solve your main problem.   I answer, however, that some things, perhaps subsidiary and unessential as you feel, must be understood first before we are in any position to arrive at a positive conclusion.   Let us admit without reserve that Tree as a personality was greater than anything he accomplished; but you must allow me to observe that that in itself is a compliment, and in the case of many artists a very great one. Moreover, it makes no little difference in the result how and in what spirit you approach the consideration of a character. To me the important point is to ask what a man can do, not to worry yourself about what he cannot do. The latter attitude leads to purely barren criticism and an enumeration of unilluminating negatives. The former gives one interesting glimpses of psychology. It is the same with other things besides men. It is true of a piece of mechanism like a bicycle or a motor-car; it is true also of a dog or a semi-personal being, like a ship. You will never get the best out of such objects, you will never get the best out of ordinary human relations, unless the positive occupies you more than the negative, what can be done rather than what cannot. Do not smile at such truisms. So far as I can judge, they are often quite curiously and wantonly disregarded by many men, most women, and a large proportion of critics.

Somewhere—I think in " The Mirror of the Sea "—Mr. Joseph Conrad remarks that certain ship-masters are like Royal Academicians. They are eminently safe, but they never startle you by a fresh audacity of inspiration or a touch of originality. There are actors of a similar kind. They are quite sure of themselves, they can be trusted to do the right thing at the proper moment, they are recognised leaders of the profession who will always give you the same sort of acting, quite good, quite reputable, quite adequate (hateful word !), but devoid of any disturbing brightness of emotion or fancy. No one could charge Tree with belonging to this solemn order of artist. He was always unexpected, daring, original. He often gave one a shock of surprise, welcome or unwelcome. He was good when you anticipated a relative failure; poor, when you could have wagered on his success. His acting was never monotonous, rarely the same from night to night. Like his conversation, it was full of quick turns and unlooked-for spurts of wit. For the same reason, his figure as he moved on the stage was vivid, graphic, picturesque, satisfying the eye, even when occasionally he failed to satisfy the mind. When he was acting Mark Antony in the Forum scene he broke off the famous speech in the middle, came down from the rostrum and finished his speech, standing on a broken pillar. I argued with him about this, suggesting that if Mark Antony was really holding his audience he would never have altered his position. Tree answered : " You forget the soon-wearied eye of the spectator : he becomes tired of one situation and demands another. Besides," he added with a whimsical smile, " change is a necessity for my nature." It was indeed. And owing to this he became tired and bored with his part, and sometimes broke off the run of a piece in the midst of a brilliant success. I anticipate what you will say, my critical friend ! You will remind me that I am describing the qualities of an amateur, not of a professional. I do not shrink from the conclusion. Tree had all the best points of an amateur, and some of his triumphs were gained just for that reason. He was a glorified amateur who dared things which a professional never would have dared, and won a shining victory. He mistrusted all talk about technique. " I have not got technique," he once said; " it is a dull thing. It enslaves the imagination." And when he established his school in Gower Street, in which I was able to render some small help, he retained some doubts, which were afterwards dispelled. " You cannot teach acting," he said. No, but you can prepare the groundwork by means of which the natural aptitude gets its chance. And this he subsequently recognised to be the case.

What were the positive contributions of Herbert Tree to the English stage ? Here there is some room for dissent and disagreement : I will only put down certain facts in the form in which they appear to me. Remember, in the first place, that he inherited a great tradition from Henry Irving who had set a magnificent example of stage-production at the Lyceum. Tree was at first content to carry on the tradition on similar lines. He produced plays with extreme care for detail and many appeals to the eye. There was never anything slipshod either in the method of stage representation or in the attention paid to what the diplomats call " imponderabilia." Indeed, it was the care taken over the minutiæ which guaranteed the effectiveness of the whole. Thanks in especial to Irving and Tree, London stage-production reached a higher level of completeness and finish than was to be seen in foreign capitals. Sarah Bernhardt and other foreign visitors acknowledged that in this respect they did not do things better in France. Gradually Tree bettered the examples of his predecessors. His critics said he over-elaborated his effects; his friends were never tired of welcoming new grades of beauty. I take only two instances out of many which offer themselves

s

in recollection.   Probably there never was a more beautiful
stage picture than Olivia's pleasaunce in *Twelfth Night*.
We talk of the hanging gardens of Babylon as of something
legendary and rare.   Here before our eyes were to be seen
Olivia's hanging gardens, a dream of exquisite and appealing beauty which seemed to bring out the more clearly
by contrast the vulgarity and coarseness of Sir Toby
Belch and Sir Andrew Aguecheek, while it enhanced the
delicacy of Viola and Olivia herself.   The other example
I will take is from the *Midsummer Night's Dream*.   You
will recall that though the scene is supposed to be laid in
the neighbourhood of Athens, the feeling, the atmosphere
of the play belong essentially to Stratford and England.
Accordingly, Tree gave us, alternately with some marble
seats and olive trees, splendid glimpses of British forests
in which the fairies ran wild and Bottom and his companions
rehearsed their uncouth theatricals.   Anything more restful
to the eye than these glades of sylvan beauty I have never
seen on any stage.   I used to drop into the theatre while
the play was going on just to realise once more the solemn
delightful effect of the old beeches sheltering the wayward
fancies of Oberon, Titania, and Puck, and providing a
rehearsal ground for *Pyramus and Thisbe*.   I must also
add something about the elaborate scene at the end of the
play when the pillars of the Duke's palace glow with internal
light to enable the fairies to carry on their domestic tasks
of making everything clean and sweet for the mortals.   It
was beautiful, but perhaps too elaborate.   One missed in
this case the note of simplicity, the wise sobriety of an
accomplished artist who would not strive " to do better
than well " lest he should " confound his skill in covetous-
ness."   There were charming pictures, too, in the *Tempest*,
little sea-fairies peeping round the edges of the rocks, while
Ariel sported in the pools, which one remembers with
gratitude.   But, indeed, the time would fail me if I were
to recount half the wonders which the magician Tree dis-
played before our eyes in play after play.   You may call
him a consummate decorator, if you like, *le Tapissier du
notre Théâtre*, as Luxemburg—was it not?—was called by
reason of his conquest of flags and other costly stuff,
le Tapissier de Notre-Dame.   But I maintain that he had
the eye, the feeling, the touch of an artist.
    It would be a small matter to decorate the outside of
the vase if it did not contain within itself rare and exquisite
essences.   Tree soon realised that decoration in itself could

only please the groundlings or the dilettantes, and that the main matter of consequence was the spirit in which the whole adventure was attempted. What was the character of the adventure? It was to give the British stage dignity as well as charm, high seriousness as well as æsthetic adornment. It was for this reason that from time to time he put before his public—a *clientèle*, by the way, which was always steadily growing—stately performances of Shakespearean plays, incidentally proving that our great English dramatist did not necessarily spell bankruptcy, but, judiciously treated, might be made to yield a fair percentage of profit. He varied his programme with lighter fare, as a matter of course : a man who had undertaken the responsibility of so large a theatre as His Majesty's was bound to keep a steady eye on the booking-office and replenish his coffers now and again by popular appeals. Unfortunately, our public is not always spurred and exalted to finer issues; and though Shakespeare under special conditions can become almost popular, a certain melodramatic blatancy—or at least insistence—has a more distinct pecuniary appeal. Where theatres are not supported by municipalities or the State, the lessee and manager is forced to " go here and there and make himself a motley to the view " for base considerations of solvency. But Tree did not forget the higher obligations of the position he had attained. As head of the profession he realised his responsibilities. He was full of the idea of the importance of the theatrical art, as a main instrument of culture and as a most necessary element in civic and social life. He did not work merely for his own hand, but upheld the claims of his calling. He instituted a Shakespearean week—a most costly undertaking—in order to keep alive our indebtedness to the Elizabethan stage. He presided at meetings, made speeches, inaugurated movements, pushed and encouraged various policies, in order to prove that actors were important elements in the community who had their proper functions in the body politic. You know how many speeches Tree made in the United States, not because speaking was easy to him—it never was—but because he felt it to be his duty to represent British interests and ideals in this appalling universal war. Only a week or two before his death he told me that he often composed the speech he was presently going to deliver while he was declaiming Wolsey's long " farewell to all his greatness " before his audience in *Henry VIII*.

There is no doubt that the career of this well-equipped actor and most competent manager and lessee had a beneficial effect on the English stage; for Tree had a great organising ability and admirably quick and valuable intuitions. But you will naturally ask me a question which has long been on the tip of your tongue—I am writing to you as though I actually saw and witnessed your impatience—the question as to Tree's attitude towards the future of the dramatic art. Granted that his influence on his contemporary public was all to the good, what about his relation to novel movements and to those efforts which zealous innovators have made to " reform " the drama? The future of the English stage! Ah, but will you tell me what is the future? There was a movement some few years back, to which I will return presently. But what is the prospect now? Looking superficially at existing facts, one might give several replies. Apparently the tendency at the present moment is in the direction of light, frivolous entertainments, only intended to amuse and distract men's minds from the horrible preoccupation with the war. American comedies have had their chance, and succeeded in proportion to the farcical elements they have contained. Revues flourish as much as ever—perhaps rather more than they used to. Composite entertainments, musical, droll, heterogeneous, are in vogue, especially if they have enlisted in their company at least one clever woman and one reputedly clever man. Mr. H. B. Irving with admirable boldness tried *Hamlet*, but it had to be withdrawn for want of support. Serious plays seem to be at a discount, unless, like M. Brieux's plays, *Les Avariés*, and *Les trois filles de M. Dupont*, and Ibsen's *Ghosts*, they make an appeal which is not mainly histrionic. Doubtless some of these phenomena are due to the unreal conditions of the time; they are symptomatic not of currents of artistic or inartistic fashion running below the surface, but of our unrest, our weariness, our irrepressible feeling that, set against the lurid background of ceaseless warfare, no artistic effort matters very much. Meanwhile our theatres are full— when they are full—of officers and soldiers on leave accompanied by their sisters or cousins or lovers who only want their military friends to be happy—and this is not the kind of theatrical audience which cares for dramatic art or even desires to think at all. Tree brought back from America a piece in which he strongly believed. *The Great Lover*, I think, was its name. He had every intention of producing it forthwith; but what success it might have secured under present conditions is an unsolved problem. The great success in London is, of course, *Chu Chin Chow*, a piece beautifully presented and full of elaborate and admirable pictures. But it is hardly a play in the sense in which you and I understand the term.

Still, you remember that there was a movement going on a few years back, which we associate with Granville Barker and with a competent body of actors—Ainley, Nicholson, Leon Quartermaine, Lillah McCarthy, and others.[1] It was an effort in the direction of greater simplicity of stage presentation and the abolition of long waits between scenes and acts. It revealed to us, for instance, that some of Shakespeare's plays could be given in three hours without any cuts and omissions—so that we might be seeing the plays more or less as the author intended that we should. Time was gained by making the actors speak faster, without wearisome pauses and unimpressive silences. I don't think I have ever heard an actor speak with such rapidity as Ainley achieved as Laertes in *A Winter's Tale*. The movement included some elements of mere freakishness, as when Barker gave the fairies in *Midsummer Night's Dream* gilded faces. But the scenery, though elementary, was to a sufficient degree picturesque, and the acting was persuasively good. A similar method applied to *Macbeth* or *Othello* would have been very instructive. Meanwhile *Twelfth Night*, so treated, had a real effectiveness of its own. And the daring experiment of putting Mr. Hardy's *The Dynasts* on the boards was, within the limits prescribed, a triumph.

I do not think that Tree had much sympathy with this movement. He took a great interest in it, of course, just as he did in the Russian Ballet, which he visited as often as he could. But so far as I could make out he preferred older methods. With regard to the Russian Ballet, he once remarked with no little acuteness that it struck him as " the gilded plaything of an effete autocracy " ; and with regard to Granville Barker's productions he seemed to feel —though I do not remember a definite statement—that they were bizarre, freakish experiments which could only appeal to a section of the public and not to the great mass of theatre-goers. For himself, remember that he had the vast auditorium of His Majesty's resting on his shoulders,

---

[1] Mr. Martin Harvey tried similar experiments in *Taming of the Shrew* and *Hamlet.*

and that he was bound to consider the tastes not of sections, but of the public at large. He always insisted on this fact. " I have to find something which will be agreeable to stalls, upper circle, pit, gallery—all at once." And directly we think of the many-headed public who keep theatres going, and the difficulty there is in finding a common focus for their ardent, unsophisticated enthusiasm and their uncritical approval, we shall begin to recognise the burden laid on theatrical *entrepreneurs* and the necessary contrast between their point of view and that of irresponsible dramatic critics.

I do not know if I have satisfied your curiosity in these few remarks of mine. I recognise that yours is a legitimate curiosity from the standpoint of a man like yourself who stands outside our more intimate interests and desires to view a situation in its broad and general features. To you Herbert Tree is an actor and a manager who has done certain large things in a large way, and has either succeeded or failed. To us he is a many-sided personality, in whose case mere histrionic success is only one element in a complex and varied whole. On one point I think you may feel confidence. If you admit that Tree fills a conspicuous space in our admiration and regard, you will also have to accept this as a solid fact—even though it may surprise you—with which you have to reckon. He has had many admirers and no few devoted friends. He was believed in as a force in our dramatic world, as a man who consistently held a high ideal for our stage, and employed his sympathy, his energy, and his own remarkable powers in a valiant attempt at its realisation. That is a simple fact which cannot be gainsaid; and it must enter into your general estimate on the other side of the Atlantic, as it has already done and will increasingly do into ours on this side.

A high ideal for the stage? Perhaps you stop over this phrase and feel some hesitation in adopting it. But if you do, you are up against one of those baffling points in psychology, which affect many other men besides Tree. How much of the ideal must be sacrified in daily practice if anything whatever is to be achieved? Does the ideal cease to be an ideal if it ever be forgotten? Can one worship the ideal in secret and deny it in the open light of day? Is compromise a reputable, even if necessary, policy? Ah, who shall scrutinise his conscience without many pangs of self-reproach in questions like these! That Tree produced some unworthy pieces it would be absurd to deny.

He did, and he knew he did—just as he knew also that he
must keep up a great theatrical establishment and transact
a vast business, for which the possession of funds was obliga-
tory. I remember one occasion at a club after the production of a gaudy melodrama—I will not mention its name for
fear of getting into trouble with the author—when some of
us were chaffing—I think you call it " chipping "—Tree
concerning some of its banal effects and its " popular "
character. He loved being chaffed, or, at all events, he
bore it with unflinching good humour, and riposted gaily
on his critics. As a matter of fact, the piece was a pecuniary success. But Tree by himself was in a different mood.
He knew what he was doing, and was not proud of it.
" Compromise, the god of the shiftless," he used to say.

You remember Henry James's ironical little story, " The
Lesson of the Master "? In that you will find the philosophy of the matter. An older novelist preaching to a
younger novelist, warns him against being seduced from
his high ideals by such encumbrances as a wife and children
and the obligation of keeping up a costly and hospitable
house. The young writer is duly impressed until he discovers that his mentor—even after his melancholy experience of what marriage can do to deaden aspiration—
deliberately marries again, and marries the very girl with
whom the young disciple of the master was in love ! How
shockingly cynical, one says, and then, after a moment's
deliberation, how abominably true ! It is true, my friend,
and true of all of us. A little clearer vision and then the
clouds come down again. A glimpse of the pure high
æther of heaven and then the rain-splashed earth. We do
what we must and not always what we can. Let him that
is without sin cast the first stone. I, at all events, have no
wish either to bombard you with truisms or to cast stones
at Tree. His was a fine, courageous, indomitable character;
and over and over again, for his delight and ours, he drew
from his intellectual instrument the finest music that
nature had hidden in it, and played it as it should be played.
Peace be to his ashes—he will be much and widely missed.
Multis ille bonis flebilis occidit.

INDEX